DATE			

"I think there is something more here. I wish—" He looked at her with such pain in his eyes that she gasped.

"What is it?"

"I wish you had come back before my wife died. I wish Faith had been here to save her and the baby."

"Cleanliness," Amy said. "That's all that was needed. Your horrible old doctor delivered some twins in the village and didn't bother to wash his hands before or after. Then he went to your wife and delivered her with his filthy hands. It's called childbirth fever and no one will find the cause of it until Victorian times, about a hundred years from now."

"It could be that simple?" Tristan said.

"Yes, it could. Tristan, I'm sorry. It's not as though my world has found cures for everything, but we have found out about washing our hands. I've seen old paintings of men wearing suits while they operate on someone."

"And what do the men in your time wear?"

"The men *and women* who operate wear specially made sterile gowns and thin rub-

ber gloves on their hands. They work in a sterile environment."

Tristan put out his hand to pull her up to stand beside him. "I want you to tell me everything about this." His voice lowered. "I want to prevent what was done to my wife and my uncle from happening again."

"You want to be a doctor?"

"No, I just want to take care of my family."

"Will you keep a guard with you?" she asked. "At all times? I want to keep you alive until . . ."

"Until you leave?"

He looked at her, then pulled her into his arms and kissed her. For a moment he held her in his arms, her head against his chest, his heart beating against her cheek. "Do not tell me that I cannot touch you. He will have you for the rest of your life. You will go back to him and it will be his children that you have. I have only now, these few days with you."

"Tristan . . ." she said, but she didn't push away from him.

It was he who put her at arms' length. "You and I are going to do what the others are doing. We are going to learn. You are going to tell me what you can that will help me in my world. Never again do I want to have a woman die in my arms, her blood flowing out of her like a stream of death. Never again do I want to see someone I love lie in a bed and waste away when all he needed was a bath and some good food. Will you help me?"

"Yes, of course. I'll do what I can, but I still must save your life. Someone here hates you and wants you dead."

He smiled at her. "I will find him even if I have to sit up all night and watch for him. Come! We must go to the house and get food, then you must tell me everything."

THE
OTHER
MACDONALD
REPORT

Twenty-one

"You look horrible," Zoë said.

"Thanks," Amy said. "You've made my day."

"If you're having trouble sleeping I could give you something," Faith said.

They were in the main house, sitting at the round table in the south parlor, a full tea in front of them. It was the first time they'd all three been together in nearly a week.

"Do you know that you're beginning to sound like a drug dealer," Amy said to Faith. "Are those things you're giving people legal?"

Zoë and Faith looked at each other.

"Don't look at me like that. Yes, I know where I am. I haven't forgotten. A few days ago I told Tristan everything."

For a moment neither Zoë nor Faith could speak.

"You did what?" Zoë said at last. "What do you mean by 'everything'?"

"Time travel, the works."

Both Zoë and Faith fell back against their chairs and stared at her.

"I had to explain why he and I couldn't . . ." She looked down at her plate, then up at Zoë defiantly. "Why we couldn't do what you and Russell are doing all over this estate."

Instead of being embarrassed, Zoë smiled. "Lusty man is my Russell. Think I could take him back with me?"

"You don't fool me," Amy said, her eyes narrowed. "When we leave here you're going to leave your heart behind."

"And you aren't?" Zoë shot back. "The way you and that gorgeous babe look at each other could melt the silver. I hope you aren't trying to make us believe that you aren't bouncing around in his bed every night."

THE CONSENSUS ON CANADA'S FUTURE
THAT THE MACDONALD COMMISSION LEFT OUT

THE
OTHER
MACDONALD
REPORT

EDITED BY
DANIEL DRACHE AND DUNCAN CAMERON

James Lorimer & Company, Publishers
Toronto 1985

Cover design: Don Fernley

Canadian Cataloguing in Publication Data

Main entry under title:
The other Macdonald report

Submissions to the Royal Commission on the Economic Union and Development Prospects for Canada.
ISBN 0-88862-901-X (bound). — ISBN 0-88862-900-1 (pbk.)

1. Canada — Economic policy — 1971- *2. Canada — Economic Conditions — 1971- *I. Cameron, Duncan, 1944- II. Drache, Daniel, 1941- III. Royal Commission on the Economic Union and Development Prospects for Canada.

HC115.086 1985 330.971'0647 C85-098935-3

James Lorimer & Company, Publishers
Egerton Ryerson Memorial Building
35 Britain Street
Toronto, Ontario M5A 1R7

Printed and bound in Canada

6 5 4 3 2 1   85 86 87 88 89 90

For a second Amy's eyes blazed with anger, then she let out her breath, put her elbows on the table, and her head in her hands. "I should be so lucky. It was easy when all he wanted from me was sex. I could get away in ten minutes, then go cry myself to sleep. But now he wants information about the future."

"What kind of information?" Faith asked. "About cell phones and that sort of thing? Or who's going to win the next election?"

"The stock market?" Zoë asked.

"No," Amy said tiredly. "He wants to know all I can dredge out of my tired brain about modern medicine."

"Good thing he didn't ask me," Zoë said, "or he'd be out the door in five minutes. Why don't you send him to Faith?"

"He's already sent the village to me," Faith said. "How can I take on more? Most of what I do is tell them to take a bath and brush their teeth. If I stayed here . . ." She looked at them. "I think I might end up being burned as a witch."

"Wrong time period," Zoë said. "I think. When did that happen in Salem?"

"Could we get back to the problem at

hand?" Amy said. "We only have three more days."

"Yes," Zoë said, and there were tears in her voice. "Three more days. How will I live without him?"

Faith put her arms around Zoë and hugged her. "And I don't know how I'll be able to return to a life of uselessness."

"You both have your times to go back and change your futures," Amy said. "Remember Madame Zoya whom neither of you believed in? She said you will have your own lives to fix."

"What good will that do?" Zoë asked, sitting upright and out of Faith's embrace. "Russell is here, not there. Even if I take another three weeks with him, that's all I'll get."

"I think you need to find out what happened to you in our time," Faith said in a motherly way.

"Look who's talking. I think you should find out who killed your boyfriend."

As soon as she said it, Zoë clamped her lips shut. "Sorry, I didn't mean to say that."

Faith looked at Zoë, then Amy. "What is it that you two know that I don't?"

"I don't think now is the time to go into this," Amy said. "I called you two here to talk about Tristan."

Faith stared at Zoë. "I want you to tell me what you know."

"Go ahead and tell her," Amy said, frustrated that she could never seem to get the women to talk about what she thought was their reason for being there.

Zoë took a breath. "I saw it on the Internet. Six months ago a skeleton was found at the bottom of a cliff in your hometown. He was identified as Tyler Parks."

Faith looked as though she'd been slapped. "Ty is dead?" she whispered. "When did it happen?"

Zoë looked at Amy as though asking her for help.

"Tell her all of it," Amy said.

"He didn't just die," Zoë said as she reached for Faith's hand. "He was murdered about fifteen years ago."

"How?" Faith whispered.

"A blunt instrument," Zoë said. "Maybe a . . . a rock."

Faith got up from the chair and walked to the far end of the room. "That's why Ty never came back," she said. "After we had

Contents

IV: An Alternative Vision of Canada   167

our fight I never saw him again. We all thought he left town. The money he made from the sale of the land was given to his mother. I talked to her once and she also thought he'd run off. I always thought it was because of me, because of our argument. And because I married Eddie soon afterward."

When Faith looked back at them there were tears in her eyes. She put her hand to her mouth. "But he didn't leave me."

"Is that better than death?" Zoë asked.

"Yes. I mean, no." Faith sat back down. "I . . . He didn't leave me."

Zoë looked at Amy.

"Someone murdered him," Amy said. "It was a long time ago, so I doubt if they'll ever find out who did it, but—"

"My mother," Faith said. "She killed Ty."

"What?"

"I didn't understand it until now, but on her deathbed she told me she'd killed him. I thought she meant she'd killed the love that Ty and I had. It looks like she meant she actually killed Ty. She so wanted me to marry Eddie that she killed to attain it."

Amy raised her eyebrows to Zoë.

"I can go back," Faith said. "Just like you

Acknowledgments

In the course of preparing this volume, we received assistance and support from various groups and individuals. We wish to thank the organizations that were willing to make their briefs to the Macdonald Commission available to us for publication, all of which responded quickly and positively to our request. We are grateful to Ginette Rozon, Louise Clément and Phuong Chi Hoang of the research secretariat of the Faculty of Social Sciences, University of Ottawa, for word-processing assistance. We wish to acknowledge the cooperation of staff members of the Macdonald Commission library who greatly facilitated our research. The students of the School of Translation, University of Ottawa, who operate the translation service *Tranglia*, are to be thanked for providing the translations of two briefs originally written in French. The staff of the Social Affairs Commission of the Canadian Conference of Catholic Bishops generously provided us with assistance at an early stage of our research. The Department of Political Science, University of Ottawa, provided some much needed material support. Ted Mumford of James Lorimer and Company was always available for greatly appreciated editorial counsel. Finally, we owe a special thank you to Katherine Farris for her help and encouragement.

went back to change your past, I can go back and change my life with Ty. When he climbs in my window, I'm going to be packed and ready to leave with him. We're going to live in that old farmhouse and I'm going to have a ten-acre herb garden. If I could figure out a way to take Beth's seeds back with me, I might make some of her products."

"Put them in your hair like Amy's ribbon," Zoë said, and Faith's eyes widened as she remembered that the ribbon Amy had been wearing was still in her hair when they arrived in the eighteenth century.

"What a great idea," Faith said. "I could—"

"Would you two mind if we talked about why we're here?" Amy said. "We have three days left and I'm worried about Tristan being killed."

"I'm sorry, Amy," Faith said, "but I have to leave now and think about all this. This is a big change in my life and . . ." She didn't say anything else as she seemed to float out of the room.

"Wow," Zoë said. "I thought she'd be angry to hear that her old boyfriend had been murdered."

"Better dead than to have dumped her," Amy said. "I think we just released the source of Faith's lifelong depression."

"Let's send Jeanne a whopping great bill," Zoë said.

"Let's talk about what we need to do to keep Tristan alive."

"When you saw him dead in your dream wasn't he in his bedroom in this house?"

"Yes," Amy said.

"So why don't you move him to that greenhouse Faith lives in and let lots of people sleep around him?"

"I don't think Tristan would agree to that. He has a real stubborn streak in him."

"Then get Faith to drug him. Or tell him you'll sleep with him if he'll do it." She raised her eyebrows at Amy's look. "We all have to make sacrifices."

For the first time, Amy smiled. "This meeting has not gone as well as I hoped it would, but it has certainly been interesting. I think you're right and I'll do everything short of sex or murder to get Tristan out of this house."

"Good," Zoë said, standing up. "Then we're done. I'm—"

"Everyone in this village, and probably

for about three over, know what you're going to do today and have been doing since you arrived here."

"Celibacy can sure put a woman in a bad mood," Zoë said.

Amy ignored that remark. "Is it too much to ask if you did what you said you were going to do and talk to the maids about anyone who might be harboring a grudge against Tristan?"

"I did better than that, I asked Russell. He put the word out to the women and they're to tell him anything they hear. So far, there's been nothing. Now, if you don't mind, I have something else to do." She left the room.

Amy put her head in her hands. "Oh, Stephen," she moaned. Just three more days, and she'd be back with him. Just three more days.

Twenty-two

"Are you feeling all right?" Faith asked Amy. "You look—"

"I don't need another person to tell me how bad I look." They were standing in front of the orangery and Amy was studying the glass walls. "I don't think this place is safe."

"If it were a prison it wouldn't look safe to you." Faith took her hands. "Amy, everything that can be done is being done. Tristan will have Thomas to look after him. He's going to sleep in a dormitory with lots of other people." It was all Faith could do not to let her displeasure show. In these

Introduction

On November 5, 1982, the Macdonald Commission on Canada's future was launched with a broad mandate, a large budget — and not much public confidence in the entire exercise. How could a government commission be expected to cure unemployment, inflation and recession, when solutions had evaded governments and business throughout the industrialized world? With the aging Trudeau government reeling from the worst recession since the 1930s, the enlistment of former finance minister — and Liberal heir apparent — Donald S. Macdonald had the markings of an act of political desperation.

What Donald Macdonald was asked to do was nothing short of proposing a new social consensus on economic policy. This was an extraordinarily political task to hand a supposedly nonpartisan commission. Given the persistent media clamour of dozens of different interest groups all announcing top priorities for the nation, Canadians can be forgiven their skepticism about the likelihood of the commission's finding a consensus.

The fact is, however, that such a consensus exists, expressed in the views the commission was to hear from what we call "the popular sector": churches, trade unions, women's groups, social agencies and organizations representing Native People, farmers and the disadvantaged. This fundamental regrouping of forces represents an alternative to the rigidities of Canada's two-and-a-half-party system and the simple two-class model of society. In a period when Canadian society is supposedly shifting to the right, there are more forces ready for social change than either the general public or the traditional left can recognize.[1] The proof of its existence is the coalitions that have been built in the Solidarity effort in British Columbia, the court challenge to cruise missile testing, the defence of abortion rights, the Eaton's boycott and the Social Policy Reform Group. The groups active in these coalitions are Canada's counter-institutions, and they draw on a counter-discourse of political economy.

The popular sector groups contradict the urgings of business that government reduce its role in the economy and give free rein to "market forces." The economy must serve human well-being rather than corporate balance sheets, the popular sector says, and for this end a fundamental break with the conventional value system of policymaking is the only means available. They reject a view of economics that separates ends from means and that is based on having people adjust, accommodate and lower their expectations to the short-term profit considerations of business.

This alternative view was voiced by labour's sole representative on the Macdonald Commission, Gérard Docquier. In a dissenting statement, he condemned the final report "for having endorsed market-based fantasies as a solution to [Canada's] nearly two million unemployed." He stressed that there were four key areas of disagreement with the commission. "These are: the lack of a serious effort to eliminate unemployment; the advocacy of U.S.-Canada bilateral free trade; proposals to roll back the unemployment insurance program; and some recommendations on labour management relations." His most fundamental disagreement was over unemployment. "In this way the Commission has failed the people of Canada." As to the commission's major recommendation, he called free trade with the U.S. "a blind and imprudent act" that does not represent a solution to Canada's problems. On the whole, Docquier said the commission was "obsessed with Canada's competitiveness," when its commitment should have been to "full employment and social justice." Indeed, the popular sector proposes a radically different economic order in which democratic control of the economy and the state is strengthened by creating new forms of participation.

It is the potential and ultimate failure of the Macdonald Commission to grasp this consensus that is the inspiration of this book. The bulk of the book reproduces many of the key popular sector documents submitted to the commission at hearings across the country. In this introductory essay we fill out the context of how these two ships passed in the night, beginning with a look at how royal commissions work; then turning to a critique of the "business agenda" that dominated the deliberations of the commission; and finally, a brief analysis of the popular consensus.

I: Royal Commission Politics

Whether Donald Macdonald had any chance of success had much to do with the *realpolitik* of royal commissions.

In theory, a royal commission is a useful device for shaping public debate and creating a consensus on divisive issues.[2] Critics charge that in practice many commissions are a waste of time, if not because the commissioners are disinclined to question the status quo, then because the ultimate recommendations are ignored. Of the four federal commissions that reported between 1981 and early 1985, in only one instance has the government acted on most of the short-term recommendations. In the case of two of these inquiries, none of the long-term recommendations has been acted upon.

On the rare occasion when a commission has been too independent, the government simply commissions a counter-report. Ottawa initially sat on the McDonald Report on RCMP "dirty tricks"; then it hired Justices Ritchie and Wright of the Supreme Court of Canada to write a second report. In effect their opinion was that the McDonald Commission was wrong about the law and the government needed to take a second look at many of its recommendations to reform the Mounties. A similar fate met the Carter Commission in the 1960s. That commission's pioneering suggestions for reforming Canada's inequitable tax system were shelved on the advice of "government experts."

Thus, either from the beginning or in the end, royal commissions are rarely an exercise to get to the bottom of things. Nor are they primarily established to educate the public, as many political scientists suggest. In fact, royal commissions serve an explicitly political purpose.

Governments need to defuse explosive issues. Since royal commissions are perceived to operate impartially, they are the ideal instrument of brokerage politics. In contrast to the theoretical purpose of *producing* a consensus through a formal process of fact-finding, the job of a royal commission is to *appear* to have produced a consensus.

A royal commission can change not only the focus of public discourse but also conventional wisdom, by generating an "expert" body of knowledge. For this reason the commission must be headed by a high-profile, supposedly neutral person, often an ex-politician or judge, who is seen to be acting in the national interest. Commissioners are not necessarily experts in fields such as law, political science, economics or sociology. Rather, they are usually appointed because they have a general knowledge of policy or a policy area, and represent (despite the image of impartiality) a region and/or special interest group.[3]

This legitimization is completed by the hiring of leading academics to research and write background studies and the final report. Here, rather than in the commissioner's office, is the actual source of "expertise." Lawyers figure prominently within the expert group, giving the commission the air of legal authority.

With mandate, commissioners and staff in place, the public can be consulted, usually in stage-managed hearings.

By contrast, the Macdonald Commission had an admirable model, in the Berger Commission into the Mackenzie Valley Pipeline, for carrying though the true spirit of public inquiry.[4] The Berger Commission financed research by Native groups that, unlike the oil companies, did not have the means to make themselves heard in a sophisticated way. Berger's empowering of these groups was undoubtedly an influence on the commission's landmark decision to slow down resource development in the North. As we shall see, the Macdonald Commission did not find the Berger model worthy of emulation. Instead they adopted the elite model of inquiry.

The Organization of the Macdonald Commission

Apart from the chairman, there were twelve people — nine men and three women — on the Macdonald Commission (formally known as the Royal Commission on the Economic Union and Development Prospects for Canada). The members were: Clarence Barber, a University of Manitoba economics professor; Albert Breton, a university of Toronto economics professor; Gérard Docquier, Canadian director of the United Steelworkers of America; William Hamilton, president of the Employer's Council of B.C.; John Messer, a Saskatoon resources expert; Angela Peters, chairperson of Bowering Brothers Limited of Halifax; Laurent Picard, dean of McGill University; Michel Robert, a Montreal lawyer; Daryl Seaman, chairman of Bow Valley Industries of Calgary; Tommy Shoyama, a University of Victoria professor and former Ministry of Finance mandarin; Jean Wadds, former Canadian high commissioner to the U.K.; and Catherine Wallace, a retired educator and executive from New Brunswick.

As for Donald Macdonald, he is a Toronto corporate lawyer who took a significant cut in pay by accepting the chairman's $800 per diem.

While this list covers Canada's regions and makes a token nod to ethnic diversity, its social and economic makeup is awry. The members are mostly older and well-off; government, academia and business are well represented in a sort of plurality of the establishment. But farmers, churches, the voluntary sector, the arts community, social agencies, Native Peoples, the young, the poor and the unemployed are all absent. Labour is clearly underrepresented, and while there are three female members, there is no representation from the women's movement.

The first order of business for the Macdonald Commission was to devise a plan of attack for the most complex mandate handed any royal commission in the last two decades. The commission decided on a three-pronged approach of public hearings, private consultations and a global review of government policies. This scheme was to enable the commission to identify, as its chairman boldly announced, "a reasonable degree of consensus among Canadians" on the challenges and prospects facing the country. In order to develop this consensus, the commission asked for the participation of all three levels of government. Canadians were invited to prepare briefs and present their views in public hearings.

The commission tackled its review of government policies by establishing a secretariat in Ottawa. True to the usual style, the policy review took the form of a research program under the direction of leading scholars in economics, political science and law.[5] Studies were contracted from yet other academics to provide the theoretical and empirical basis for the commission's work.

For three months in the fall of 1983, the commissioners took to the road to find out what Canadians thought about their country's future.

past weeks her life had become very comfortable. True, it had been hard on her to
see the line of people who came to her
with diseases that she couldn't cure, but
aside from that, she and William and
Thomas had formed a nice life. William
was very easy to live with. His constant
good humor had kept a smile on her face,
and as he healed, he began to help her
with the herbs. One morning, in a moment
of honesty, he'd told her that his life had
never been useful.

"I am sure my nephew has told you that
I have never achieved much. I was much
younger than my ambitious older brothers,
and I was my mother's favorite. I stayed
with her until she died, but by that time I
had no inclination to marry and burden
myself with children. She left her money
to me and I spent years traveling about
the world. I even went to that America of
yours."

"You didn't tell me that."

"If I had, I might have missed out on the
stories that you have told me. I did not see
it as a place of great advancement that
you seem to know it as."

Faith had to turn away to hide her red

face. She'd joined Zoë in coming down hard on Amy for telling Tristan the truth, but she realized she'd told William a great deal more than she thought she had.

"I know you plan to leave here," he said, then held up his hand when she started to speak. "I listen more than you think and I hear you whispering with the other two women. I know that the time is coming soon. I was wondering . . ."

Turning, Faith looked at him.

"If you feel that you need to leave because you have no real place in this world, I would like to make you an offer. The old house, the one you have ranted about having cows in it, is mine."

She smiled at his use of the word "ranting." She wanted to protest that she'd done no such thing, but she had. Good! she thought. Maybe she'd made enough of an impression on him that after she was gone they'd take care of the house and not let it fall into ruin.

"I can offer you the house," William said softly. "And me."

She realized that he was offering her marriage and a comfortable life with him. It would be nice, she thought, to live here.

She would love to oversee the remodeling of that wonderful old medieval house, and she'd like to continue working with the herbs and applying what she knew while learning more.

She looked at William. He had gained a lot of weight in the last weeks and she was beginning to see the man he once was. He was handsome, intelligent, and wonderfully good company. He would make fine husband.

She looked down at the big white marble mortar and pestle that was filled with ajuga leaves. She was pounding them to make an infusion to use on mouth ulcers. No, she thought, she'd had a life of comfort with a "fine husband." Eddie had been good company and he'd had more money than they could spend. If he hadn't been ill and had a mother from hell, he would have made a great husband.

Except for one thing, she thought: passion. She and Eddie had never once had passion. When she looked at Tyler, her knees had weakened. She'd never felt that with Eddie.

"I'm going to hold out for passion," she said aloud, then looked at William in horror.

What an awful thing to say to a man who'd just proposed to her!

William surprised her by letting out a loud laugh. "You are a wise, wise woman," he said, then he looked at her in a way that he never had before. "Give me a bit more time and I think I can fulfill your wish."

Faith returned his smile. She wanted love with her passion. Not a one-night stand, but true love and passion that made her knees weak. "It would take you more than a bit of time to take *me* on," she said to William.

He laughed again and reached for her, but Faith eluded his hand. "Sit down and eat," she said in the motherly voice she usually used with him.

Since that day there had been an easy, teasing camaraderie between her and William that she'd enjoyed immensely. But now Amy was moving into their cozy glass house with Tristan and probably half a dozen retainers.

"Do not look so down," William said. "My nephew is a man of humor."

"Yeah, but does he pick up his socks?"

William smiled at her ill humor and went

In twenty-eight towns and cities the commission met with more than 700 groups and individuals, and gathered more than 1,100 briefs, totalling some 40,000 pages.

What did the commission hear as it toured Canada?

There were three political philosophies vying for the commission's attention. The first came from the corporate sector, through organizations such as the Canadian Manufacturers' Association, the Canadian Bankers' Association, the Canadian Federation of Independent Business and the Fraser Institute. Stated simply, this view held that Canada should reduce the scope of government: the public sector, social welfare programs and government economic intervention should all be reduced, freeing the market to create jobs and growth. As well, the market must be allowed to identify "loser" industries so that more productive "winner" industries can break through to a new era of rigorous international competition and revised trade relations with the United States.

The second agenda, less clearly articulated, reflected the views of state agencies such as the Science Council. This agenda envisioned a new mandate for the state and a starring role for Canada's "high-tech" industries. It called for the creation of a new social accord between workers and their employers, featuring European-style mechanisms of cooperation. But neither the labour movement nor the major business organizations supported it.

The third agenda is embodied in the contributions to this book. It represents the views of groups who speak for ordinary Canadians. Theirs is a subordinate view of Canada, Canada as seen from the factory, office and farm; as seen from the unemployment line and the welfare office. Their briefs gave the Macdonald Commission the opportunity to encourage, examine and develop the critiques and proposals of Canadians who actually have borne the brunt of failed economic policies and weathered the ravages of the recession (see Table I-1).

However, the academic consultants chosen by the commission held views that largely coincided with those of the business agenda. This reflects the fact that the social science disciplines naturally take their agenda from the dominant concerns of society — and in a liberal democratic society, business concerns are dominant.

In economics, the current obsession of Canadian economists is making the market work by getting rid of "imperfections." This translates into proposals to eliminate minimum wages and social benefits, and to reduce the power of trade unions. In political science, the latest wisdom suggests that since the tension generated by the aspirations of Quebec is at a thirty-year low, Canadian federalism has proven its maturity and is strong enough to enter into a new economic relationship with the U.S.[6] In ways such as these, the research being done for the commission dovetailed with what the commissioners were hearing from businessmen at public hearings.

Frank Underhill warned that academics working for royal commis-

TABLE I-1
Economic Decline in Canada

	1980	1984
Jobs created	1.23 million (1976-80)	290,000 (1980-84)
No. unemployed	860,000	1.4 million
Rate of unemployment	7.5%	11.3%
Inflation	10.2%	4.4%
Balance of trade	$8.78 billion	$17.70 billion (1983)
Increase in fixed investment (excluding residential construction)	62.4% (1976-80)	14% (1980-84)
Business investment as % of GNP (constant dollars)	16.2%	13.3%
Federal deficit	$10.40 billion	$29.2 billion
Direct personal taxes	$23.47 billion	$38.40 billion
Direct business taxes	$ 8.57 billion	$11.71 billion
Official poverty rate (excluding farm population) of active population	15.1%	16.3%
Prime interest rate	18.1%	12%
Real interest rate (prime rate less inflation)	8.05%	6.85%
Total GNP growth in four years (constant prices)	9.9% (1976-80)	7.3% (1980-84)
Average family income in constant dollars	$34,550 (1979)	$34,080 (1983)
Average individual income in constant dollars	$14,013 (1979)	$14,090 (1983)

Source: Statistics Canada, Labour Canada and the Bank of Canada.

sions become "the garage mechanics of capitalism." Despite this, some of Canada's most eminent scholars agreed to provide the expertise for the Macdonald Commission. They were put to use in three ways. First, leading figures such as Alan Cairns, Richard Simeon, David C. Smith, Ivan Bernier and Bruce Doern made the commission credible simply by participating in directing research. A second group developed the commission's policy orientation in key areas such as labour markets, Canada-U.S. relations, productivity and industrial stategy. Of these, the most important field was labour markets, where contributors to the commission's work included Craig Riddell (coordinator for this section), Morley Gunderson and S.F. Kaliski. Finally, there were people hired for their particular expertise, which was put to use in writing key chapters of the report. This group included Jack Quinn, an internationally recognized expert in free trade areas; André Blais for industrial strategy; and Keith Banting on the role of the state.

Research was broken into two broad categories: the appropriate policies for economic development in a fast-changing world; and the viability of government programs and their capacity to respond to the changing needs of Canadians. From this we can see that the research program
is designed to be forward-looking: How best can Canadian political
economy adapt to change? The range of topics covered far more than
could possibly be considered in the overall drift of the report: from
"political elite opinion and federalism" to "regulation, overregulation
and economic efficiency"; from "the role of caucuses and regional
caucuses in Parliament" to "contemporary developments in liberal
constitutionalism."

Popular participation in the commission was limited to tightly
managed appearances at public hearings. Typically, there was a short
statement from the group, followed by some perfunctory questions
from the commissioners. Then the submission was filed away. But the
appearance was of genuine consultation: the popular sector groups were
co-opted into a process where their views were sought but not heeded.

One might well ask why the commission should bother soliciting views
if the briefs are only indexed and not followed up or treated seriously.
Not one of the 300-odd research contracts called for by the commission
was directed at deepening or refining the views presented by the popular sector organizations. This fact seemed lost on the commission. Its
executive director, Gerald Godsoe, said the inquiry process produced
"the deepest picture of what Canadians think about themselves, their
country and the world that has ever been taken." The Canadian public
— which, after all, is footing the bill for this "picture," the most expensive public inquiry in more than two decades — has a right to know
why the commission did not go beyond the mainstream in hiring its
experts. These are the sort of thinkers, largely wedded to the status
quo, who are responsible for the economic policies that the Macdonald
Commission was supposedly founded to replace. Only a handful of
academic dissidents — Robert Martin, David Wolfe, Leo Panitch, Daniel
Latouche — were asked to do studies.

The lack of confidence in the style of the commission may explain
the reception to its 1984 interim report, "Challenges and Choices,"
which set out the issues and options that had been presented during
the course of consultations. The public reaction was overwhelmingly
negative.[7] Many journalists charged that the commission was a colossal
waste of money, time and effort. One national columnist remarked that
the report could have been done by two students working at a medium
pace for a week. To a skeptical eye, the entire endeavour was another
example of government avoiding urgent economic matters by studying
them until they went away.

Even when the commissioners rebutted their critics by promising a
final report that would make fundamental recommendations about
Canada's political institutions, federal-provincial relations and a new

back to taking the flower heads off the chamomile that Faith had given him to work on.

Since Zoë had told her about what happened to Tyler, Faith had not been the same. She was restless now. There were only two days left, then what would happen? Would the three women disappear in a puff of smoke? And if they did, would they end up back in Madame Zoya's sunroom? Would Faith and Zoë be given second chances at their lives?

Turning, Faith left the walled garden and headed for the tower. Yesterday she'd confronted Zoë about her and Russell being in there.

"Keep your shirt on," Zoë said. "We didn't hurt anything."

"It's a matter of privacy," Faith said. "And where did you get a key?"

"Russell said he borrowed it."

"Stole it, more likely," Faith said. "I want that key." She had an idea that Russell had had a duplicate made from Beth's key, and he'd probably done it while she was in London. She didn't blame him. The tower would be an excellent place to paint when

economic policy framework, it was open to question whether the
commission could ever win the respect of the public.

II: The Business Agenda: The Real Issues?

The business community presented the Macdonald Commission with a
powerfully argued program for revitalizing the economy. The underlying theme of the briefs was that private enterprise alone produces
this country's wealth. Thus, Canada's political institutions, which have
developed largely as a framework to promote the interests of private
enterprise, should continue in this role.

Business made three policy arguments that appear to have captured
the attention not only of the commission but also of the Mulroney
government. The first is that public policy is insufficiently attuned to
the need for efficiency and increased national productivity. This means
that the market must be allowed to decide which firms will be winners
and which will be losers. The second is that since Canada's international
competitive position is being eroded by the massive global changes in
trade and production relations, Canada needs to seek not only new
markets but also a new trade relationship with its major trading partner, the United States. The third is that the size of the public sector
deficit is choking private initiative and enterprise. This calls for a
fundamental re-examination of the role of the state in the economy.

These arguments are presented as the rationale for the development
of a dramatically different public policy to resolve the economic crisis,
restore the confidence of the business community in the state, and,
most important, promote the interests of private enterprise. It is this
focus on private sector confidence, according to the business briefs,
that must be the number one priority of public policy in Canada today.

Even though the popular sector briefs regrouped in this book were
written without the benefit of coordination, they present a trenchant
critique of the business agenda. In the following we will focus on three
issues — productivity, free trade and the resilience of the U.S. economy — that were at the heart of the business agenda and the work of
the commission.

Productivity

In its simplest sense, improving productivity means producing more
for less by using capital, labour and technology more efficiently. Business perceives "productivity" as being synonymous with profits. And
since business aims to lower unit costs of production and increase output
per person in order to earn higher profits, it has three preferred solutions to the productivity "problem." It trys to substitute machines for
labour; cut labour costs; and introduce new techniques to reorder the
production processes and the workplace. (Quantum leaps in productivity come particularly from introducing new technology.) All these

it rained. And a place to escape the girls who made eyes at him every minute of the day.

The truth was that Faith wanted to use the tower as her own private sanctuary, a place where she could go to be alone. It seemed that soon she was going to be faced with a great many decisions in her life and, this time, she wanted to do what was right for her. Not for Ty, Eddie, her murderous mother, or even for Eddie's battle-axe of a mother. Faith needed to figure out what was right for *her.*

As she went through the quiet forest, she stopped once because she thought she saw a shadow move. She waited, but saw no one, then went on to the tower quickly. Beth had told her about wolves in the forest and she didn't want to meet one of them.

In the days since Beth had shown her the plants in the tower, Faith had asked every question she could think of about them and the recipes, the "receipts" that Beth had written out for her. Beth had shown Faith how to cut the bark of the shrubs to get the sap out, then how to use it to make the ingredient in the face cream, the shampoo, and the soap. They were simple recipes with one, single, extraordinary ingredient.

Since working with the balsam plants, Faith felt as though they'd become her friends. She felt honored to be near something so old as they were, plants that had had so much written about them. Even in the ancient world it was said that they grew in only one place on earth: Jericho. She would spend hours in the tower looking at the plants, inhaling their divine fragrance, and wondering what catastrophic events had caused the plant to become extinct.

Faith went to the stone where she knew Beth kept seeds hidden. She'd said that her ancestors had done everything they could to get the plant to grow in their gardens but it wouldn't. It had taken years to find out that it liked the dryness inside the tower, the heat reflected off the stones, and the small amount of water poured onto its roots.

Faith had written down every word that Beth told her about the plants themselves and her family's history with them, then Faith had memorized it all. She knew that since the plant was extinct in her time, that

meant the Hawthorne women's preservation of it had not survived. One lightning
strike to the glass roof, one flood, and the
plants would die, Faith thought. If it was
at all possible, she was going to preserve
the precious plants. She had spent hours
sewing tiny tubes that would hold the
seeds. On the last day she planned to tie
them in the hair of the three women.

When she left the tower it was nearly
nightfall and the woods were growing dark.
As she walked quickly down the path, Faith
looked from right to left, remembering the
shadow she'd seen on the way in. She
was almost to the gate when she stopped.
Hadn't that shadow been where she'd seen
the poisonous mushrooms? When Eddie
was alive and they'd spent their days reading about herbs, he'd made jokes about
that brilliant red mushroom. In the sixties
and seventies, the hippies made psyche-
delic drugs from it.

She was musing on this when it occurred to her that wanting to get high was
not just a modern desire. She overcame
her fears of whatever was lurking in the
woods, turned off the trail, and went into
the darkening forest to look for the mush-

methods allow business to lower costs and, theoretically, pass on the benefits to the consumer. Increased profits from productivity gains also allow for new investment, which, in turn, triggers new growth industries.[8]

The popular sector groups reject this narrow, conventional view of economic growth. They believe it has little to do with economic reality and is unacceptable as social policy. What is the worth of economic logic which only acknowledges that, in the words of the Vanier Institute brief, "production is performed solely by firms rather than households and community groups"? When a company invests, the economy, as measured by the gross national product (GNP), grows. When a household invests, it is regarded as a consumer expenditure and its productivity activity goes unrecognized. Economics based on accounting principles are unreliable in telling us what a real rise of productivity means and are even more subject to error in explaining the alleged slowdown in productivity growth. In an economy that increasingly consists of services rather than goods, the concept of productivity systematically underestimates real productivity growth. A growing number of economists are openly skeptical about the recent figures indicating Canada's supposedly poor productivity performance.

It is not hard to understand why business has used the "quest for productivity" as the reason for reducing the number of jobs, intensifying the work process and/or replacing full-time workers with a part-time work force. As Mel Watkins says in *The People's Report* (an inquiry into the B.C. government's program of budgetary restraint), this neo-conservative view "will cause people to lose their jobs and others to fear that they will, thereby destroying consumer confidence, lessening consumer spending and creating an environment inimical to new business investment."[9] A recovery doesn't come from laying people off, but, in the words of one B.C. resident who appeared before the B.C. People's Commission, "only by putting them back to work."

The fundamental difficulty with business's view is that Canada's productivity slowdown can't be explained in terms of soaring labour costs. We must look elsewhere. For every dollar companies pay out in labour costs, they spend three dollars on materials. Since the 1970s, studies have shown that how management organizes work is a key factor in the hunt for greater efficiency. It is estimated that under a conventional factory management system, three-quarters of production time is spent transporting materials between work stations. New management techniques can slash the time spent handling materials so that the majority of an operator's shift can be used in machining and assembly. Finally, in North America, 30 to 40 cents is now spent each year to maintain every dollar of inventory.[10]

Business continues to minimize the influence of high levels of foreign ownership on Canada's potential for growth through productivity increases. Branch plants may not be cost-efficient, but they can be profitable nonetheless because of pricing agreements with their parent companies. In an economy dominated by branch plants, productivity is going to rise more slowly than economic models based on competitive market forces predict.

In any event, so-called gains often turn out to be illusory. One of the largest gains in productivity ever experienced in Canada came in 1983, in the midst of the worst recession since the 1930s and despite minimal growth in GNP, double-digit unemployment and the prevalence of plants operating at 70 per cent of capacity! In this instance, business's productivity increases are simply the result of cutting the size of their work force and reducing labour costs and benefits.[11]

In arguing that labour restrains Canadian productivity, the corporate sector — and the neo-classical economists hired by the Macdonald Commission — point in particular to Canadian labour costs being out of line with those in the U.S. The nub of the issue is that "because of the greater increase in costs in Canada since the 1970s than in the U.S., manufacturers in Canada have been unable to fully pass along these greater increases to consumers without losing market shares domestically, internationally, or both."[12] Even if we accept the view that labour costs are a causal factor, this view errs by overlooking the fact that for almost the entire postwar period, Canada has had a lower wage structure in manufacturing than the U.S. and that in recent times fluctuating currency rates have often given Canadian producers a distinct selling advantage (Table I-2). With a cheap dollar and labour's income declining every year since 1980, Canadian capital can hardly blame soaring wage costs for its sluggish performance. From an international perspective, Canadian wages were declining even in the late 1970s. Of ten industrialized countries, Canada recorded the smallest increase in hourly wages between 1975 and 1980. American wages in manufacturing rose 56.2 per cent, compared with 48.3 per cent in Canada. In Japan they rose by 92.8 per cent, Belgium 99.7 per cent, France 104.3 per cent, West Germany 91.3 per cent, Italy 93.8 per cent, Holland 84.5 per cent, Sweden 75.5 per cent, and Great Britain 116.2 per cent.[13]

Beyond all this, a high level of capital investment in manufacturing shows that Canada has been considered to be a productive place to invest. Throughout the postwar period, Canada has had more capital invested in machinery and equipment on a per capita basis than the U.S.[14]

On the face of it, given plenty of capital, a lower wage structure and a better record in productivity growth per person employed than in the U.S., over time Canadian industry should have become cost-competitive.

Business had nothing new to tell the Macdonald Commission on this crucial question. Indeed, much of what it did say obscured the real reasons for the long-term decline of Canadian industries, which is more

rooms. She'd knocked down all of them she'd seen but she could have missed some.

Within minutes, she saw that she'd missed several of them and that someone had taken the trouble to hide them under leaves. There was one freshly broken stem in the earth, showing that within the last hour or so, someone had broken off one of the poisonous mushrooms.

Annoyed, Faith stood up and destroyed the rest of them, but it looked as though someone were using them. For what? A trip?

Her head came up as she looked back toward the trail. People did things on drug trips that they didn't usually do in life. Sometimes it was silly; sometimes it was violent.

"Tristan," Faith said out loud. In the last weeks Amy had lost weight, had pretty much given up sleep, as she tried to figure out who hated Tristan enough to kill him. What if no one hated him? What if someone on a drug trip went berserk and stabbed him?

For a full minute, Faith's mind's eye could see the inside of the orangery. Tristan's big

TABLE 1-2
Average Rates of Change in Canadian and American Labour Costs in American Dollars
(per cent)

	1960-73	1973-83	1973-80	1981	1982	1983
United States	1.9	7.2	7.6	6.1	6.6	-0.8
Canada	1.9	6.9	6.4	10.9	10.2	0.5

Source: U.S. Department of Labour Statistics, *News*, December 31, 1984. Adapted from Table 1.

due to the wastefulness and inefficiency of private enterprise than to any other one factor.

The Manitoba Political Economy Group (chapter 3) adds up the costs of "the waste burden" — including idle labour and productive capacity, speculative investment and labour-management strife — and arrives at a 40 per cent loss in potential GNP. A clear-eyed explanation of decline must begin with the recognition that assertions of the conventional supply-demand model of modern economic theory aren't very useful in understanding the vicious circle of slow growth, rising unemployment and the weak performance of Canadian manufacturing.

Popular sector groups appearing before the commission presented the basic elements of an alternative view of Canada's productivity crisis that shed light on the way markets work in Canada and the economic behaviour of business.

First, a large part of the productivity gap between Canada and the United States is due directly to the weak link between Canada's mass production industries and mass consumption. Because Canada tends to import mass consumer goods rather than manufacture them, Canadian industry is not able to develop sufficient economies of scale.[15]

Second, slow growth is directly tied to idle plant capacity.[16] Since the branch plants are not aggressively seeking export markets, Canada's reduced share of world trade has held back capacity utilization rates and not led to a significant reduction of production costs on a per unit basis.

Third, many of Canada's problems stem from the nature of investment in manufacturing noted above. By the 1970s, Canada had one of the most capital-intensive manufacturing sectors of any nation. This was due "to past corporate tax incentives (such as fast write-offs of capital assets through depreciation allowances), and tax encouragements to personal savings."[17] Business invested because it was a quick way to improve corporate balance sheets, not because it cut production costs. Despite the presence of what has been called "the most generous tax and subsidization system available to the private sector in the

bed had been moved in there that morning. Amy had posted guards at the entrances to the walled garden, but their instructions were to allow no strangers in. She'd even shown them how to search people to make sure they carried no knives.

Zoë had laughed at Amy for her paranoia, but now Faith seemed able to see it all. It wouldn't be an enemy who killed Tristan, it was someone he knew, someone who thought it was fun to eat a bit of a poisonous mushroom and feel like he was flying or . . .

Faith didn't take time to think any more. She'd left her big knife on top of the cabinet nearest Tristan's bed. She grabbed her skirt up to her knees and took off running as fast as she could. As she ran, cursing her out-of-shape body, she wanted to hit herself for not listening to Amy, not paying attention to her. Faith had been so wrapped up in her own problems that she'd left Amy alone. She and Zoë might as well not have come to the eighteenth century for all that they'd helped Amy.

When Faith could see the walled garden, she ran even faster. Her lungs were about to burst, but she didn't slow down.

When she was still a hundred yards from the gate, she saw William saunter outside the wall.

Faith didn't know how else to get his attention but to scream at the top of her lungs.

William turned and started toward her. Faith didn't slow down but dropped her skirt and waved at William to go back. "Tristan!" she yelled, then tripped on her skirt and fell flat on her face. As she was trying to get up, she looked up at William and saw that he understood.

With all the energy he had, he hobbled back between the gates on his canes and out of sight. Faith got off the ground and started running again.

There were three people in the walled garden when she ran through. They were all trusted employees and were resting from having moved furniture for Tristan into the orangery. He's not here, Faith thought. Tristan isn't here yet. She was relieved, but she didn't slow down. The people in the garden stopped to look at her as she sped past them and into the orangery.

What she saw inside made her halt in terror. She could see the bottom half of

Tristan lying on the bed. In front of him was the young woman who brought Faith herbs twice a day. William's frail body was behind her, his thin arms around her shoulders. When he heard Faith enter, he turned the girl. Faith's largest knife was dangling from the fingertips of her right hand, and her eyes had the wild look of someone who had just taken a hallucinogenic.

Behind them Tristan, eyes open, was lying on the bed in absolute stillness.

Faith put her hand to her mouth. "He—"

William, still tightly holding the girl to him, moved aside and Faith saw Tristan. His eyes were open and, best of all, there was no blood on him.

Faith ran to him. "Are you all right?" Her hands were running over his chest, down his legs. "Did she hurt you?"

"I am fine," he said, looking a bit dazed. "I fell asleep. The sun and . . ." He waved his hand about the beautiful room, then looked at his uncle. "What is wrong with her? She looks mad."

Faith stood up and looked at the girl William was holding, his face white from the exertion. She took the knife out of the girl's hand.

Western World,"[18] Canada's expenditures on research and development have been declining for more than a decade and have failed to reach the modest goal of 1.5 per cent of GNP that the government committed itself to at the commencement of the decline. Not having our own capacity to innovate does much to explain Canada's lower productivity performance.

Finally, a large chunk of Canada's productivity problems have been incurred by what Thomas Maxwell, chief economist for the Conference Board, one of Canada's major business organizations, calls the poor use of "non-productive capital investment" by Canadian business, the most important being the quality of management. According to Maxwell, "faults attributed to Canadian management include preoccupation with short-term financial gains, lack of concern for productivity in the workplace and a failure to create an environment in which non-management ideas are welcome. These management problems are said to account for almost half of the productivity decline experienced by Canada recently."[19]

Beyond all this, the popular sector groups point to the waste of "paper entrepreneurialism" and a growing body of literature showing that productivity is driven down by labour-management antagonism, but (echoing Maxwell) enhanced when workers are allowed input.

Free Trade

Powerful groups such as the Business Council on National Issues and the Canadian Manufacturers' Association have assessed the structural problems of the economy and are convinced that the only solution is a policy of free trade with the U.S. Their statements give the appearance of business unanimity. The free-traders have used their clout and access to the commissioners to convince them of the validity and reliability of their beliefs. Whether it be called trade enhancement, trade liberalization or assured access to the U.S. market, the free-traders have collected powerful allies. One is the national business press. For instance, Ronald Anderson, one of free trade's frontline crusaders, heads his *Report on Business* column with headlines such as "The exposure to free trade is manageable for Canada" or "Economic union with U.S. becoming more acceptable."[20] Day in and day out, his theme never varies: It is not inevitable that the country would be destroyed should Canada enter into a common-market type of relationship with the U.S.

Ironically, perhaps, one of the loudest and most persistent allies of free trade has been Donald Macdonald himself. Before the commission had even finished its hearings, he told an audience in the U.S. that he was now committed to a comprehensive free trade agreement. Macdonald said that this would require a "leap of faith" but would be good for Canada.[21] His action of publicly committing his commission to this option before it had even finished its fact-finding is without precedent — analogous to a judge commenting on the merits of a case before all the evidence is heard. Surprisingly, no one in the media or Parliament, nor any of his fellow commissioners, called for Macdonald's resignation.

Essentially, the free trade argument holds that with access to the larger U.S. market, Canadian industry will finally develop economies of scale and a satisfactory level of productivity and competitiveness. Though there will be some "loser" industries, Canada will be a net winner in the continental market, creating a higher standard of living and a rising level of real GNP. By abandoning those products in which Canada has no comparative advantage, we will be able to acquire them at less cost by importing from the U.S. This basic reasoning has inspired various claims regarding the benefits of free trade. These deserve closer scrutiny.

The economic case for free trade that corporate Canada made to Macdonald was derived from econometric models originally developed some fifteen years ago by Paul and R.J. Wonnacott and periodically updated by other neo-classical economists. These models claim that gains in productivity from across-the-board free trade would lead to between an 8 and 13 per cent increase in Canada's GNP.

The prognosis is mere conjecture. As Mel Watkins has observed, these models "pretend that economics is a science with laws we must heed. In fact, the present state of economics, like the present state of the economy, is one of disarray; it does not permit anyone to speak with certainty."[22] Any up-to-date economist knows that the Wonnacotts' work has an essential flaw: it is based on a static model that has little ability to determine the future impact of technology on production costs.[23]

The simple truth is that economists don't know in real terms how much Canada stands to benefit from closer ties with the U.S.[24] It is clear, however, what we have to lose. In his testimony before the Senate Committee hearings into free trade, David Dodge, a senior government economist, painted a revealing picture of the potential winners and losers. He put such industries as mining, smelting, ferrous and non-ferrous metal, lumber and plywood, pulp and paper, electrical and communications equipment, glass, nonmetallic minerals, fertilizers and some chemicals in the winners' column. Among the losers were: food processing, beverages, tobacco, textiles and cloth, some metal fabricating, household appliances, hardware and tools, aircraft, motor vehicles, paints and household cosmetics. Contrary to the predictions of Canada's orthodox free-traders, many of the losers would be in manufacturing, while most of the winners would be in resource-based industries where Canada already has a comparative advantage.[25]

In manufacturing, tariff walls, debated in Canada since the National Policy, have acquired an almost mythological reputation as the impediment to efficiency and competitiveness. In fact, tariffs have been falling during the last three decades and, as Fred Lazar shows in *The New Protectionism*, they are less important to Canada's trade perform-

"I think someone has fed her a mush-room that's made her temporarily crazy," she said as she pulled the girl out of William's arms.

"But why?" Tristan asked.

"My guess is sex," Faith said. "Some-one found out about a certain mushroom's ability to get rid of a girl's inhibitions."

William and Tristan were looking at her in puzzlement. "You know," Faith said, "candy is dandy, but liquor is quicker?"

That made the men nod in understand-ing. Faith led the girl to the door and called to Thomas to come and get her.

"Take her into the house and keep her in a room until her reason returns," she told him. "Don't hurt her and don't let her hurt herself."

In the next minute Amy came up on Tristan's big black horse, jumped to the ground, and pushed past Faith to get to Tristan. As soon as she saw him as he had been in her dream, wearing the same clothes, on the same bed, with the windows behind him, she burst into loud tears.

"I knew it all. It was all in my head," she said, crying copiously and holding on to Tristan's hands as he sat on the edge of

ance than changes in production technologies.[26] Moreover, by 1987, under arrangements already in place, roughly 85 per cent of trade between Canada and the U.S. will be tariff-free.

As the title of Lazar's book suggests, protectionism is not becoming extinct. Rather it is taking new forms. In the past, the erection of tariffs was the way to industrialize. It was axiomatic that "protectionism was the key to any attempt to change a country's position in the world economy, be it capitalist, socialist, or reactionary. Protectionism opens the economic space for choice, the necessary but not sufficient conditions for change."[27] The debate about free trade is no longer about tariffs per se but about a variety of "non-tariff barriers," including customs barriers, anti-dumping legislation, and subsidies that nations erect to protect their home industries. The United States is no exception. Even when there are no official tariffs, protectionism remains in one guise or another. This fact is reflected in the increase in trade restrictions among Organization for Economic Cooperation and Development (OECD) countries — from 36 per cent to 44 per cent since 1974.[28]

For the rest of this century, international trade is going to have less and less to do with "free trade" and market prices and more and more to do with neo-mercantilist bilateral trading agreements between nations or blocs of nations. Governments are needed to negotiate the terms of trade, because, in the words of Bennett Harrison, "we're in a new world. We didn't make it neo-mercantilist: it is neo-mercantilist." If the Canadian government does not know how to play according to the new rules, a lot of Canadian firms will fail.

Even if the network of American nontariff barriers proves surmountable, there simply aren't many Canadian firms that can benefit from free trade. Of the 110 firms in Canada with sales in excess of $400 million, only 25 to 50 are Canadian controlled.[29] As the CIEP brief on free trade (chapter 12) points out, "It is Alice-in-Wonderland economics to expect branch plants in Canada to compete with their parent companies in the United States."

Free trade would involve a heavier cost for Canada than the U.S. because Canadian firms would be more dependent on the American market than American firms would be on the Canadian market. Fewer than 5 per cent of Canadian firms have the capacity to export.[30] By comparison, in the U.S. at least 10 per cent have sufficient knowledge, finances and products to risk selling abroad. In Canada's branch-plant economy, the figure is dramatically less. It is estimated that more than 80 per cent of Canadian firms are not in a position to expand their operations in any circumstances.

For the most part, Canadian small business lacks the resources and know-how to be export-oriented. Sixty per cent of small businesses are in the service or service-related sector — which is not subject to international competition — while only 8 per cent are in manufacturing.

the bed. "I didn't put it together. In the dream I saw you and I saw the men around you. I even saw Beth. This place is so different from my dream that I thought you'd be safe. And you were so well guarded. You—"

"Amy," Tristan said as he pulled her up from the floor.

William put his arm around Faith's shoulders and led her outside. "How did you know?"

"The mushrooms," Faith said. "I saw them by the tower, but in my vanity I thought no one but I knew what they could do. Amy begged us to help her with Tristan, but I paid no attention to her. But if I hadn't come back with her, and if I hadn't taken you from that room, Tristan would have died."

"Sssssh," William said and pulled her into his arms so she could cry on his shoulder. "It has worked out as it should. It is his destiny to live."

"Yes," Faith said against his shoulder. "Maybe Tristan's destiny is back on its rails again." She smiled when William looked at her in question. "It doesn't matter. Tristan is safe now." Behind them, they could hear

Amy and Tristan talking quietly inside the orangery.

"What say you that we spend tonight in the house?" William said.

"Yes," Faith said. "I think we should. Let them have their time alone. But I'm going to send them a huge supper. Amy needs to eat."

William laughed. "I think you would like to feed the world. Tell me, in your time, do they still have poverty?"

"I have no idea what you mean by 'my time,'" she said with all the innocence she could muster. "I grew up in . . ."

"Quick!" William said. "Give me the name of an English county."

"California," Faith said. She looked around them and they were in the parkland that had been designed by Capability Brown. In just a very short time, she'd never again see this place, this time, or these people.

She looked at William. He was still many pounds under what he should weigh and there were still circles under his eyes, but he was freshly shaven and his shirt was so white it sparkled.

"Ah," he said, "I have seen that look before, but thought never to see it again."

"Do stop talking," she said.

He put his arms around her and kissed her, then held her against him. "I might not have the strength to . . ."

"That's okay, Faith said. "I'm good on top."

He laughed and they walked to the house hand in hand.

It is likely that as many as three-quarters of the firms established since 1975 are geared to the domestic and local markets. They are small, labour intensive and often undercapitalized. The vast majority have sales of under $250,000 annually. Their failure rate is so high that the actual number of new businesses is increasing only marginally.[31]

In the goods-producing side of small business, most plants are little more than assembly operations, with an average of less than twenty employees and with limited market growth potential. In the face of growing competition from the U.S., these companies have enough trouble staying in business in Canada, let alone expanding into the U.S. market. Unless the government has an industrial strategy to assist small firms and protect Canada's economic space, many of these firms won't be in business. Trade liberalization precludes this kind of government assistance.

Given the above, it is no surprise, despite what the spokespersons for business told the Macdonald Commission, that there is no viable consensus on free trade in the business community. A nation-wide survey of Canadian Manufacturers' Association members asked the question "What would be the net impact on your company of Canada/U.S. free trade?" Out of a thousand replies, only one-third expected to expand, one-third expected to contract and another third expected no change.

Free trade is also touted as the tonic to bring labour costs in line. We saw above the weakness of the argument that Canadian labour is not productive enough. Recent figures show Canada's overall cost structure to be competitive with western European economies and that productivity growth has begun to recover since the darkest days of the 1981-83 recession (see Table I-3). The question that the free-traders can't answer is: Why does Canadian business need guaranteed access to the American market? Why can't it compete like the French, the Germans and the Italians, who sell their industrial products in the U.S. despite American tariffs, transport costs, and the high wage structure of most European industrial economies?

Another refrain of free trade advocates is that Canada is a protectionist country in a free trade world. The success of the European Economic Community (EEC) is often held up to illustrate the benefits of liberalized trade relations. What the EEC example probably illustrates better is that free trade is never an end in itself. For the EEC it was only one initiative among others to make the strong industrial economies of western Europe more powerful and more efficient. A critical element was agreement on a common monetary system setting exchange rates to reduce fluctuations that distort trade and/or prevent workers from bargaining for better wages and a higher standard of living.

The success of the overall EEC program is due to the institutional framework that brought about adjustment and harmonization of poli-

TABLE I-3
Manufacturing Productivity of Leading
Industrial Countries, 1977-82

Country	1982 Output per Hour of Work (1975 prices)	Rate of Growth 1977-82 (%)
United States	$11.20	0.6
Canada	10.21	-0.3
Germany	12.39	2.1
France	11.96	3.0
Italy	11.29	3.6
Japan	10.63	3.4
U.K.	6.85	2.7

Source: DRI, *Report on U.S. Manufacturing Industries*, 1984.

cies among members. The institutional agreements all needed escape clauses allowing a country the right to opt out or adopt contingency measures to protect an industry or industries in times of national need.

As for trade barriers, various forms of protectionism continue to exist in the EEC because its members recognize that a country's ability to set policies in its own interests is indispensable to sovereignty. Within the EEC, market protectionist measures have risen from 20 to 30 per cent of the total of manufactured goods imported from 1981 to 1984.

Even if the EEC were a sort of free trade nirvana, a model involving ten partners obviously cannot be applied to the relations of two unequal partners. Indeed, a European-style common-market arrangement is the worst possible model for Canada. A full or even partial common-market agreement is next to impossible to create between a strong dominant partner and a much weaker associate with an open economy that is, despite business's claims, vulnerable to external pressures. As the Quebec Teachers Federation (chapter 11) drily notes, "In a match where one contestant outweighs the other ten to one, the outcome is easy to predict."

If the European Community is not quite the model of free trade that some free-traders make it out to be, what of the charge that Canada is clinging to narrow nationalistic protectionism while the U.S. is, by temperament and tradition, committed to the goal of free trade?

We mentioned above that the U.S., like other trading nations, has a range of nontariff barriers designed to keep out imports and protect domestic industry. The fact is that protectionism is deeply rooted in U.S. legislative and political life.[32] The U.S. Congress's enormous power over foreign commerce comes from three umbrella-like statutes that provide the authority to impose countervailing duties, to initiate anti-

Twenty-three

Just as they had dreaded, one moment they were in the eighteenth century and the next they were in Madame Zoya's sun-room. Instantly, Zoë started crying.

"I was afraid of that," the woman said. "It often happens when people want to go far back in time."

"I'll never see him again," Zoë said. "He's dead. Dead hundreds of years ago."

Madame Zoya looked at Faith and Amy. "Was it a success for you two?"

Faith's hands went to her hair and her face lit up. "Oh yes!" she said. "A great, overwhelming success. Nothing in my life has happened to equal what I learned and saw in these last weeks."

"You didn't have to leave anyone behind," Zoë said. She pulled two tissues out of the box on Madame Zoya's desk and blew her nose.

"Have you two decided when you want to go back to?"

"I have a question," Faith said. "When we went back in time we arrived there wearing clothes of that time. I want to know if we can go back in our own time and keep these clothes on."

"What does that matter?" Zoë asked, tears on her cheeks.

"Pockets," Amy said dully. "She wants to return with her pockets full." She wasn't crying, but the thought of never again seeing Tristan and Beth and the whole estate was weighing her down.

"You want to take money back with you?" Madame Zoya asked, her tone letting them know what she thought about that. "I don't think that—"

"I want to take seeds," Faith said as she ran her fingers through her hair and pulled out long, thin tubes of cloth. Her precious seeds were inside. "I want to take some very special seeds back with me."

"Ah," Madame Zoya said. "Seeds. And how special are these seeds?"

"They are from a plant that is extinct today."

"It's a plant that's in the Bible," Amy said, pulling tubes from her hair. Faith had intertwined them in her and Zoë's hair on their twenty-first day in the eighteenth century.

"Interesting," Madame Zoya said. "Would you two like to go back now or would you like twenty-four hours to recover?" She glanced at Zoë who was still crying.

"I'd like some time to think," Faith said as she put her hand over Zoë's.

"All right," Madame Zoya said. "I will see you two tomorrow at two o'clock."

They left Madame Zoya's house, went outside and walked to the main street. For several long minutes they stood there looking about them at the paved road, at the cars whizzing by, at the women wearing trousers and makeup, and the buildings with their big glass windows.

"It's another world," Faith said. "I—" She

didn't know how to tell the others that she wanted to be alone. She needed some time to think about where she'd been and what she'd done. And she wanted to think about where she was going tomorrow. Did she really want to do her life over? She had some decisions to make, and she wanted to make them without hearing the opinions of others.

"I'll see you two back at the house at about seven," Amy said, then she turned down the street, away from them.

"She wants to see what the books say her lover boy did after she left," Zoë said, as she blew her nose.

"And wouldn't you like to know what Russell did?" Faith asked. "Maybe you can't have him in the flesh, but you can read about him."

Zoë looked at her suspiciously. "What I want to know is where you disappeared to for those last two days."

"Zoë, darling, I've heard that every generation thinks it created sex, but it's not true. Now dry your eyes, dear, and go find out about your boyfriend."

With that, Faith turned and went down

dumping legislation, and/or to make use of an escape clause mechanism exempting specific American industries from existing trade agreements when Congress decides that they are in economic trouble or when it is in American military interest to do so. Since 1980, effective protection of the American domestic market from imported manufactured goods has risen from 20 to 30 per cent.[33] Canada has no equivalent tradition, and the House of Commons has no equivalent statutory authority. A recent report by the U.S. Trade Commission described Canada as "the least interventionist of the countries it has examined on industrial targeting."[34] It said that Ottawa's role falls far short of the kind of government support that Mexico, South Korea and Brazil give in protecting and subsidizing their auto and auto parts industries.

While free-traders may promise jobs, the whole point of trade liberalization is not to increase employment but to enhance the efficiency and profitability of individual companies.[35] As in the recent past, exporting firms won't necessarily be selling more timber, base metals or whatever to the U.S. but, given the cheaper Canadian dollar, they will see bigger profits when they convert their American receipts into Canadian dollars. Even business economists are skeptical about the alleged resulting good. In the words of Donald Daley, a specialist in free trade questions, "the exchange rate changes have not led to any fundamental correction of the deep-seated and continuing comparative disadvantage of Canadian manufacturing."[36]

Looking at the claims made for the free trade panacea alongside a prognosis actually based on the facts, the inevitable conclusion is that a free trade agreement is going to undermine Canada's economic space further without offering any political and economic advantages in return. With both economies growing at a snail's pace and a combined import/export trade approaching $125 billion, one has to ask how much more Canada-U.S. trade is possible. Even R.J. Wonnacott, the current ideological godfather of free trade, has recently admitted that for the Americans, measured in terms of their huge GNP, the net economic gains would not be large.[37] Given such circumstances, Canada can ill-afford to become more beholden to American policies and more reliant on the U.S. markets.

Under a free trade arrangement, Canada gives up the world for the right to be inside the American protectionist wall. Free trade is not an expression of nationalism, nor of internationalism, to cite yet another virtue claimed by partisans. Rather it is pure and simple continentalism. What proponents don't acknowledge is that free trade is only a code word for continental integration, the preferred solution of most of Canada's economic elite. This would mean aligning Canadian economic policy with the American, and reducing the sovereignty of Canada's Parliament over such matters as taxes, social benefits and industrial incentives. These would be decided by intergovernmental agreements or left alone to be determined by market forces.

Even though the facts didn't fit and the economic theorizing was little more than conjecture, business and the commission's economists were able to convince Macdonald to announce support for the free trade policy option. Their ace-in-the-hole was that free trade was preferable to a return in any form to protectionism. Despite the fact that we are now in a new protectionist era of nontariff barriers, the options were reduced to a simple choice between free trade and protectionism; the real issue — whether a country like Canada is determined to control its economic space and protect itself against sudden harm — was avoided. The present crisis has amply shown that a country that does not have its own industrial base and its own economic space is forced to accept the economic policies imposed on it by others: deflation, deindustrialization and social cutbacks. Since every country has in its economic and social structures a certain built-in level of informal protectionism, the strategic issue is the appropriate industrial policy and how effectively the state addresses the real problems posed by the power of the multinationals to shift production to wherever it is most advantageous to them. In an age where business knows no boundaries, the free market does not exist. What does exist, as the United Auto Workers' (UAW) brief (chapter 2) explains so succinctly, is the power of the multinationals to do generally as they wish.

Banking on the U.S.

The push towards trade liberalization comes from Canada's largest corporate giants. Their gamble rests on two assumptions: that the American economy is strong enough to support a Canadian recovery and that Canada won't be hurt by increased dependence on the U.S. In the preceding paragraphs we've seen that the latter assumption is on very shaky ground. The former misses the changed state of bilateral economic relations. Under the postwar system of economic regulation, Canada became more developed and more dependent, though not in equal proportions. When the economy faltered, the state looked to a leaner and meaner version of staple-led growth to get the economy back on track. This meant more foreign ownership to stimulate the economy, a tough, restrictive system of industrial relations and, until 1970, industrial wage levels well below those in the U.S. In the 1980s, wrinkles are appearing in the relationship between Canada and the U.S. With the decline of mass production industries on both sides of the border, Canada and the U.S. are on a collision course as each country seeks to protect its standard of living and increase exports to the other.

The repercussions of these circumstances have yet to be acknowledged by Canadian business, and the Macdonald Commission's research studies are equally unrealistic about the future of Canadian-American economic relations. Instead of taking a hard look at what is happening to the American economy and its effects on Canada, Canadian businessmen continue to believe that American foreign capital will show enough goodwill to sustain a Canadian recovery, and they hope to ride on the back of the American business cycle as they have in the past. Remarkably, the Macdonald Commission seemed to ignore the vigorous debate about the American economy carried out in the mainstream press and fuelled by such important studies as Bluestone and Harrison's *The De-Industrialization of America*, Piore and Sabel's *The Next Industrial Divide*, Reich's *The Next American Frontier* and Lawrence's *Can America Compete?* The controversy centres on the structural weaknesses of the American economy and the failure of the Reagan administration to address them.

The recent "recovery" of the U.S. economy is illusory.[38] Except for inflation, the economy's performance has been worse under Reagan than under Carter (see Table I-4). Unemployment has risen sharply (almost twice as many jobs were created under Carter than Reagan); interest rates have skyrocketed; individual savings are at an all-time low; the median after-tax income of Americans (measured in 1974 dollars) is lower in 1984 than in 1980; business investment has declined; the budget deficit has grown like topsy; and the percentage of those of the active population living in poverty has increased from 13 per cent in

TABLE I-4
The State of the American Economy under Reagan and Carter

	Carter 1976-80	Reagan 1980-84
No. of jobs created	10.5 million	6.5 million
No. of unemployed	7.6 million	8.5 million (1984)
Rate of inflation	12.4%	4.8% (Sept. 1984)
Four-year average	11.4%	6.5%
Commercial trade	-$24.3 billion	-$130 billion (est.)
Business investment as % of GNP (four-year average)	5.4%	0.2%
Increase in industrial investment in plant and equipment in real terms (four-year average)	28.6%	3.5%
Federal deficit	$50.7 billion	$174.5 billion
Prime interest rate	2.5%	11.5%
Official poverty rate as % of active population	13%	15.2%
Median income after federal taxes in 1974 dollars	$10,282	$10,175

Source: The original table appeared in *Le Monde Diplomatique*, janvier 1985, p. 6, from which the above table was adapted.

1976 to 15.2 per cent in 1984. Fuelled by military spending, the federal budget has grown from 22 per cent of GNP under Carter to a record 24 per cent under Reagan.

In trade, the picture is equally grim for U.S. industries. With the exception of computers, American industries have suffered a dramatic decline in their share of international trade over the last ten years (see Table I-5). In machine tools alone, sales have plummeted from $5.7 billion in 1979 to $1.7 billion in 1984. Imports captured 36 per cent of the domestic market in 1984 (see Table I-6). In terms of new businesses, only 1.5 per cent are in the field of high technology, while the rest have been largely in the service sector.

The ravages of deindustrialization can be seen in changes in the wage and occupational structure of the labour force. "During the last four years alone," writes Barry Bluestone, the co-author of *The De-Industrialization of America*, "twenty of our twenty-five basic manufacturing industries posted declines in total employment during a period that includes a very strong economic recovery. What's more, this loss of production jobs has been going on for fifteen years."[39] Between 1973 and 1980, in household appliances one job in every five had disappeared. The shrinkage of the basic sectors of the American economy has left in its wake thousands of abandoned plants, millions of people without jobs and hundreds of communities without industry. "Overnight, ghost towns are created in one set of communities and boom towns spring up in others."[40]

The deterioration of the traditional industrial base has created a shift to lower-paying jobs within the economy's total job pool. In 1961, six out of ten jobs were in the middle-wage occupations. By 1982, there were only five. The number of production workers had fallen by 7 per

TABLE I-5

American Industrial Decline in the World Economy

(U.S. % share of world trade in industrial end-products)

Sector	1973	1983
World trade in industrial activity	26.1 (1972)	24.4 (1982)
Exports	13.4	12.1
Motor vehicles	31.7 (1972)	19.2 (1982)
Steel	19.6	11.6
Civil aviation	78.3	66.8
Electrical conductors	58.1	55.4
Construction engineering	50.0	30.0

Sources: *U.S. News and World Report* (September 10, 1984) and *Business Week* (September 24, 1984).

the street in the opposite direction of Amy.

❧

Faith didn't get back to Jeanne's summerhouse until nearly nine. She'd spent a lot of time walking and thinking about what her life had been and what she'd been through in the last three weeks. She kept thinking about what Amy had told them that Primrose had said about destiny. If destiny was like a train and it could be derailed, then Faith's train had been pushed into the mud a long time ago.

She tried to boil it down, but it seemed that what she'd learned in the eighteenth century was how important it was to be useful. In a mere three weeks she'd become a person who was needed by others and it had fulfilled some need in her that she hadn't even known was empty.

Zoë had teased Faith about having come out of her depression because she found out that Ty hadn't jilted her, but Faith knew there was more to it than that. All her adult life she'd felt that she'd had a choice between two men and that she'd chosen the wrong one.

What she'd asked herself today was whether either man was right for her. It was easy to say that her mother had forced her into marrying Eddie. And it was easy to blame her mother-in-law for all the misery in her marriage, but what part had Faith played in it all? She liked to think of herself as an innocent bystander, but she hadn't been.

By the time she got back to the summer-house, she was glad to see that the lights were off. She was afraid that Amy and Zoë would be up with a bottle of wine and wanting to spend the night talking.

Instead, there was a note from Amy on the breakfast table saying that she and Zoë had gone to bed, hope she didn't mind.

"Ready?" Madame Zoya asked Faith and Zoë the next afternoon.

"Yes," Faith said. Her hand was on the seed capsules in her pocket, and she'd given Madame Zoya three capsules. It was the least she could do.

"I'll see you two tomorrow," Amy said when they left the house. "I'll make us a nice dinner and you'll tell me everything that happened in your new lives."

All morning they'd talked about the idea that if they went years back into their pasts then when they returned their entire lives would be different. Amy said that if Faith went back and married Tyler, then lived a new life, maybe when she returned she'd have children at home waiting for her.

Faith hadn't replied because she had some other ideas about what she'd like to do with her life.

As for Zoë, she made it clear she didn't have much hope. She said she'd run away from her hometown and avoid the car crash, but then what? Whatever she'd done would still be there. "And Russell wouldn't be," she said.

Amy didn't say anything. She'd been so tired yesterday that she'd slept all afternoon and through the night. For the first time in weeks she'd been able to relax because Tristan was safe. As far as she could tell, saving him hadn't changed her life at all. She'd called home, listened to the same message in Stephen's voice saying that Amy and their two sons were out, please leave a message. It was all exactly the same now, but today she hoped to search the Internet to find that Tristan or his descendants had done something great.

Whatever she found out, she was determined to be cheerful and not let Faith and Zoë see her true feelings.

"And when we return, you can tell us about Tristan," Faith said.

"I will," Amy said, but she had volunteered no other information. She closed the door behind them.

"Is it me or do you think that under her fake cheeriness she looked disappointed?" Zoë asked.

"I think she has to be going through a bad time. She was in love with Tristan and she had to leave him. That must have hurt."

"What I want to know is what the two of them did those last two days. I know you were in bed with William. I just hope you didn't kill him."

"He managed to live," Faith said dryly. She was glad to see that Zoë hadn't put on her dark makeup again. Now she looked like a pretty young woman who wanted to live.

"And I—" Zoë looked into the distance.

"Zoë," Faith said as she put her hand on her arm.

TABLE I-6
Growth of Import Penetration of the American Economy

(foreign sales as % of domestic consumption)

Sector	1974	1983
Shoes	24	46
Clothing[1]	8	22
Television[1]	10	40
Steel[1]	10	25.4
Cars[1]	16.1	27.8 (1982)
Machine tools	13	36
Textiles[1]	15	31
Wood products	12	40
High technology	—	16 (1984)

[1] Products benefitting from some form of protection.

Source: Marie-France Toinet, "Les risques de la seconde phase reaganienne," *Le Monde Diplomatique*, janvier 1985. Toinet has drawn this data from a variety of American sources.

cent. And those who lost better-paying jobs but were able to find new employment took an average drop in pay of 30 per cent. Bluestone and Harrison call this phenomenon "occupational skidding": workers lose their jobs in the mass production industries and then are reabsorbed into the economy as part of a rapidly growing low-wage labour pool.[41]

According to leading American economists such as Lester Thurow, the "recovery" is based largely on military spending and on the creation of small, short-lived, labour-intensive firms in the field of business and personal services. But the real strength of the "recovery" is also due, paradoxically, to the fact that both U.S. business in particular and American society in general are grossly undertaxed. The combined effect of tax cuts, a drastic decline in personal savings and business savings and unpaid bills from the Vietnam War has pushed the American deficit to record levels. With its sky-high interest rates, the U.S. is racking up foreign debt at the rate of $2 billion (U.S.) a week to finance a recovery which, when it falters, economists now believe could result in financial havoc. Essentially, the rest of the world is financing the American recovery. The U.S. has become a debtor nation, and the burden could soar to one trillion dollars by the end of the decade.[42] The deficit is currently growing at such a pace that the outflow of interest and dividends will be greater than the backflow of profits generated by American investments abroad. This can only increase the need for foreign borrowing.

Unlike Canadian business, which sees the American economy on the road to a strong recovery, many American economists are not seduced by the massive inflow of foreign capital. They believe that relatively little of this capital is being put to good use. (Only about a third is going into productive investment.) The other fear shared by a growing number of American economists is that imbalances in the system will cause the American dollar to plunge, leaving Americans to service this debt with a reduction in their domestic standard of living under conditions of inflation and recession.

The question one must ask is how is Canada, with its weaker economy, going to cope with the massive changes that are radically transforming the economy of its largest trading partner. Canada doesn't have an arms industry capable of pulling the Canadian economy out of the doldrums. Nor can Ottawa cut business taxes by 30 per cent and expect the rest of the world to finance Canada's capital needs.

Rather than face the realities of the U.S. economy, Canadian conservatives are inclined to look to the U.S. as their model for tough new policies to promote economic growth. The preferred solution of business is to build a strong recovery by cutting wage costs, forcing down the price of labour through institutional means such as radical changes to the labour market and restrictive labour practices. In this crucial area, Canadian business objectives are mirror images of Reagan's.

What makes Canada so vulnerable is that the shift from a high- to a low-wage economy is occurring much faster south of the border, where unions have been routed and business, with the support of government, has been able to push down rates faster than in Canada. The danger, especially in a more continental economy, is that Canadian wages will follow the stateside trend, and/or investment in Canada will decline.

The popular sector briefs explain that in the race to become competitive, labour markets have become industrial war zones, on both sides of the border, as workers are forced to compete against each other to protect their collective-bargaining rights. They also outline why the pool of better-paying, secure, skilled jobs is shrinking and will continue to shrink for the rest of this decade. By 1990, if not sooner, Canadian economists are predicting that we shall have an enormous number of young people "with no significant experience with steady work or employment."[43] In short, the popular sector makes it clear that in place of a job-oriented society, Canada and the U.S. are building unemployment economies.

III: The Popular Sector Consensus

For the popular sector it is not productivity, nor the lack of a "sunny" climate for investment, that is Canada's number one problem. It is the growth of the unemployment economy — which also serves as the most visible symptom of the bankruptcy of government policy.

Government and business rarely acknowledge the full dimensions of the employment crisis (outlined in Table I-1). "Official" unemployment stands at more than 11 per cent, but as the Toronto Social Planning Council indicates in chapter 1, this figure excludes the underemployed, the part-time worker, the involuntary part-time worker, those working in the informal economy, those forced to work a shorter work week, and those who are working only because the government is subsidizing part of their salary by paying employers to create jobs. If the people who are encouraged to take early retirement, unpaid workers in the home and job seekers who have given up looking are all added to official figures, the rate of all forms of unemployment and underemployment is closer to 25 or even 30 per cent of the potential work force. The resulting toll in the mental health of Canadians is nothing short of a national tragedy (see, in particular, chapters 3 and 7). Unless an innovative response to the sweeping changes in Canada's labour markets can be found, we face a future characterized by an army of unemployed, no job security for a majority of the population, and a virtual absence of permanent jobs in many communities. The traditional working class will be no more than a privileged minority, while the rest of the work force will be engaged in part-time, casual and temporary labour. In the stark vision of André Gorz,

> any employment [will] be accidental and provisional, every type of work purely contingent. [The neo-proletariat] cannot feel any involvement with "its" work or identification with "its" job. Work no longer signifies an activity or even a major occupation; it is merely a blank interval on the margins of life, to be endured in order to earn a little money.[44]

Technology may transform not only the nature of jobs, but also labour's means of resistance. With the microchip revolution letting management split up their work force and contract out work, the Ontario Public Service Employees Union (chapter 13) asks, "How do you call a union meeting of workers who never meet and have no opportunity of seeing or talking to each other?"

Industrial Policy

A key theme of the popular sector briefs is that Canada should be pursuing a coherent industrial strategy to create jobs rather than putting its faith in resource exports or free trade. What precisely constitutes an "industrial policy" of course depends on who is talking. The European experience has shown that an interventionist industrial policy, embracing concerns as diverse as trade, monetary policy and industrial relations, can chart the course of the economy and strengthen the industrial sector by encouraging new industries.

The question of industrial policy consumed much of the Macdonald Commission's hearings and research budget. The commission heard advocates of both an interventionist style of policy, in which the state plays a large role in setting investment, trade and export goals, and controlling the allocation of resources; and a noninterventionist approach, which generally leaves these decisions to the initiative of the market. Basically, the commission had to decide whether the existing market-based strategy of economic growth could be reworked and continue for the decades ahead, as business groups argued, or whether a more interventionist approach, advocated by the popular sector, was called for. Both sides deserve scrutiny.

Since the Second World War, Canada has relied on an export strategy of development, based on its comparative advantages in resources.[45] It was assumed that trading Canada's unprocessed resources to more developed countries in exchange for manufactured goods would expand domestic demand and eventually create a large manufacturing sector in Canada. In practice, as the labour groups stressed to the commission, what happened is that since resource industries are less labour-intensive and create fewer "multiplier" jobs than manufacturing, jobs effectively have been exported.

For government planners, the key to prosperity in an advanced economy has been the strength of the industrial side of the economy. Given a strong industrial base, a good economic performance was said to consist of fast growth, low inflation, a surplus or equilibrium in external trade and moderate to low unemployment.[46] Now, however, it is fashionable to suggest that high-tech industry has replaced the industrial side of the economy as the main engine of growth. If this is true, is the service economy becoming the new centre of gravity of the Canadian economy? French economist Robert Boyer replies, with good reason, that "the new generation of high-tech capital goods will lead to new growth in the goods-producing industries once the effects are diffused to other sectors, particularly services."[47] This means that far from relinquishing its leading role as many futurologists predict, the industrial sector will play a great part in determining our modern living standard and the growth of social services because of its importance to income formation.

The concept of "high tech" forging ahead in splendid isolation while production industries decline is also rejected by the popular sector groups. The UAW notes in chapter 2, "Auto, for example, is often presented as a declining industry and is contrasted to high tech. But, in fact, auto is a major *user* of high tech." The union notes that explicitly high-tech jobs are forecast to account for less than 3 per cent of job growth to 1990 in the U.S. In isolation from an overall industrial strategy, the smaller, weaker Canadian high-tech sector, which employs less than 3 per cent of the work force, would be a very long shot as the country's economic salvation. (The downside of high tech — its

"I'm okay," Zoë said. "Really I am. I spent some time on the Internet last night."

"And?"

"Let's just say that I memorized some things too."

"What does that mean?" Faith asked.

"I'll tell you later—if it works out, that is," Zoë said. "So tell me, was William good in bed? As good as Tyler?"

"Different," Faith said, smiling. "All three of my men were different from one another."

"You're the one who's different," Zoë said. "I wouldn't recognize you from the woman I first met here."

"Really?" Faith said. "And what about you? Did they run out of industrial-strength eyeliner?"

They had reached the road to Madame Zoya's house. Zoë turned down it and started walking backward. "Since my portrait is hanging in the Louvre, I thought I ought to have a face that matches it."

Faith stopped walking and stared at her. "Zoë! Is that true?"

Zoë just shrugged, laughed, and raced ahead to Madame Zoya's house.

Part Three

negative effects on labour — is the subject of the Ontario Public Service Employees Union's brief, chapter 13.)

Given the high-tech/production industry dynamic, Boyer stresses that the key question for any country is how to find a policy that is both growth-oriented and aims at price stabilization — in other words, how to avoid "choosing" between growth and inflation. This is why an industrial strategy is so crucial for Canada. It is the most important tool available to a government for making fundamental decisions about income distribution and for changing Canada's economic priorities.

At one end of the industrial strategy spectrum is the market-based model.[48] Basically, the business briefs advocated a strategy comprised of tough monetary policies, government cutbacks, increased incentives to business and a reduced role for the state in the economy. They clearly opposed any attempt by the state to coordinate industrial restructuring. In other words, the business briefs did not offer an industrial strategy in the true sense of the term.

The business sector proposals stem from neo-conservative philosophy, which has very particular ways of resolving the related issues of government deficits, interest rates and inflation. Governments are to spend less in order to eliminate fiscal deficits, cause interest rates to drop by borrowing less, and cut back expenditures, thereby freeing up the market to provide growth without inflation. In its purest form, the neo-conservative vision is based on a return to the market as the optimal means of allocating sources, unhampered by state intervention, a liberation that would leave workers without minimum wage legislation, women without fair employment protection and disadvantaged regions without special assistance programs.

Apart from the fact that such a strategy seeks to revert to the survival-of-the-fittest style of capitalism that Canada has long outgrown, it doesn't make economic sense for a country that has a small industrial sector, an open economy and a history of government involvement in the economy. Nor is it likely, as we've seen, that the reliance on high-technology industries that some business groups advocate is going to solve our immediate problems.

For Canada, business's market model of an industrial policy is the worst possible option. With 200,000 jobs lost between 1981 and 1984 in the mass production industries thanks to "market forces," a noninterventionist industrial policy would accelerate deindustrialization. It would limit Canada's economic space and would likely mean an economic future based on falling wages, a deteriorating social fabric and minimum social justice. And if free trade were to be the chosen vehicle for implementing this option, it would increase Canadian subservience to the U.S.

While business's idea of industrial strategy seems inspired by misplaced nostalgia, the popular sector groups are forward-looking. Their central, and most radical, message to the Macdonald Commission

Twenty-four

"Okay," Amy said after she'd poured the wine. "I want to hear every word of it." She'd spent the morning in the library and the afternoon making a dinner for the two returning women.

It had taken all she had to overcome what she feared could become a deep depression. She had saved Tristan, yes, but she'd also lost him. That emotion was understandable, but the one she didn't like in herself was a feeling of disappointment in the fact that, as far as she could tell, nothing had changed in her life. But hadn't she said that her life was perfect?

was that an industrial strategy must be more than a plan to restore vitality to the economy. These organizations do not ask for further tinkering with economic policy that will bring benefits to their membership in the short run. They assert that unless the underlying assumptions of government policy change, little else matters. Despite the range of viewpoints and concerns of women's organizations, unions, the churches, Native People's groups, and social service and health associations, they all arrived at this conclusion: not only must there be a significant role for government in the economy, but there must be *new* forms of government intervention, based on grass-roots involvement in government planning outside the traditional channels of public service and private industry. In the words of the United Church (chapter 17), "the role of government, as the arbiter of the common good, is not going to fade with the years . . . . Rather the challenge becomes ever more acute to develop in government the capacity to constantly respond to new developments," and "to do this in a manner which is discrete, nonpartisan, flexible and accountable." What this requires is reformulating the basic principles of political life so that it is possible to build a viable consensus among all members of society. This entails rejecting the idea that consensus can be arrived at by majority rule, which "has traditionally implied that there is always one winner." Rather, the major operating principle of social, economic and political democracy has to be founded on a consensus that "there will be many winners, and a society in which the well-being of the whole community is paramount." In building for the future, Canada has to seek a form of democracy where, as the United Church brief stresses, "the needs of the poor must take priority over the wants of the rich; the freedom of the dominated must take priority over the liberty of the powerful; and the participation of marginalized groups must take priority over the preservation of an order that excludes them."

The popular sector believes in enlarging Canada's economic space by exploring "the very real possibilities which public ownership provides for democratic control by citizens." In the words of the Canadian Union of Public Employees' (CUPE) brief (chapter 19):

There are many reasons why public ownership should be the central component of an alternate economic strategy. The first, and most important, is that it is necessary to break the stranglehold of the large multinational corporations over many areas of the economy. Public ownership provides the means to challenge the power of private corporations, limit their monopolistic practices and ensure that profits generated in our economy are used for further investment in socially desirable projects.

The other vital component in the strategy is to expand employment in the service sector, since even an enlarged manufacturing sector can

So she should be glad that she'd not changed any of it.

She'd called home, talked to her father-in-law, and he was the same gruff man she'd always known. What had she expected? That if she kept his ancestor alive, Lewis Hanford would turn into a gentleman? It hadn't happened.

Stephen and the boys were still camping, but they'd be back in time to meet Amy's plane tomorrow. She was looking forward to seeing them again, although she knew she'd never tell Stephen or anyone else what had happened to her. Stephen would tell her she'd been reading too many romance novels, then he'd laugh at her.

As Amy had been cooking today, she realized that the only people she could talk to about what had happened were Zoë and Faith. It was ironic that these two women whom she'd feared for being strangers might be her friends for life.

Amy left the women at the table and went into the kitchen to get the bread she'd baked. No jealousy! she told herself. Whatever had happened to Zoë and Faith in their three weeks in the past—but just minutes in this time—had certainly changed them a great deal.

Amy remembered the Faith she'd first met, a stooped-over old woman who looked as though she expected people to be mean to her. The woman who was in the summerhouse now stood up straight and looked like she owned the earth. What in the world had happened to her?

As for Zoë, she looked great. She was wearing some New York–type outfit that could have come off a runway. Her eyes were alight and she laughed at everything.

Both women were wearing wedding bands.

Amy took a deep breath and went back into the dining room. "Tell me!" Amy said as she sliced the bread. "I want to hear it all." The only thing they'd told her so far was that they had both wanted to remember everything in both lives, the new one as well as the old one.

"It all seems so long ago," Zoë said, turning to Faith. "Doesn't it?"

"A lifetime. Whereas we were only gone three weeks to the eighteenth century, and when we returned, our lives were the same, this time my life has been totally different," Faith said. "What about you?"

"Completely different," Zoë said.

They looked at Amy.

"The same," she said. "Not one change that I can tell."

Faith and Zoë looked at her in sympathy.

"What happened to Tristan?" Faith asked.

"He lived. Remember that I told you I had him go to London and hire a genealogist? Well, it seems that he did find relatives of mine, and he married a young woman who was an ancestor of mine and they had four children. And guess what?"

"What?" Faith asked politely.

"His two sons became doctors, and his two daughters married doctors."

"Goodness," Faith said. "A whole family of them. That's wonderful."

"But the bad news is that the title was dissolved right after World War I, and the estate was sold. We didn't save his family forever, but it lasted longer thanks to us."

They were silent for a moment.

"This looks great," Zoë said, staring at the food. "I'm starving."

provide neither full employment, nor satisfy the social needs of Canadians. Therefore, expanding public rather than private services should be the cornerstone of an industrial strategy. This requires first recognizing that the problem is not that we have too much public spending, but rather we have too much of the wrong kind, whose purpose is to bolster business development. Expansion of education, day care, medical services and the arts will not only create new employment but will be far more valuable "to improving the lives of ordinary Canadians than alternate private sector spending." (See also chapter 11, the Quebec Teachers Federation's "The Need for an Industrial Strategy.")

For groups such as the Vanier Institute, any plan to restructure the economy must recognize that it does not only consist of a public and private sector. There is also the informal economy, which consists of production and services "for one's own use or for exchange within one's family or community." This includes mutual aid, barter and skills exchange and, frequently, the work of cooperatives and collectives. Though it has been largely ignored, this economy, if the household production sector is included, is roughly equivalent to 50 per cent of the GNP. It is this informal economy that represents a significant alternative to both the market and the state and "the blind pursuit of the GNP which has become the raison d'être of the nation."

The growth of the informal economy offers a channel for the economic democracy that many of the popular sector groups find critical. Finding alternative arrangements is of crucial importance, not only because the economy is in crisis but also because the existing institutional arrangements are trapped in a closed circle of ideas.

Apart from exploiting the potential of public services and the informal economy, industrial policy must address the structural weaknesses of the economy: corporate concentration, foreign ownership, and over-reliance on raw resource exports. Strategies must avoid mistakes that have characterized economic policy and government finance in the past: relying on handouts and tax breaks to corporations to stimulate economic growth; an unfair tax system that starves the state in general, and the poor and social programs in particular; and the automatic cutting of social programs in hard times — the very time they are most needed to protect the fabric of Canadian society. In short, the popular sector groups are calling for an approach that, while it seeks to broaden Canada's economic space in terms of investment, production and trade, goes beyond market criteria as the basis for economic decision making. Only with a creative industrial strategy can government go beyond the traditional policy of crisis management, which, in the words of the Canadian Mental Health Association (chapter 7),

serves to reinforce the instabilities to which our economic system is structurally prone. . . . Clearly our choice is between policies that encourage decision making which is responsible to the community as a whole and those that emphasize profits and corporate power. This includes participation of workers in the plant and the participation of local political representatives in the decision making of enterprises.

An industrial strategy must have the capacity to link the fundamental need for economic growth with a sense of community, freedom and self-respect, the very essence of what public policy should be about.

Real change means innovations in employment patterns: work sharing, a shorter work week, co-determination in plant management, local initiatives, and income supplements through expanding tax credits or negative income tax mechanisms for the "working poor." In government, it requires a fundamental reform of the disjointed and unplanned nature of intergovernmental arrangements. The present reality is that

> as one government adds a benefit, another subtracts a like amount. Some overlap. And several operate with conflicting objectives. Some supplements, credits, or allowances had their origin in political motivation. The system is so fragmented that some clients receive benefits from as many as six or seven different sources.

Untangling federal and provincial responsibilities in social policy has to be a priority. The real issue is not, as is often alleged, people ripping off the system, but rather the waste, inefficiency and rigidity of government organization.

In terms of closing the income and wealth gap, a key step is reducing the gulf between those who presently profit because of tax shelters, loopholes and write-offs and those who don't. The tax system should be reformed along the lines proposed by the Carter Commission in the Sixties. For a society that perceives economic and social life as an extension of self, and is committed to creative social change, this requires

> pensions and income support pegged generously to average income levels so as to guarantee to every Canadian a life above the poverty line. Income support from the present social assistance category should be a right and delivered through the tax system in tax credits or a negative income tax.

More generally, Canada's existing institutional order is inadequate to articulate a new spirit of openness and internationalism that must permeate our relations with the rest of the world. Canada cannot afford to limit its horizons to a North American isolationism which, in terms of foreign relations, entails a return to Cold War policies, the continuation of the arms race and beggar-thy-neighbour policies towards the Third World.

"So?" Amy said. "Are you two married? Kids?"

Faith and Zoë nodded, their heads bent down in silence.

Amy slammed the wooden cutting board down on the table. "That's it! I'm not going to have you two feeling sorry for me. Do you remember what my husband looks like? And my kids? Just a day ago, that's right, just one day ago in real time, you two were feeling sorry for yourselves because I had it all. Now here you are feeling sorry for *me* because you two have it all. You cannot have it both ways!"

Faith and Zoë looked at each other and began to laugh.

"She's right," Faith said.

"Perfectly right. So who goes first?"

"Zoë," Faith said. "I want to know why that town hated you."

"They didn't," Zoë said, then paused to hold the suspense. "They did hate the person who made a man kill himself, but they just *blamed* me." She put her hand on Faith's arm. "You'll love this: The whole thing was caused by my sister."

"Damn my waistline, give me more

pasta!" Faith said. "I want to hear everything. Don't leave out a word."

"You have to understand," Zoë said, "that when I went back, I didn't know anything more than I did when I arrived here. My memory didn't come back until—"

"The night of the car wreck," Amy said.

"That's right. How did you know?"

"That's what would make the story good," she said, then waved her hand. "Go on. Sorry for interrupting."

"I went back to two weeks before the crash," Zoë said, "and everything was fine. No one hated me. No one paid much attention to me. I was just an ordinary girl in an ordinary town where nothing much happened. I'd graduated from high school but I had no plans to go to college."

"With your talent?" Faith asked. "Were you crazy?"

"That's the odd thing," Zoë said. "I was so ordinary that I didn't know I had any talent. You guys may be too old to remember this, but funding has been cut in schools so much that we don't have art classes anymore. My teachers used to tell us to draw a farm and we did. No one ever told me to draw the faces of my classmates, so I never tried. And at home I wasn't exactly surrounded by creative people."

She ate a bite of food. "I have to backtrack a bit. When my parents died, I was just thirteen, so I was sent to live with my sister. She was ten years older than me, married and had two kids, so she didn't exactly welcome me. All she talked about my last year of school was how glad she was going to be when I could get a job and help with the expenses."

"Nice woman," Amy said.

Zoë said nothing for a while. "Back then, while I was in it, I didn't see how bad it was. When I went back, knowing what I do now, I saw how truly horrible it was. My sister had been the prettiest girl in the school. She was on the local floats and she won every beauty contest there was. The whole town celebrated when she married her male counterpart, the best-looking guy, captain of the football team, all that."

"The golden couple," Amy said, and looked away. It sounded like her and Stephen. "But the real world is different, isn't it?"

"Right," Zoë said. "She was pregnant when she got married and he got a job selling used cars. It's amazing how soon that high school glory can disappear. When I went back, my sister looked old and haggard."

She looked down at her plate. "Well, maybe she didn't look too old or too haggard."

"What did you do about the car crash?" Faith asked.

"You once told me that if you had it to do over again, you'd just leave town," Amy said.

"That's what I did," Zoë said. "I figured that whatever was going to happen would happen whether I was there or not, and I wanted no part of it. I had access to a hundred and fifty dollars, so I took it, a few pieces of clothing, and I left town without saying a word to anyone. I went to New York."

"And it's my guess that you looked up someone you'd found on the Internet," Amy said softly.

"I did," Zoë said, grinning at her.

"You two are leaving me out," Faith said. "What man did you find on the Internet?"

"Who said it was a man?" Zoë asked.

"Oh, sorry," Faith said. "I'm sure you

Taken together, the popular sector briefs offer an alternative not only to liberal and conservative social thought but also to social democratic and even socialist thought, all of which, in one way of another, have fallen victim to the economic crisis. In its candid confrontation with tomorrow, the popular sector has arrived at a profoundly innovative vision of what could become of this country. On the question of technology and society, it breaks with the humanistic pessimism of Canada's leading philosophical thinker, George Grant, who sees only a bleak future for the country. It equally rejects the unfulfilled utopianism of McLuhan, who saw only good coming from the "electronically-wired" society and from technological progress, the harbinger supposedly of a better future.[49] It opts for a rethinking of the relationship between ethics, the economy, culture and society by going beyond the boundary of conventional political discourse. The popular sector does not propose piecemeal change *tout court*. Nor does it have any illusions that even if workers are to receive ten cents an hour more, if social services are liberalized, and if somehow the leash on corporate Canada can be tightened by one inch, any or all of these measures are going to change Canada fundamentally. The briefs point to the conclusion reached by Rudolph Bahro, a leading German social theorist, who has said, "We must think of quite new combinations if we are looking for the mass social force for a solution to the crisis at the general social level, and the form in which this is to be found."[50]

The popular sector critique builds on the pioneering analysis of the Canadian Catholic bishops' 1983 New Year's Day statement, *Ethical Reflections on the Economic Crisis*. Like the bishops, the popular sector insists on looking at society from the standpoint of the marginalized, giving the needs of the poor priority over the wants of the rich, and promoting the view that the bias of modern economics ethically violates the principle of the "priority of labour over capital." In chapter 20, the bishops reiterate their belief that Canada suffers from a lack of social imagination. Despite a wealth of human and material resources, "the people of this country have seldom been challenged to envision and develop alternatives to the dominant economic model that governs our society."

The critique and vision of the popular sector's briefs challenge all Canadians by asking us to put aside our past images of the industrial world and instead seek to create a new, ethical and more equitable framework free of the tyranny of markets. This is a bold vision on which to plan the next economic era and, in a world dominated by special interests of the powerful, our only real alternative for the future.

An Overview of the Briefs

The twenty selections that follow were culled from scores of written submissions to the Macdonald Commission. Each piece is preceded by a brief introduction by the editors, in italic type. Editing has been restricted to some condensation, the requirements of stylistic conformity and the deletion of some overlaps.

The careful reader will easily detect divisions among the contributors. A prominent example is the answer to this question: Is growth in itself an objective for economic policy? An organization like Quebec's Confederation of National Trade Unions, with many production workers in its membership, may urge "a policy aiming at the constant growth of overall demand." Other organizations, like the United Church, assert that the future economy "should be based on a conserver mentality rather than a growth mentality."

These splits cannot be denied. A possible explanation is that the individuals and committees writing these submissions did so in isolation from each other and they tailored their texts to the narrow function of the commission hearings. But the real reply is the simple fact that more binds the briefs together than separates them. Their critique of the status quo and their vision of the future derive their power from the popular will, which, as forceful as it may be, is not monolithic. The only cause for regret is that the Macdonald Commission did not see how well it would have suited its mandate to develop the common ground.

The contributions are organized in four broad sections.

Part I, "The Economic Crisis," lays out a sobering analysis of Canadian society. The contributions in this section share the view that considering only the short-term interests and needs of corporations is an inadequate basis for establishing public policy. They explain the bias of economic markets that benefit the rich and the powerful, and outline why the common interests of Canadians are ill-served by a market mechanism that treats individuals as if they were commodities to be bought and sold without regard to human need.

Part II, "Equality: Still a Canadian Principle?," presents the views of women, the poor and those who live in the disadvantaged regions of Canada. What the briefs show is the failure of existing policies to address the real issues that face Canadians and the dangers of adopting a neo-conservative strategy advocated by Canada's business elite. In the economic crisis, it is these millions of people who are subsidizing the Canadian economy through their ill-paid work.

Part III, "Challenges for Economic Policy," focuses on obstacles in the way of using our human and natural resources for the good of all Canadians: regional inequality, the failure of business to invest creatively in the economy and the loss of jobs due to the microchip revolution, the failure of Canada's labour relations system, the precarious situation facing Canadian farmers, and the destructive effects of new technology on the labour force. In terms of public policy, the briefs address the effects of restraint on public sector workers and analyze the free trade option so touted by business.

Part IV, "An Alternative Vision of Canada," shows how ethics and nonmaterial concerns must be integral parts of the debate on Canada's economic future. The briefs present a different way of understanding the relationship between the economy and culture and society, and make practical suggestions for transforming this country. The risk Canada faces in not accepting this vision is that Canadian citizenship will perpetually be devalued. Canadians will be captives of powerful interests whose very existence makes most Canadians strangers in their own land. In the words of the Catholic bishops, "What is required, in the long run, is a dynamic process designed to stimulate social imagination, develop alternative models and forge a new cultural vision in this country."

Daniel Drache and *Duncan Cameron*

found out you had a half sister whom you'd never met, so you looked her up, and she's the one who's made you smile like that."

Amy looked at Zoë. "You stole my idea, didn't you?"

"Yes," Zoë said. "I ripped off your idea completely. That night when we came back from the eighteenth century, I looked for Russell Johns on the Internet. I'd read a lot of art history books but I didn't remember hearing his name. But after we came back here, he was all over the 'Net. You know what for?"

"His paintings of common people," Amy said. "In Tristan's time, he was always sketching us as we pulled bread out of the oven. He loved the washerwomen. Hey! Do you think we're in any of his pictures?"

"I don't know about you two, but I saw several nudes of me," Zoë said, and the three of them laughed.

"In the Louvre," Faith said, and that made them laugh more.

"So what happened to him?" Amy asked as she buttered a slice of bread. "He was such a talented man."

"He married and had some children,"

PART

I

The Economic Crisis

Zoë said softly. "I cried in jealousy when I read that."

"But not now," Amy said as she nodded toward Zoë's wedding ring.

Zoë turned the ring on her finger. "No, not anymore. You see, I took Amy's idea about descendants and I searched until I found Russell's family tree."

"Don't tell me!" Amy said. "You found out that one of his descendants lives in New York, you memorized the address, and when you left your sister's you went to him. Is he a painter?"

Faith and Zoë were looking at her in astonishment.

"When did you get so good at stories?" Faith asked.

"I think I'm like Zoë and her art. I think maybe I've always been good at stories, but I didn't know it. So, am I right?"

"Yeah," Zoë said, "but he's not a painter, he's—"

"A photographer," Amy said, then when she looked at their faces, she said, "Okay, I'll shut up. You tell your story, Zoë."

"Thank you. But, yes, he's a photographer. He does some commercial work but he's made his name by . . ." She looked at Amy as though daring her to say a word.

Amy made a zipper sign over her lips.

"Russ photographs people in ordinary situations doing ordinary things. He's won a lot of awards."

"Russ?" Faith asked.

Zoë shrugged. "Last name is Andrews, but the first is the same."

"And you are madly in love with him," Amy said, then looked at them. "Am I allowed to say that?"

Zoë laughed. "Of course. You want to hear something weird?"

"I don't know if I can stand weird," Faith said. "I shock easily."

"When Russell and I were together, back in his time, he asked me a lot of questions about my life. I couldn't tell him about Oregon because, well, it didn't exist back then, so I told him as much as I knew about my early family history."

She looked at Amy as though challenging her to finish the story. Amy frowned in concentration for a moment, then her face lightened. "You didn't! He didn't!"

"I'm lost," Faith said.

Zoë smiled. "It seems that the great

painter, Russell Johns, sailed to the American colonies in the fall of 1797. He settled in Williamsburg, and today you can see his portraits of some of our forefathers."

"I hope he got Amy's friend Thomas Jefferson," Faith said, deadpan.

"Who told you that?" Amy said. She looked at Zoë. "Who did he marry?"

"A young woman with the last name of Prentiss."

"Your family's name, I take it," Amy said.

Faith frowned for a moment. "If you're related to Russell's wife and your husband is descended from their children, does that make you and your husband cousins?"

"Just like royalty," Zoë said, and they laughed.

"Okay, so now tell us what made the town hate you," Faith said.

"Ah, that," Zoë said. "The entire memory of that came to me at what I think was exactly the time that my accident happened. I'd meant to pay attention to the date and take care of myself, but when I got to New York, I went to Russ's that first day, and we hit it off rather well, so, uh . . ."

"You were in bed with him when the

1

Economic Decline in Canada

SOCIAL PLANNING COUNCIL OF METROPOLITAN TORONTO

The Social Planning Council acts as a voluntary social planning organization in the Metropolitan Toronto community. It encourages citizen participation in the analysis of social issues, the development of social policies and the delivery of human services.

The problems and proposals for the Canadian economy are dealt with in this excerpt from their eighty-page brief to the Macdonald Commission entitled "Democracy, Equality and Canada's Economic Future" (see chapter 5 for another excerpt from this brief). The council argues that structural changes in the economy are leaving Canada weak and that an economic policy that relies on the private sector to be the engine of economic recovery is hopelessly inadequate. Problems examined here include unemployment, productivity declines, decreasing social spending, increasing poverty and widening inequalities. Yet the council finds the most disturbing aspect of economic decline is the sense in which it is treated as inevitable.

The brief was prepared for the Social Security Review program group by Leon Muszynski, who is a program director at the council. The group is chaired by David Wolfe of the University of Toronto.

In their efforts to restructure the economy for recovery, business and government are increasingly unsympathetic to the plight of the poor and unemployed. There is a real danger of a future society where large numbers of people will be marginal to the economy as the commitment to public provision for their welfare declines. Technological change and industrial restructuring are occurring at such a pace and in such a manner that the interests of the workers and the communities involved are ignored. Nor is there in place a labour market policy that would cushion this adjustment process and allow those most affected by change to have some input into the decision making that so overwhelmingly affects their future....

The truth of the matter is that tough monetary policies, government cutbacks and increased incentives for private accumulation have not and will not work to achieve economic recovery. Further cuts in social programs and real wages only reinforce the cycle of decline. Spending cutbacks, the wastefulness of unemployment, and increased reliance on private sector investment decision making are all inextricably linked to our worsening economic situation. The final result of these policies is the longest and deepest recession since the 1930s....

It is irrational economics designed in the interests of the rich and the powerful and imposed upon Canadians without adequate debate or consensus....

This brief argues that economic decline is not inevitable.

Unemployment

Unemployment in Canada is higher now than anytime in the post-Second World War period. But the problem of unemployment is not simply related to the recession we have experienced since 1981. The rate of unemployment for the decade between 1970 and 1980 averaged 6.8 per cent. Unemployment has been low in Canada for only a few short periods in the past sixty years: in the late 1920s, throughout the 1940s and for a very brief period in the mid-1960s. The proportion of the Canadian labour force unable to find work has steadily risen since the mid-Sixties.

Canadian workers are at considerably greater risk of joblessness than their counterparts in other Organization for Economic Cooperation and Development (OECD) countries. In 1982 Canada had an average rate of unemployment of 11.0 per cent, while the average of the major OECD countries was 7.1 per cent. In a twenty-four-country comparison of all OECD member nations, Canada ranked twentieth in its rate of unemployment for 1982 (Table 1-1).

In the mid-1950s Canada was on par with western European OECD countries. For most of the subsequent period European countries performed much better than Canada (Figure 1-1). There are two striking conclusions to be made as a result of these comparisons. The first is that many countries similar to Canada in economic structure have had rates of unemployment, even during the current recession, far below the rate of unemployment for Canada for at least the past decade. Secondly, Canada has been one of the worst performers in maintaining a low rate of unemployment of all OECD member countries.

Even these figures, striking as they are, do not tell the complete tale of unemployment. There are large numbers of unemployed left out of the official figures. For example, not included are the 427,000 people who, in the March 1983 survey of the labour force, reported that they were not in the labour force but wanted work and were available for work.[1] Nor do they include the over 400,000 people who are working part time but want full-time work. Adding these two groups

wreck was to happen, weren't you?" Amy said.

When Zoë nodded, Faith said, "How are you doing this?"

"I don't know, but it's like I can see it in print. I just seem to know. But I'll stop talking. Zoë, tell us what you remembered."

"I don't like to remember it even if I know it didn't really happen. At least not my part in it."

"What did your sister do to you?" Faith asked, making the others smile.

"Now you're the storyteller," Zoë said. "And you're completely accurate. It was all my sister's fault."

❧

"I don't want to hear another word," Zoë said to her sister, Karen. She put her hands over her ears. She was sitting in Karen's living room, on the old, worn-out couch, and her sister was pacing.

"You have to help me. You're the only one I can trust." Karen put her hands on Zoë's wrists and uncovered her sister's ears.

"What about Bob?" Zoë asked. "How could you do this to him?"

"Bob?" Karen said in disgust. "What does he care? The highlight of his life was when he made three touchdowns in one game. It's been downhill since then. Please, Zoë, this is for my whole life."

Zoë looked up at her sister and wondered how she'd been able to pull off an affair with the most important man in town. Alan Johnson was the oldest son of the richest man in town and he'd done nothing in his life that hadn't flourished. He was on every charity committee. He was married and had two children, a boy and a girl, who were polite and sweet-tempered. His wife was beautiful and spent the time her children were in school volunteering at hospitals and old-age homes.

"I don't understand why he was having an affair with you," Zoë said.

Karen whirled on her in a flash of rage. "For your information, underneath all of this—" She waved her hand to include the house with its aluminum windows, its stained carpets that were littered with kids' bright plastic toys, and herself in her often-washed sleeveless dress. "Underneath this I'm a very desirable woman."

Zoë was really trying to understand, but

she couldn't see it. Yes, her sister used to be quite pretty, but not in a movie star way. She was more hometown-girl pretty. And the years since she'd married had not been kind to her. The fact that she smoked two packs a day and drank Coke that was half bourbon with dinner didn't help.

"He really loves you?" Zoë asked.

"Do you find that so impossible to believe? Alan does love me, and he's going to divorce that cold bitch of a wife of his and marry me."

Zoë just sat on the old sofa and stared at her sister. Karen was always telling Zoë that she knew nothing about life, but even she knew that this was a story so old that comedians used it in their stand-up acts. But Zoë also knew that she couldn't reason with her sister. When she was like this, smoking one cigarette after another, and saying she *had* to do this and *had* to do that, she was impossible to talk to.

"I want you to go with me," Karen said.

"Where?" Zoë said and hid her crossed fingers. Please don't let it be to go see Mr. Johnson. One year he'd dressed up as an Easter bunny and had given Zoë the prize for the most eggs found. She didn't want to have to face him in this ugly affair. And, too, there was Bob, Karen's husband. Maybe he wasn't the most exciting man in the world, but he loved their children and he was totally devoted to them. Last year he'd been passed over for a promotion because he'd missed so many days at work when he stayed home with the kids because Karen couldn't "get herself together."

"To see Alan."

"Karen," Zoë said, her voice a whine. "I don't want to do that. Please don't make me do that."

"After all I've done for you!" she started, saying all the things that she'd said a million times before. It seemed that Zoë was to give her life to Karen in eternal gratitude for taking her in when she was orphaned. Never mind that Karen got a free live-in babysitter.

"I'll stay with the kids and you go. You should be alone with him," Zoë said.

"No. I want Bob to stay with the kids. That'll keep him from snooping into my life."

"He knows about you and Mr. Johnson?" Zoë asked in horror.

"Will you stop calling him that? You make him sound like a . . . a pillar of the community and I'm the slutty secretary. It's demeaning to me."

Zoë looked down at her hands and avoided her sister's eyes.

"Look, Zoë," Karen said, her tone changing. "It's just that I need to see him. I got a weird phone call from him today, and—"

"What did he say?"

"Nothing that would concern you, but if you must know, I think he's having doubts about us." She waved her hand in dismissal. "It's nothing. I told him I might tell his wife, but of course I wouldn't. Anybody who knows me knows I wouldn't do something like that. No, Alan is going to have to stand up in front of the entire town and tell them that he loves me and only me."

"What about the children?" Zoë asked.

"Don't you dare get that holier-than-thou look on your face. *You* have never been trapped like I am. Do you know that I could have gone to college? I could have had a full scholarship, but I turned it down to marry Bob. I thought he was going places, doing things. What a fool I was."

Zoë didn't dare look up. Her sister had

barely kept a C average at school. Who was going to give her a scholarship? For what? And Zoë too well remembered that Bob had tried to break up with her before they graduated. *He* had been offered a four-year football scholarship at the state university, but when Karen became pregnant and insisted on keeping the baby, he'd given it up to marry her.

Karen glared at her sister. "I've done everything for you and Bob and the kids. Now it's time for you to do something for *me.* You're going to go with me tonight and that's it. I don't want to hear anything else about it. Now go get dressed. We'll leave as soon as Bob gets home."

Which means that *he* has to make dinner for the kids, Zoë thought.

An hour and a half later, she was in the car with Karen. Her sister was wearing a short, red cocktail dress with a fake diamond necklace.

"Should you be wearing that?" Zoë asked, looking at her sister as she inhaled deeply on her cigarette. Once again, she'd forgotten to put the window down.

"I want to look my best," Karen said. "Someday when you have a real boyfriend, not that geek you pal around with now, you'll understand a woman's need to sometimes wear something other than jeans." She gave a little smile at Zoë's Levi's.

When they got to Mr. Johnson's house, Karen turned off the headlights at the top of the drive. "This is just one of the little things we've had to do," she said, smiling at Zoë as though they were in a conspiracy together. She maneuvered the car by the landscaping lights along the drive, hiding it way in the back, behind the garbage bins.

There was only one light on in the house. "That's his study," Karen said. "It's where we meet when we need to be alone." She gave Zoë a look to let her know what she meant by that.

"I'm not going in," Zoë said.

"Of course you aren't," Karen said. "I just needed you to come with me so Bob would have to stay with the kids. I didn't want him free tonight."

Karen pulled the sun visor down and reapplied her lipstick in the little lighted mirror. "Just wait here. I shouldn't be too long. Well, maybe I'll be a long time."

Zoë knew that if she said anything to that, Karen would blast her, and she didn't want to hear it. She watched her sister walk into Mr. Johnson's house, her hips swaying, her high heels tapping on the pavement.

I have to leave this town, Zoë thought as she sat in the car and waited for her sister. Karen had said Zoë owed her for all the years she'd taken care of her "for free," but Zoë was now old enough to see that she'd more than carried her weight. It occurred to Zoë that if it weren't for her taking care of the children, Karen wouldn't have had time to have an affair.

When the car door was jerked open, Zoë almost fell out. Karen had a frantic look about her and her eye makeup was running down her cheeks.

"You have to talk to him," Karen said. "He's crazy."

"Me? What can I say to him?"

"I don't know," Karen said, "but he won't listen to me. He keeps talking about money, but what does that have to do with me? He's bought me a few measly presents, but not much. Zoë, he's always liked you, so maybe he'll listen to you."

"I can't—" Zoë said, but Karen grabbed her arm and pulled her out of the car. "I'm not going in there! I can't." For once Zoë felt strong. It seemed that all her life she'd been intimidated by her older sister. Karen was the pretty one, the social one, the one who was going to make it in the world. Her parents had never said it, but they thought Zoë was "the weird one." The girl who stayed to herself and rarely talked to anyone. The loner.

"I'm not going in there," Zoë said again. "This is your problem, you made it, and I'm not getting involved in it."

"It's not me," Karen said, and put her hands over her face. "It's something else. I don't know what it is, but he's . . ." She looked at her sister with pleading eyes. "I think he's going to kill himself."

"Call the police," Zoë said, and reached inside the car for her cell phone.

"No!" Karen said. "Listen, Zoë, I'll do whatever you want if you'll help me on this. I can't let the town know about this. I can't let Bob find out. Or the kids. Did you think about them?"

"You're not going to turn this around on *me*!" Zoë said. "You—"

"Please?" Karen begged. "Please. Just go talk to him."

"If I do this, then I'm going to leave," Zoë said. "You're always saying I owe you my whole life, but this will pay it off."

"Of course," Karen said. "I'll give you anything you want. I'll help you find an apartment and I'll help you decorate it. And Bob will get you a car. How about a nice BMW convertible? You'd like that, wouldn't you?"

Zoë wasn't so naïve that she thought Karen would actually help her, and when she said "leave" she hadn't meant an apartment two miles away from Karen. No, helping her sister in this crisis would get rid of the burden of gratitude that Zoë lived under.

Karen stepped aside so Zoë could go into the house. Her heart was beating hard as she went inside. She left the door open in case she wanted to run out. The house was dark except for a light shining around a half-closed door to her left, and it seemed eerily quiet.

"Mr. Johnson?" she called out, but he didn't answer. She went to the door and pushed it open. The room was his study, with bookshelves around two walls and big glass doors leading out to a patio. There was a blond oak desk and behind it sat Mr. Johnson. He was holding a gun to his head.

"Please," Zoë said. "Mr. Johnson, please don't do this."

"Zoë, I can't live like this anymore," he said, then he shot himself through the temple.

For a moment she couldn't move. She just stood there staring at him.

In the next second, his wife ran into the room. She looked from her husband, his bloody head slumped on the desk, then she looked at Zoë. She raised her hands in fists as she ran toward her.

"You killed him!" she shouted. "You killed my husband."

"I . . . I didn't," Zoë stammered, backing up toward a wall of bookcases, her arms across her face to protect herself. When Karen appeared behind the woman, Zoë had never been so glad to see anyone in her life. Karen ran to Zoë, put her arm around her shoulders in a protective way, and led her out of the house while the wife ran to the phone.

"He shot himself," Zoë said, her whole body shivering. "I saw it."

"That's what I was afraid would happen. Look, I have to do something, so you take the car, and—"

"Karen, you can't go back in there. There's a loaded gun in there. She'll kill you."

"I have to get some things. Look, Zoë, you take the car and go. Meet me at that drive-in on Fourth. I'll be there as soon I can get there. All I ask is that if the police question you, you say I was with you."

"You can't—" Zoë began, but all she could see in her mind was that man shooting himself.

"Trust me," Karen said as she led Zoë back to the hidden car. "I know I've not always been the easiest sister in the world, but you don't want to see me in jail, do you?"

"Jail?"

"There are some things of mine in that house that could make people think I had something to do with his death."

"Things?" Zoë asked. She couldn't seem to think very well.

"Letters. I have to find them and get rid

of them, and I have to have an alibi. Remember! I was with you all night. Now go." She shoved Zoë behind the steering wheel and put her hand on the key. When Zoë didn't react, Karen started the engine for her, then closed the door. She didn't stay to wave goodbye, just ran back into the house.

❧

"So I left," Zoë said to Faith and Amy, "and about a mile away, I drove into a tree. When I woke up, I was slathered in bandages, I couldn't remember anything, and the whole town hated me."

"She put you behind the wheel of a car after you'd seen something like that," Faith said in wonder.

"Your sister told the town the man was having an affair with *you,* didn't she?" Amy said.

Zoë shrugged. "When all that was going on, I was in a hospital bed unconscious, and when I rewrote history, my accident hadn't happened, but, yes, I think that's what she did."

"An all-time low," Faith said. "Even for a sister."

Zoë nodded. "As you pointed out, on

the night I was supposed to be in the car wreck, I was in bed with the man I was to marry."

"So what happened this time around?" Faith asked.

"After I left Russ's apartment the next morning, I realized what day it was and I wondered if Mr. Johnson had still shot himself. Or had I changed things so much that he didn't do it? I checked the Internet and he had, indeed, killed himself."

"Was your sister there?" Amy asked.

"Yes," Zoë said. "She told me she hadn't really needed me that night, that I was just her cover, so when I wasn't there, she went alone. She left Bob with the kids, put on her red dress, and went to see Alan Johnson."

Zoë looked down at her empty plate. "I found out some things later, but I knew nothing that day in New York. When I got back to my apartment, I had four frantic messages on my phone from Karen. She said I had to call her, that I had to come home, that she needed me. She said I couldn't abandon her after all she'd done for me."

Faith put her hand over Zoë's wrist to calm her.

"It took me a while to piece together the story of what happened the first time, but . . ." She looked at Amy.

"I don't think it would have taken much on your sister's part to make the woman believe that her husband was having an affair with you rather than the worn-out mother of two kids," Amy said.

"I don't think it did," Zoë said, "and when I had the wreck and was conveniently in a coma for a while, I think my sister did everything she could to sully my name, and save her own skin."

She smiled. "But the second time around, things happened in a very different way. When Mrs. Johnson came home, there was her husband dead, and my sister was tearing through the study trying to find the letters. Mrs. Johnson immediately called the police, and they . . ."

"They what?" Faith asked.

"Put my sister in jail for a few days."

"Serves her right!" Amy said.

"I guess so," Zoë said, "but she begged me to come back and be with her, but I wouldn't. Thank heaven, this time around I'd had time away from her, not to mention three weeks in the eighteenth century, so

I could tell her no. If it had happened right after I left—"

"You would have been stuck there for the rest of your life," Amy said.

"Probably."

"So what happened this time around?" Faith asked.

"They let my sister out of jail when they saw it was a suicide, but of course everyone wanted to know why such a great man had killed himself."

"And of course they blamed a woman," Faith said.

"Completely. The police found the letters my sister had written him, so everyone knew about the affair."

"Why did he really kill himself?" Amy asked. "I don't think that men of this century kill themselves over love."

Zoë couldn't help smiling. "How diplomatic of you. They certainly don't kill themselves over trashy women like my sister." She took a sip of wine. "It seems that the man had a gambling problem and was up to his ears in debt. It took a year for all the ugly details to come out, but everything he was involved in was a fake. He had no money, nothing. His wife lost everything and had to get a job."

"And your sister?" Faith asked.

"Bob divorced her and kept the kids. Karen moved away and the last time I saw her . . ."

"What?" Faith asked.

"She visited me in New York and she thought I'd be the same little girl she'd bullied all her life. But I'd changed. When she said something nasty, I just laughed at her. I kept remembering that while I was lying in a hospital fighting for my life, my sister had been letting the town believe that Mr. Johnson and I had been having an affair."

"It makes more sense that he'd want a gorgeous dame like you than a Tobacco Road girl," Faith said.

Zoë laughed. "You two are good for my ego."

"And what about Russ?" Amy asked. "Did she make a pass at him?"

"She's doing it again," Zoë said to Faith. "Yes, my sister in her polyester dress, with her four-pack-a-day habit, made a pass at my boyfriend. And when he pushed her away, she got so angry she tried to make me believe he'd come on to her."

"Classic," Amy said. "I bet she went away in a rage."

"Oh, yeah," Zoë said. "In a fury. But it didn't bother me. In my head were the years of hurt I'd suffered at her hands. I didn't realize it then, but I was really beaten down by what that town had done to me. There I was in a hospital with my cracked skull and they hated me without even trying to find out the truth."

"Do you think she felt any guilt? I mean the first time," Faith asked.

"Some. I remember her face when I saw her when I burned the car on the town square. She couldn't get away from me fast enough. The truth is that I'm ashamed of myself because I can't forgive her."

Amy looked at Zoë. "Primrose said that there was always true love involved in anything Madame Zoya did. Where was your true love?"

"I'm not sure," Zoë said. "I know I had a boyfriend of sorts. We'd gone together all during high school, but he turned on me as soon as there was a hint of scandal. I didn't miss him."

"I think your true love is that art of yours," Faith said. "When you thought you'd lose your talent, you were willing to keep the hatred of an entire town and the damage to your body. If that isn't true love, I don't know what is."

"I never thought of that," Zoë said, "but it makes sense. I think my true love has now expanded to my husband and daughter, but, yes, if I had a true love back then, it was the talent I'd been given. And art led me to the two men in my life."

"So how much like Russell is the new guy?" Faith asked.

Zoë laughed. "Wait till we get to you. I'm going to ask you nothing but personal questions."

"Like who's the better lover of all my three men?" Faith asked.

Zoë laughed.

"What did you answer?" Amy asked Faith.

"I didn't," Faith said, and the women laughed together.

"I have a blueberry cobbler," Amy said. "How about if we have it in the living room?"

"And hear Faith's story," Zoë said.

"My thoughts exactly," Amy said.

Twenty-five

In record time, the three women had cleaned up the dishes, put everything away, and were ensconced in the living room, ready to hear Faith's story.

"I think that you should guess," Faith said.

"That's not fair," Zoë said. "I'm no good at stories."

"I like the idea," Amy said. "Let me see." She stared hard at Faith. "I'm not sure that what we think happened, did."

"You didn't marry Eddie," Zoë said. "That's for sure. And I don't think you were in love with William enough to want to find his descendants, so that means you married Tyler."

Faith just smiled and looked at them over her wineglass.

"I don't think so," Amy said. "I think that your time in Tristan's world changed you. I think that if you'd gone back in your time before that, you would have married Tyler, but . . ."

Zoë was looking from one to the other of them, then she got up, went to Jeanne's cabinet and withdrew drawing supplies. "I'm glad to see that some things haven't changed. Did I tell you two that some of *my* drawings have survived from the eighteenth century? They say they were done by a student of Russell Johns."

"Any of the nudes of him?" Amy asked.

"How did you know about those?" Zoë asked.

"Tristan snooped through Russell's room."

"You're kidding," Zoë said. "He didn't have the right to do that."

"He owned the place and I think he felt that he could do what he wanted to," Amy said. "So did any of those beefcake nudes survive the ages?"

"Actually, two of them did. Both of them

are of Russell, but no one knows who they are. They think they're of the local blacksmith. No one can believe the artist looked like that."

"I know," Amy said. "People today think we have the market cornered on beautiful men."

"Speaking of which," Faith said, "how did you and Tristan spend your last two days together?"

Amy smiled. "I want to hear how you've spent your last sixteen years. I see you're married but, somehow, I don't think it's to either Eddie or Tyler."

Zoë looked up from her drawing pad. "Don't tell me she's right."

"She is."

Zoë lifted her glass to Amy in tribute.

"Okay, that's enough about me," Amy said. "I want to hear about you."

"If Tyler hadn't died—"

"Been killed by your mother," Zoë said.

"All right, but I don't like to think about that," Faith said. "My mother was a woman of deep passions and I'll never know what really happened that day, but I'm sure it was spur of the moment. I'm sure she didn't plan to kill him."

"Dead is dead," Zoë said, her eyes on her drawing.

"Yes, and that's why I went back," Faith said. "If it hadn't been for Ty's premature death, I wouldn't have gone back to change anything."

"You're kidding," Zoë said.

"No. After I came back from living in a place where I was a useful woman, I knew what I wanted to do with my life," Faith said.

"And there were the seeds," Amy said. "You were concerned about them. They'd made it through one transport, but you weren't sure they'd stand another one."

"Exactly!" Faith said.

Zoë looked at her. "Are you telling me that you would have given up a chance to take away all the dreadful things that had been done to you just for a plant?"

"Yes," Faith said.

Zoë shook her head at her. "I'm almost glad Ty was killed if only to make you go back and rewrite your life."

"Me, too," Faith said. "I needed my youth to give the balm time to grow."

"Start when Ty came through your window," Amy said. "You told us that if you had a chance to do it again, you'd be packed and ready to leave with him."

"I was packed all right, but I wasn't leaving with any man." She looked at Amy. "Can you figure it out?"

"I think . . ." she began, then looked up. "I think the problem was that you thought you had only two men to choose from. One was a motorcycle-riding hillbilly, and the other was a tea-drinking rich boy."

Zoë looked at Faith.

"Is she right?"

"Perfectly," Faith said. "After we returned from the eighteenth century, I realized that I could never be happy with either man. If I married Ty, even knowing what I do now, I knew I wouldn't be happy with him. I had a vision of his working fourteen-hour days, seven days a week."

"All to prove that he was as good a man as Eddie," Amy said.

"Yes," Faith said. "I'm not sure what made me see it, maybe it was that back in Tristan's time, as Amy calls it, it was the first time that I was truly free. That sounds funny when you think of the centuries involved. We think women are free today, but were subjugated back then. For me, it was the opposite."

"But then, in this time, you had two mothers telling you what to do—for your entire life," Zoë said.

"It's going to be hard to believe, but I think the mothers had very little to do with it," Faith said. "I think I grew up loving that two boys were in love with me. I thought about my childhood as best I could without wallowing in emotion and sentimentality."

She took a breath. "I think that I've always looked at my life entirely wrong. I always saw myself as a victim of my mother and later as the punching bag for Eddie's mother. But when I looked at things from afar, I saw that I was the one who caused the problems."

"You'll have to explain that to me," Zoë said, but Amy said nothing.

"I spent my whole childhood with two boys, Tyler and Eddie. I think it's just possible that I was the strong one when we were kids, and I think I may have adopted them in a motherly way."

"It's easy to mother the men in your life," Amy said. "It's one of my great faults."

"I didn't realize how motherly I was until I was in that orangery with William. I thought I was a martyr for taking care of Eddie all those years, but William made me realize that I like helping people."

Faith looked down at her hands. "I used to think that I overlooked the awful circumstances that Ty and Eddie lived in, but I came to realize that that's what I liked about them."

"They needed you," Amy said.

"Yes, they did. Ty was trapped in horrible circumstances in his family life, and even though Eddie looked to be better off, he wasn't. He just had more money."

"You thought you had to marry one of them out of guilt," Amy said.

"Right," Faith said. "I had taken them out of their bad families and we'd formed our own family."

"That doesn't sound so bad," Zoë said.

"Someday, you have to push your children out of the nest," Amy said. "I dread it. I want to buy houses for my sons that are next door to us. Even the thought of their going to college makes me ill."

"I agree," Faith said, "but I also know you well enough to know that, when the time comes, you won't hold your children back."

"No," Amy said, sighing. "I'm sure that when I have to, I'll get my courage together and let them go. However, I feel sorry for any girl who wants to marry one of *my* sons."

Faith and Zoë laughed.

Faith continued. "I knew that if I was going to give Eddie and Ty a real chance at life I had to leave them. I didn't plan to explain, just leave."

"Like me," Zoë said.

"Exactly. Sometimes words can't fix anything," Faith said, "and I knew this was such a case. If it had come to the point where my mother was willing to kill to make me marry the man of her choice, then I had to change everything."

"So what did you do?" Amy asked.

"You can't guess?" Zoë said.

"Maybe," Amy said, "but I'd rather hear what actually happened."

"When Ty climbed in my window that night, I wasn't there. And I wasn't there when Eddie came in and threw his jealous little fit. Instead, I went to Eddie's mother."

"You did what?!" Zoë said, her eyes wide. "I thought you hated her."

"I did. I knew all the awful things she'd done to me over the years I was married to her son. It hadn't happened yet and wasn't going to, but I still remembered them. But I also knew that she'd been right."

"You didn't love Eddie," Amy said.

"Yes she did," Zoë said. "She loved both of them."

"True," Faith said. "I loved Eddie like a brother, and I loved Ty like a sex machine. I had fun with him, but in the end I married Eddie."

"Why did you go to his mother?" Zoë asked.

Faith looked at Amy. "Do you know why?"

"I would think that you went to her for money."

"Don't tell me that's true," Zoë said. "I would have walked the streets before I asked her for money."

"That's because you can go into a gallery, show them your work, and instantly, you have a job."

"Not quite," Zoë said, looking up from

her drawing. "It takes more work than that and I have a lot of supplies to buy."

Faith and Amy looked at her.

"Okay, so Russ bought them and, yes, I did sell rather quickly to a gallery. Stop staring at me! It just seems to me that going to Eddie's mother to ask for money would be like my going to my sister to ask for money."

"Where did you get the hundred and fifty dollars that got you to New York?" Faith asked.

"Stole it from my sister," Zoë said, grinning. "But didn't she owe me?"

"And so did Eddie's mother," Faith said. "But I didn't just borrow money, I gave her a piece of the business I wanted to start."

"And what business was that?" Amy asked.

"Right," Faith said, "you've been in this house and haven't seen how I've changed the world."

"You changed the world?" Amy asked.

"Changed it a bit," Faith said as she got up and went to get her bag on the hall table. She reached inside and pulled out a jar of what looked to be face cream. It was a jar of dark blue glass, about two inches high, with a silver lid and silver writing on it. She handed it to Amy.

"I've never seen this before," Amy said. "Indigo," she read on the label. She unscrewed the lid and smelled it, then her eyes widened. "Beth. The seeds."

She glanced at Zoë and saw that she was staring at Faith with a look of astonishment on her face.

"Did I miss something?" Amy asked.

"Indigo?" Zoë asked. "You don't know about this stuff? No, right, you've been in here. That company is yours?"

"All except the seven percent that Eddie's mother owns. I tried for five, but she held out for seven. She uses her millions to do charitable works in Eddie's name. He died on the same date he died when I was taking care of him."

"Destiny," Amy said, then, "Millions?"

Zoë laughed. "More like megamillions. It's hard to believe that you haven't seen these bottles on the store shelves. There's shampoo, face cream, you name it. It's a whole line and they're everywhere, on TV and in magazines. There isn't a movie star who doesn't use it." She looked at Faith. "If you run this company, how do you have time for a life?"

"I let a bunch of people in New York who wear suits all day run it. I just stay home with my kids. And . . ." She hesitated. "I run the charity part of my company. We give a lot of money away. And—"

Faith seemed to pause, as though for a drumroll. "One of the first things I bought was Tristan's house and the old medieval house next to it. I found out that after we left, William ran the cows out and restored the house, so it's still there today." Faith smiled. "I read that he never married, but he lived to be ninety-five. If you look deep in obscure books on landscaping, you'll see his name."

"That's great!" Zoë said.

"The houses are mine and I've spent a lot on putting them back to the way they were. When my kids are out of the house, I hope to have the time to oversee the re-creation of an eighteenth-century estate and open it to the public, but for right now, it's private housing. I don't get to stay there very often, so maybe you two would like to visit. Amy, would your kids like that?"

"They'd love it. All of us would. What about the tower?"

Faith shook her head. "Part of it was still there, but the glass roof was gone and of course there were no plants."

"You really did save them," Amy said.

"I want to know what happened between getting money from Eddie's mother to becoming a multi-millionaire."

Faith smiled in memory. "I talked to Eddie's mother and I told her the truth, that I had come by some seeds from a plant that is extinct today and was mentioned in the Bible, and I wanted to grow it and make cosmetics with it. She wasn't interested until I told her I planned to move to California to grow the plant there."

"So she was paying you to get out of town," Zoë said.

"More or less. Actually, that's exactly what she was doing. The night before, she'd found the receipt for the engagement ring Eddie had bought me, and she knew what was going to happen. I took the ring off its chain and said I'd throw it into the deal. Gave her the diamond, I kept the chain." Faith reached under her collar and pulled out a pretty little gold chain. "I always wear it to remind me of Eddie and what might have been."

"What you escaped," Amy said.

"So how much did she give you?" Zoë asked.

"We put the money in a revolving account. She'd support me for the seven years I figured I needed to get the plants to a good size, and of course I had to buy land. In the end, it was quite a lot of money, but she's been repaid many times over."

"What happened in your personal life in California?" Amy asked.

"I met a man who I hadn't spent my childhood with and who I didn't mother. We got married, started Indigo, and along the way I had six children."

"Six!" Zoë said in horror.

"Six," Amy said in envy.

"We live in a beautiful house in the Napa Valley," Faith said, "and it's surrounded by acres of the Balm of Gilead. I've given the plant back to the Holy Lands," she added as though it meant nothing, even though it had been the happiest day of her life when she'd presented plants to their country of origin.

"What happened to Tyler?" Amy asked.

"He got married a few years after I left and he became a successful contractor. He built some very nice houses."

"Children?"

"Three," Faith said.

"And did you see him again?" Amy asked.

"Many times. My family and I visited my hometown often and we always saw him and Eddie and my mother. You won't believe this, but Eddie's mother and I became friends. She was great at business. I thought all her money came from her late husband, but I found out that that shrewd old woman was a whiz at the stock market. She's stayed at my house in Napa a dozen times. My kids love her."

Faith paused for a moment, then looked up. "One evening we were sharing a bottle of wine and she told me she wished she'd had a daughter-in-law like me."

"Did you strangle her?" Zoë asked.

"No, actually, her words made me cry. She didn't remember it, but I'd spent years working myself to death to try to make her like me, but she hadn't. But when I stopped trying, it happened."

"Too bad you could never tell Ty that you'd saved his life," Zoë said.

"I nearly forgot!" Faith said. "At my mother's funeral, he told a story that sent chills down my spine. He volunteered to give the eulogy and he told how my mother had saved his life. A few days after he crawled through my window—"

"And you weren't there," Amy said.

"Yes, by that time I'd already made my deal with Mrs. Wellman and I was getting ready to leave for California."

"How did Eddie and Tyler take your news that you were leaving town?" Zoë asked.

Faith shook her head. "Very well. In fact, they took it too well for my taste."

"As long as neither one of them got you," Amy said.

"You're right! I think I was the bone those two dogs had fought over for most of their lives, and as long as neither of them won, they were okay. I don't like to think this, but in some ways I think they were relieved when I said I wasn't going to marry either of them."

"So what was your creepy funeral story?"

Zoë asked. "How had your mom saved Tyler's life?"

"Ty said he went out to the cliffs as we used to call the local make-out place. I look back on it and I'd panic if my kids went there. It was really dangerous. There was a turnaround that was on the edge of a huge drop-off. We used to dare one another to look over because there were three cars at the bottom. It must have been a thousand feet down. Really scary."

Faith looked at Amy. "Ty got too close to the edge and fell over. He said it was the middle of the day, nobody was there, and he was hanging on to the edge with his fingertips. By a one-in-a-million chance, my mother showed up there. He yelled and she used a rope and Ty's truck to haul him up."

"Wow," Zoë said. "That makes my hair stand on edge."

"When your mother thought you might marry him, she hit him with a rock, and . . ." Amy said.

"Watched him fall to the bottom," Zoë said. "It's a good thing you went back."

"Yeah," Faith said. "A very good thing.

You want to know something even more strange? After I left town, and after she saved his life, my mother and Ty became friends. He introduced her to his mother and when his construction company got going, he built them a new house, and I paid to furnish it. The two women lived together until my mother died. And Ty's friendship with Eddie stayed strong. He was a pallbearer at Eddie's funeral, and, yes, I was there too."

Faith looked at her watch. "I don't know about you young people, but I'm exhausted. I have a plane to catch tomorrow."

"Me, too," Zoë and Amy said in unison, then the three of them laughed.

Zoë turned her pad of paper around and showed what she'd drawn. It was Faith and Amy laughing together, glasses of wine in their hands. They looked as though they were the best friends in the world.

"Wonderful," Amy said. "Could I have a copy?"

"I'll have it framed and send it to you. We do plan to exchange addresses, don't we? I mean our new addresses."

"Mine's the same," Amy said, then looked

away before she saw a look of sympathy cross their faces. She bid them good night and went to her bedroom.

As she showered, she thought about going home. It would be exactly the same, but Amy knew that she wasn't the same. She tried not to let it hurt her feelings, but the fact that neither Faith nor Zoë had said thank you to her for taking them back to the eighteenth century did hurt. If Amy hadn't insisted that they go back with her, Faith wouldn't have the seeds for her multimillion-dollar cosmetics company. And Zoë wouldn't have found her husband— and her backbone, Amy thought. It had taken a lot to make Zoë able to stand up to her bully of a sister.

But they hadn't said a word to Amy. That's all right, she thought. If they wanted to be selfish, let them. Amy had nothing to complain about. Tomorrow she was going to go home to her husband and sons, and she was going to be as happy as she had always been.

"I don't even know why I bothered to come here," she said as she got into bed. "Except that I saved Tristan. I did what I wanted to and that's what was important."

In spite of three glasses of wine, she had a difficult time going to sleep.

❦

"She doesn't know a thing, does she?" Zoë whispered to Faith in the bathroom they shared.

"Nothing," Faith said, "and I felt bad for not telling her. She deserves to know."

"She'll find out, but I think her husband should tell her, not us."

"I'm sure you're right. If I didn't believe that, I wouldn't have agreed to keep my mouth shut."

Zoë dried her hands on the towel. "By the way, you were brilliant at not giving anything away. 'When did you get so good at stories?'" she said in a mocking tone. "I nearly lost it then."

"Quiet," Faith said. "She'll hear you. If you'd dealt with as many big shots in the business world as I have, you'd be good at lying too. We just have to remember to not give anything away tomorrow. We'll have a few hours together in the morning, then she belongs to her husband."

"Who knows nothing," Zoë said. "Didn't you find it unsettling that no one remembered what had happened? I asked my sister several questions about when I was in the hospital, but she just thought I was crazy."

"I feel sorry for Jeanne. This time around, she didn't have you and me as patients. I didn't hit my mother-in-law at the funeral of her son, and you didn't set fire to a car."

"No, this time it was all about Amy. Jeanne lent this summerhouse to a world-famous—" Zoë broke off at the look from Faith and lowered her voice. "Do you think Amy went to bed with Tristan?" Zoë whispered.

"I don't think we'll ever know that," Faith said, "and I don't think it's any of our business."

"Faith," Zoë said, "I know that Madame Zoya said that we weren't allowed to contact each other until we came here, but . . ."

"But what?"

"When I saw Amy's name, I couldn't help it. I sent her a gift."

"What kind of gift? No, wait, don't tell me. A picture of someone."

"Yes," Zoë said. "You don't think that will mess up anything, do you?"

"It doesn't seem to have. The truth is that I had to work hard not to contact her—and you. I wanted to jump up and down and say 'I know her' whenever I saw one of your paintings. I saw that you married a man named Russell, but I had no idea that he was a descendant of—"

"The man I loved?" Zoë said. "He's so much like him that sometimes it's freaky. I'm mad about him. But you! You're the great success! I had no idea that Indigo was yours. I'm truly impressed. But it's a good thing I didn't know or I would have looked you up on the Internet and found out who you married."

"Who I didn't marry," Faith said. "Zoë, I don't know how you'll take this, but my company has a new product line coming out and I've named it 'Amy.' I'm giving her a lot of the proceeds to do with as she wants."

"She'll give it to charities," Zoë said. "I hope you didn't think I'd be jealous of that. You and I owe Amy everything. If she hadn't taken us back with her . . ." Her eyes widened.

"I don't want to think about it," Faith said. "I would have married Tyler and had a second miserable life."

"And I would have spent my life feeling

sorry for myself. By the way, I already sent Amy a letter saying she gets a portrait of her family from me every five years for life." She raised an eyebrow at Faith. "What if I start to do a portrait and see that she has a son who looks just like a certain famous American author?"

"I know just the herb to give you to keep you from laughing," Faith said. "I've had to use it at several board meetings."

Laughing together, they went to their bedrooms.

Twenty-six

"I will not be disappointed," Amy said to herself as she waited in line to get off the plane. "I won't be disappointed or feel cheated. I did what I went there to do and that was all I needed to do. If I were a selfish person, I would have asked for something for myself, but I'm not so I didn't."

The man in line in front of her turned to glare at her.

"Sorry," she said, apologizing for talking out loud to herself.

When she got to the airport, as soon as she saw Stephen and the boys, all thoughts of getting "more" left her mind. The boys ran under the guard tape and nearly tackled her. She fell back against her rolling bag, and threw her arms around them, kissing them profusely.

"Can I get in here?" Stephen asked as he gave her a quick kiss, then took her bag and ushered the three of them back under the tape. "Is this it?"

"Are you kidding?" Amy said. "I have three more bags full of . . ." She leaned down to the boys who were clinging to her. "Presents!" They yelled so loud that people frowned at them.

Stephen put his lips close to her ear. "I'd tell them to calm down but I feel just as they do. I'd like to yell with joy that you're home at last."

"I was gone just a few days," Amy said.

"I know, but for some reason it seemed like you were gone forever. It's like it's been a lifetime since I saw you."

"I'm here now," she said. "And I'm not going to leave again."

Stephen laughed. "That would mean you'd have to go camping with us next year and you know how you hate that."

Amy's mind filled with images. She had cooked over an open fireplace for over a year. She could stick her hand inside a wall oven and tell the temperature within a few degrees. She'd had to deal with weevils in the flour and maggots on the meat. She'd had to use an outhouse.

"I think I might be persuaded to go camping with you guys next year." She smiled at the expression on Stephen's face. "If I'm not a good camper, you can send me back after one day." They had reached the baggage claim area. "There are my bags," she added before he could say anything.

They got the luggage to the car and Amy opened one of them to give the boys what she thought of as "car toys." They'd keep them quiet on the trip home. This time they were those plastic boxes filled with hundreds of dull-tipped nails. The boys could make images of their body parts.

When they got in the car, Stephen took her hands in his to kiss them, then he drew back. "What in the world have you been doing?" He turned her hands palm up and looked at them in horror. There were cuts, half-healed blisters, calluses, scars, and skin so rough it could have been used to sand the paint off the car.

She pulled her hands out of his grasp.

"Just because I went ridin' without my gloves one day . . ." she said in imitation of Scarlett O'Hara.

Stephen started the car and backed out of the parking space. "Wasn't the truth that she'd been working like a field hand?"

"And that's what I've been doing," Amy said as she reached in her bag and got out the jar of Indigo cream Faith had given her. When she'd handed it to her, Faith whispered, "All my products will always be free to you."

"You look different," Stephen said, driving and glancing at her. "Besides your cotton picker's hands, that is. Have you lost weight?"

"I lost weight before I left, but you never noticed," she said, lying. "I've had time to get over my sadness, and that's a big change."

"No, it's more than that. There's something different about you. I can't quite put my finger on it, but it's there."

"I'll let you try later."

"What?"

"To put your finger on it."

Stephen blinked at her a couple of times. "You didn't just make a sex joke, did you?"

"Maybe," she said, smiling enigmatically.

He seemed to be so shocked that he was silent, watching the road with intensity.

Was I such a prude before? Amy wondered, and the idea that what she'd been through had changed her made her smile. She remembered how shocked Faith had been at the state of William's bedroom. Bedbugs, head lice, fleas. When Faith told Amy about them, she'd expected her to be outraged. Now Amy remembered saying something about there being a problem, but she certainly hadn't been shocked.

"Are you laughing?" Stephen asked.

"Just at something one of the women I stayed with said."

"You got along with them then?"

"Yes, very well."

"The last time I saw you, you were acting like I was sending you to the guillotine. You didn't want to stay in the same house with a bunch of strangers."

"You know, I don't think I'll ever again worry about meeting strangers."

He glanced at her in puzzlement, then turned back to the road. The boys started yelling that she had to look at what they'd made, so she gave her attention to them.

When they got home, the boys tore into their other presents and Stephen took the fishing rod she'd bought him into the backyard to try it out, while Amy walked around her house. It was the same but it was wondrous to her. She ran her hand over her huge cookstove. Stainless steel burners that turned on with a knob. No one had to clean it, or keep the fire going all day. Her oven even had a rotisserie and she remembered the fire dogs they'd had at Tristan's house. They were iron cages that were powered by little greyhound dogs that ran around for an hour at a time. When Amy had first gone there, the dogs were made to stay in the cages for many hours. She had liberated them, and, like everyone else, they were given proper working hours.

Dishwasher, big mixer, food processor. She looked in wonder at an electrical socket, and turned the blender on and off a few times. Marvelous.

"I'm glad you came home, Mom," her oldest son said and threw his arms around her waist.

"Did you think I wouldn't?"

"I had a bad dream," he said, his face buried against her stomach.

Kneeling, she pulled him to her. "Were we in a strange house and was I searching for you and telling you to get up, that we had to get out of the house?"

He nodded against her shoulder.

"I had the same dream, and you know what? It was just a dream. You woke up and I'm here. Right?"

He nodded, but still wouldn't lift his head. "I love you and I'm glad you didn't stay there."

"Me too," she said.

He grinned at her, pushed out of her arms, and ran away to go yell with his brother.

When she stood up, Stephen was standing at the end of the counter. "He sees it too. Something about you is different."

"Maybe it's just that I'm clean," she said. "How long has it been since those boys had a bath?"

"How long were you gone?"

"Oh, Stephen," she said in mock disgust, "I expected more of you. Really! This is too much." She had her hands on her hips as she started out of the kitchen to get the boys.

He grabbed her about the waist and pulled her to him to give her a thorough kiss. "I missed you."

"I missed you too."

His hand wandered down the back of her. "Did Davy tell you about his dream?"

She nodded, her face buried in his shoulder. She'd nearly forgotten the smell of him. No one smelled like him.

"We were in the tent and he woke up screaming. He said that you were telling him to get up, to get out of the house. Even after he woke up, he kept saying that Mommy was lost. He hasn't been the same until now when he saw you here with us."

He pulled back to look at her. "Did something happen up there in Maine?"

"Yes and no," she said. "Nothing bad. I heard the life stories of some other women, and I realized that I like my life as it is."

"I hope so," he said. "I'd hate to change it just because of something that happened at some summerhouse in Maine. Why are you laughing?"

"Because I'm glad to be home. Now let

me go so I can get those boys in the tub. I'm going to have to use lye soap on them."

"Lye soap?" he said. "Where did that come from?"

"It's great against fleas and bedbugs," she said as she grabbed one boy and ran after the other one.

❧

Amy was searching for Stephen. It had taken over two hours to get the family fed (Chinese takeout) and the boys scrubbed, then she'd had to wrestle them into pajamas. It took forty-five minutes of reading to get them settled. But after they'd at last fallen asleep, she'd spent thirty minutes just snuggling with them, holding their sleeping bodies. She hadn't realized how much she'd missed them.

When she went downstairs, Stephen was nowhere to be found.

"Stephen?" she called.

"In here."

She heard his voice but didn't know where it was coming from. It seemed to be coming from outside the dining room, but she didn't think he'd gone out.

It wasn't until she called him again and heard his voice a second time that she saw a door in the dining room that wasn't there before she went to Maine.

Tentatively, and a little bit concerned about what century waited behind the door, she opened it. She saw a large room, a study, that was done all in dark green and maroon. On the walls were photos she'd never seen before, of Stephen with people she didn't know.

Her husband was standing behind a huge, carved desk that looked as though it would fit in the White House, and he was going through a pile of mail.

"Sorry, babe," he said. "I promised myself I'd wait until tomorrow to do this, but it piled up while we were away."

Amy walked across a thick-piled Oriental carpet and looked at what he was throwing away. Every envelope was addressed to Dr. Stephen Hanford.

She picked up an envelope, sat down on the leather chesterfield, and looked at it. "Stephen?" she said softly.

"Yeah?"

She looked about the room more carefully. There were plaques on the wall, the kind that are given as awards. "What do you do for a living?"

"That's a funny question."

"Humor me," she said.

He looked up at her. "You know what I do as well as I do, since we married right after I finished my internship."

"Internship?"

"Amy, what's wrong with you? Okay," he said, but shaking his head at her. "I'm a cardiologist and you know that as well as I do. You've been with me every step of the way."

"A cardiologist," she said. "What about your father's trucking company?"

"Trucks? Amy, what were you girls smoking up there?" He put the mail down and went to sit beside her. "Okay, I'm game. What is it that you don't remember? My father is retired, but he was once the best cardiologist in the state. And no, being a great doctor didn't mellow him. He's still a pain in the neck. However, whenever I run into a problem I can't figure out, I still call Dad."

"Your father is a doctor?"

"Amy, you really are acting very strange. All of the men in my family are doctors. It's sort of a family tradition and has been for, oh, a few hundred years now. I can't vouch for what kind of doctors my ancestors back in England were. They probably did blood-letting and used lots of leeches."

"Your brothers are doctors?" she whispered. "Your beer-drinking, thrill-a-minute brothers are doctors?"

Stephen gave a sigh. "You know all this. Okay, so maybe it's like one of your books. My three brothers are all doctors and they travel all over the world. They helicopter in, climb mountains. If there's a disaster in the world, you can bet that one of my brothers will be there. They like excitement as much as they like life."

"Children? Wives?"

"Lots. There are so many ex-wives and children and stepchildren and half siblings that I can't keep track of them. But you've always been able to. Every year, you put on a Thanksgiving dinner for about fifty. You know all their names and relationships and you send them birthday gifts."

"I hope I can live up to my reputation," she said. The truth was that so much was swirling around in her mind that she couldn't seem to grasp it all. Tristan, doctors; doctors, Tristan. And she *had* changed her life. No, she'd changed Stephen's life.

Somehow, her going back to one of Stephen's ancestors and saving his life, and, through Faith, introducing him to medicine, had filtered down through the centuries so that it was now a "tradition" in Stephen's family that all of them were doctors.

She had done exactly what she'd hoped to. She looked at Stephen. "Are you ready to go to bed?"

"Yeah," he said, then gave her a look that let her know what he had in mind.

At least some things haven't changed, she thought.

"I have to make one call, then I'll be up."

"Okay," Amy said as she started for the door, then she turned back. "Did you say 'your books'? As in *my* books?"

"Sure." He was looking down at the mail again. "Your books. The ones you write out there in your studio."

His words put Amy in such a state of shock that she couldn't say anything. She went to the kitchen, to the back door, and turned on the outside lights. There, at the back of their three-acre property, was what looked to be a little Victorian house. Beside the door were hooks with keys on them. The only one she didn't know had a key chain that said it was good to be queen. Amy knew that that was hers.

She took the key and went out to the house. She wasn't surprised to see that it was very much like the one in Maine owned by Primrose and Madame Zoya. When she opened the door, she smiled. The living room, down to the last fabric, was a duplicate of the room where she'd had tea with Primrose. Through an archway was another room and it was an exact copy of the room at the store where she'd found the book about the Hawthorne family. The only other room was the "with plumbing" one, the bathroom with a kitchenette in front of it. The bathroom countertop was covered with blue bottles and jars that said "Indigo."

She went back to the living room. In a bookcase to the right of the door, she found what she was looking for. There were eight books there with the author's name as Amy Hawthorne. Quickly, she read the blurbs and saw that they were books set in the eighteenth century. Inside were reprints of some reviews. One of them said that Amy's descriptions of the time period were so vivid that it was as though she'd been there.

She looked around the beautiful studio, and as she did, memory seemed to flood into her mind. It was like when she'd suddenly found herself in the eighteenth century. She had been a newcomer there, yet she knew people and places.

She took one of the books with her name on it, her pen name, and held it to her. Yes, she was beginning to remember writing it, and even remember how many weeks it had spent on the *New York Times* Bestseller List. She glanced down and saw that the hero's name was Tristan.

When she looked back at the fireplace, she saw a portrait over the mantel. She knew where to turn on the light above the mantel. There was a portrait of Tristan, smiling at her in the way she'd seen a hundred times. The signature on the picture was, of course, Zoë's name.

"They knew about my books," Amy whispered. "They knew all the time." She smiled in memory of the way Zoë and Faith had kept secret what they must have known about her. In their relived lives, they'd seen her books on the stands, and Zoë had painted a portrait of Tristan and sent it to her. Amy looked at the little brass plaque on the bottom of the frame. It said "Nathaniel Hawthorne" and she laughed at the lie.

She had not only changed Stephen's life but her own as well. Maybe it was because in this second life her husband had a job that he was happy with, and it had released something inside her so she felt confident enough to write down the stories that ran through her head.

"I thought you wanted to go to bed," Stephen said from the doorway. "Don't tell me you're out here drooling over that guy again."

"I never drool," she said.

"Ha! I've never been jealous of any man except him," he said as he put his arms around her. "Sometimes I think that if he walked into this room you'd leave with him."

"Of course I wouldn't," she said as he bent to kiss her, and she knew that they'd never make it to the bedroom. "I would choose you over him."

As Stephen pushed her shirt off her shoulder, Amy glanced up at Tristan's portrait and she could swear he winked at her. She winked back, then gave her attention to her husband.

Turn the page for a preview of
Jude Deveraux's newest novel

Secrets

From Atria Books

Prologue

CASSIE HAD HEARD that drowning was the easiest form of death. She had no idea how anyone could know that, since whoever said it had lived, but as she drifted down in the deep end of the pool, she decided they were right. She could feel her long hair floating upward, and all weight left her twelve-year-old body. She wasn't trying to kill herself. No, she was just waiting for *him* to rescue her. But dying was interesting to think about. What if this really were the end? Smiling, she let her body relax into her thoughts. Never again would she have to hear her mother declare how easy Cassie's life had been while her mother's had been so difficult. "We stopped a war!" her mother, Margaret Madden, loved to say, referring to Vietnam. "No one else in history has ever done that!" Until she was ten, Cassie believed that her mother had single-handedly made the president of the United States remove the troops from the war that was never declared to be a war.

But when Cassie was ten, an old college friend of her mother had visited them, and when she'd heard Margaret bawling out her daughter, the friend started laughing. "Maggie," she said, and Cassie looked up in wonder because no one ever dared to call her mother "Maggie." "You never left your classes and you told us all that we were idiots to sit around on the grass smoking pot and protesting."

Needless to say, that was the end of that friendship, but it had been an enlightening experience for Cassie. That was when she found out that not every word that came out of her mother's mouth was the truth. She learned that just because someone delivered a statement with force and volume, didn't make it a fact. From that time on, she began to see her mother for what she was: a bully and a tyrant who believed that there was only one way to do anything, and that was the way *she* had done everything. To her mind, if her daughter wanted to grow up to be a successful person, then she had to conduct herself exactly as Margaret Madden had. That meant going to a top school, getting the best grades, then working her way up to the head of some mega corporation.

One time Cassie asked, "What about a husband and children?"

"Don't get me started," Margaret said, then said nothing else. But she had piqued Cassie's curiosity, so she began to secretly listen in on her mother's conversations. Most of the discussions revealed nothing of interest, but one day Cassie had the horror of hearing her mother say that her daughter had been conceived from a one-night stand with a man she hardly knew while she was on a business trip to Hong Kong. "Defective condom," Margaret had said without a hint of sentimentality. She was so disciplined that she hadn't realized she was pregnant until she was nearly five months along and it was too late for an abortion. Margaret said she'd done her best to ignore the pregnancy, and that she'd meant to turn the baby over to a childless colleague, but then her boss—the person she most admired—had said he was glad Margaret was going to be raising a child. It made her seem more human. When he gave her a sterling silver rattle from Tiffany, she decided to keep the kid.

As she did with all things, Margaret planned it carefully. She bought a house in upstate New York, hired a live-in house-keeper and a nanny, then turned the child over to them while she stayed in the city and clawed her way to the top.

Cassie saw her mother only on alternate weekends, and had spent most of her life terrified of her.

It was when her mother had been invited to a weeklong seminar at Kingsmill Resort in Williamsburg, Virginia, that Cassie's life changed. She knew about her mother's career because Margaret Madden thought it was her duty to inform her daughter how to get ahead in the world. Margaret loved to tell how she had been raised in a middle-class household full of "morons" but that she had "risen above" them. She'd put herself through college, studying business administration, then got a job as a junior manager with a big office supply chain. In her sixth year there, the company was bought by a fledgling computer business, and Margaret was one of only three upper-employees kept. Within four years she was at the top of that company.

By the time she'd been out of college for fifteen years, she'd been in five corporations and had moved near the head of each one. She was creative and dedicated, and every waking second of her life was given to the company where she worked.

The trip to Williamsburg was to be pivotal. The company where she was second in command was about to be bought by an enormous conglomerate, and at the end of the week she was either going to be jobless or made executive vice president.

The only problem had been that Cassie's latest nanny had broken her ankle and the housekeeper was on vacation, so there was no one to take care of the child. Margaret had used the inconvenience to her advantage when she'd called her boss and said she so rarely got to see her beloved daughter, could she please take the child with her? The man had been pleasantly impressed and agreed readily.

Cassie and her mother were given one of the many pretty, two-bedroom guest condos, and Cassie had been left on her own. Her mother was busy "making contacts" as she called it, never friends, never anything just for pleasure, so she was unaware of where her daughter was.

It was the first time Cassie had really seen her mother's colleagues, and for a whole day she'd been fascinated. There were over three hundred people at the conference and within hours they had assembled themselves into little groups where they put their heads together and whispered. When Cassie got near them, she heard "Madden," then they broke apart. It was as if they thought the girl had been brought there to spy for her mother.

Cassie spent her time wandering about the beautiful resort and watching and listening, something she was good at.

By the second day, she saw that there was one person who seemed to be differ-

rons" but that she had "risen above" them. She'd put herself through college, studying business administration, then got a job as a junior manager with a big office supply chain. In her sixth year there, the company was bought by a fledgling computer business, and Margaret was one of only three upper-employees kept. Within four years she was at the top of that company.

By the time she'd been out of college for fifteen years, she'd been in five corporations and had moved near the head of each one. She was creative and dedicated, and every waking second of her life was given to the company where she worked.

The trip to Williamsburg was to be pivotal. The company where she was second in command was about to be bought by an enormous conglomerate, and at the end of the week she was either going to be jobless or made executive vice president.

The only problem had been that Cassie's latest nanny had broken her ankle and the housekeeper was on vacation, so there was no one to take care of the child. Margaret had used the inconvenience to her advantage when she'd called her boss and said she so rarely got to see her beloved daughter, could she please take the child with her? The man had been pleasantly impressed and agreed readily.

Cassie and her mother were given one of the many pretty, two-bedroom guest condos, and Cassie had been left on her own. Her mother was busy "making contacts" as she called it, never friends, never anything just for pleasure, so she was unaware of where her daughter was.

It was the first time Cassie had really seen her mother's colleagues, and for a whole day she'd been fascinated. There were over three hundred people at the conference and within hours they had assembled themselves into little groups where they put their heads together and whispered. When Cassie got near them, she heard "Madden," then they broke apart. It was as if they thought the girl had been brought there to spy for her mother.

Cassie spent her time wandering about the beautiful resort and watching and listening, something she was good at.

By the second day, she saw that there was one person who seemed to be different from the others. He was a tall young man with blue eyes, black hair, and a tiny cleft in his chin. She didn't know who he was or what he did, but he seemed to run the place. The CEOs of the two merging corporations both talked to him. He'd listen, then go away, and later he'd nod toward someone that something had been done.

Cassie thought he was the quiet in the eye of the storm. Tempers were high that week. There were big negotiations of who was going to stay and in what position, and who was leaving. Little cliques of men and women were everywhere, plotting and planning.

In the midst of it all was this young man, who was very calm. She watched him step into the middle of angry people, and within seconds, whatever he said to them made them quit shouting. Maybe it was a reaction to her hyper mother, who was always living in the future, constantly scheming about the next product that would sell millions, the next takeover, the next position up the ladder, but Cassie really liked this quiet man who could settle others down.

By the third day, Cassie began to study

the young man. As much as possible, wherever he went, whatever he did, she was there. When he spoke, she put herself close enough to listen. Several times he turned quickly and winked at her, but he never once addressed her directly, and she was glad. She had no idea what she'd say if he did speak to her. What she liked the most was that he seemed to be at peace with himself and the world. She never once heard him talk about a "five-year plan."

By the fourth day, she knew she was in love with him, and as a result, her watching of him became more secretive. She hid in bushes as he played tennis and laughed with the other guests. On Saturday when he went sailing, she was nearby when he left and watching when he returned. She saw that every morning he went swimming before it was quite daylight, so early on Sunday, the last day, she waited for him by the pool. The fact that she couldn't swim very well was, to her mind, an asset. If she did begin to sink, he could save her.

Six came and went but he didn't show up. Cassie was in the deep end and she was getting tired. She hadn't had much sleep in the last few days because she'd been keeping vigil over him.

By six thirty, she knew she should get out of the pool. She'd decided he wasn't going to come, but then she heard voices from the direction of the house and she relaxed. He'd be there soon. She smiled in anticipation as she let her muscles go limp and sunk toward the bottom.

It was never her intention to actually drown, but as she waited for him to come, as she thought about her mother, she forgot about time and place.

The next thing she knew, she opened her eyes and she was being kissed by . . . him. His lips, his eyes, his chin, his body were all near

hers and he was kissing her. Or giving her mouth-to-mouth, which was very nearly the same thing.

"She's alive!" Cassie heard a woman say, but she couldn't concentrate because she began coughing up a lot of water.

"Are you all right?" he asked, his hands on her shoulders, holding her as she choked and spit.

Cassie managed to nod that she was

fine. As long as he was near her, she was sure that she'd always be all right.

Someone put a towel around her, and she looked up to see a pretty woman kneeling beside her. "You shouldn't go swimming alone," she said softly, tenderness in her eyes.

The man looked across Cassie to the woman. It didn't take much to figure out that they were together, a couple. If Cassie hadn't still been choking she would have burst into tears. She wanted to shout at the woman that he was *hers*! Hadn't she nearly died to prove that?

But Cassie said nothing of what she really thought. Life with her mother had taught her to keep her true feelings and emotions to herself. If people didn't agree with her mother, there were punishments.

"Don't tell my mother," Cassie managed to say at last, looking at him and avoiding the eyes of the woman.

Puzzled, the woman glanced at him.

"Margaret Madden," he said.

The woman let out her breath in a sympathetic sigh. "I didn't know ol' Maggie could have—" She cut off her sentence. "We won't tell," she reassured Cassie. "But maybe we should have a doctor look at you."

"No!" Cassie said, then jumped up to show them that she was all right. But she got dizzy and would have fallen if he hadn't caught her. For a moment she had the divine pleasure of feeling his arms around her. She was glad she hadn't died in the pool because if she had, she wouldn't have felt his lips on hers and his hands on her body.

The woman cleared her throat and he released Cassie.

She backed away, looking at them. They were a beautiful couple, the woman tall like he was, with her dark hair cut short and close to her head. She had on a swimsuit that showed off her long, lean, athletic body. She also probably played tennis and swam. *She* would never drown, Cassie thought, backing away from them. She was embarrassed now and afraid they'd ask why she was in the pool alone if she couldn't swim very well.

"I, uh . . . I have to go," she mumbled, then turned and ran toward the house. Behind her, she heard the man's baritone voice say something. The woman said,

"Hush! She obviously has a crush on you and she deserves respect." Cassie heard the man say, "She's just a kid. She can't—"

Cassie heard no more. She wanted to die from the humiliation and embarrassment. She couldn't will herself to die, but she could stay in her room for the rest of the day.

She and her mother left the resort that evening, but while her mother said her farewells, Cassie had skulked in the corners, fearful of running into him again, afraid he and his girlfriend would laugh at her. She didn't see them. But as soon as she and her mother got into the company car, her mother launched into a lecture about how she'd been embarrassed by Cassie's rudeness. "You'll never achieve anything if you don't put yourself forward," Margaret said. "Lurking about in the shadows will achieve nothing. It's possible, even probable, that someday you'll be asking one of those people for a job. You should see that they remember you."

Cassie kept her head turned away. Her heart nearly stopped when she saw *them* strolling across the lawn, hand in hand. She was sure they'd already forgotten the child who had nearly drowned just that morning.

"Him!" Margaret said, looking at the handsome young couple. "He's part of the security hired for this meeting and he stuck his nose in where it didn't belong!" she said, a look of disgust on her face. "He told a senior VP that if he didn't contain his anger, he'd have to leave. I don't know who he thinks he is, but—"

"Shut up," Cassie said, her voice calm and quiet, but fierce. It was the first time in her life that she'd stood up to her overbearing mother. Cassie had survived because she'd figured out the meaning of "passive- aggressive" when she was three. But now she couldn't bear for her mother to say something against *him*.

As they drove by, he raised his hand to her and smiled. Cassie smiled back and lifted her hand in return. Then the car turned a curve in the road and they were out of sight.

Margaret started with, "How dare you—" but when she caught the look on Cassie's young face, she stopped talking and picked up her briefcase from the floor.

When Cassie glanced up, the driver was

looking at her in the rearview mirror and smiling. He was proud of her for telling Margaret Madden to back off.

Cassie turned to look out the window, and she smiled too. She wasn't sure what had happened but she knew that the week had changed her life.

Economic Decline in Canada

SOCIAL PLANNING COUNCIL
OF METROPOLITAN TORONTO

The Social Planning Council acts as a voluntary social planning organization in the Metropolitan Toronto community. It encourages citizen participation in the analysis of social issues, the development of social policies and the delivery of human services.

The problems and proposals for the Canadian economy are dealt with in this excerpt from their eighty-page brief to the Macdonald Commission entitled "Democracy, Equality and Canada's Economic Future" (see chapter 5 for another excerpt from this brief). The council argues that structural changes in the economy are leaving Canada weak and that an economic policy that relies on the private sector to be the engine of economic recovery is hopelessly inadequate. Problems examined here include unemployment, productivity declines, decreasing social spending, increasing poverty and widening inequalities. Yet the council finds the most disturbing aspect of economic decline is the sense in which it is treated as inevitable.

The brief was prepared for the Social Security Review program group by Leon Muszynski, who is a program director at the council. The group is chaired by David Wolfe of the University of Toronto.

In their efforts to restructure the economy for recovery, business and government are increasingly unsympathetic to the plight of the poor and unemployed. There is a real danger of a future society where large numbers of people will be marginal to the economy as the commitment to public provision for their welfare declines. Technological change and industrial restructuring are occurring at such a pace and in such a manner that the interests of the workers and the communities involved are ignored. Nor is there in place a labour market policy that would cushion this adjustment process and allow those most affected by change to have some input into the decision making that so overwhelmingly affects their future....

The truth of the matter is that tough monetary policies, government cutbacks and increased incentives for private accumulation have not and will not work to achieve economic recovery. Further cuts in social programs and real wages only reinforce the cycle of decline. Spending cutbacks, the wastefulness of unemployment, and increased reliance on private sector investment decision making are all inextricably linked to our worsening economic situation. The final result of these policies is the longest and deepest recession since the 1930s....

It is irrational economics designed in the interests of the rich and the powerful and imposed upon Canadians without adequate debate or consensus....

This brief argues that economic decline is not inevitable.

Unemployment

Unemployment in Canada is higher now than anytime in the post-Second World War period. But the problem of unemployment is not simply related to the recession we have experienced since 1981. The rate of unemployment for the decade between 1970 and 1980 averaged 6.8 per cent. Unemployment has been low in Canada for only a few short periods in the past sixty years: in the late 1920s, throughout the 1940s and for a very brief period in the mid-1960s. The proportion of the Canadian labour force unable to find work has steadily risen since the mid-Sixties.

Canadian workers are at considerably greater risk of joblessness than their counterparts in other Organization for Economic Cooperation and Development (OECD) countries. In 1982 Canada had an average rate of unemployment of 11.0 per cent, while the average of the major OECD countries was 7.1 per cent. In a twenty-four-country comparison of all OECD member nations, Canada ranked twentieth in its rate of unemployment for 1982 (Table 1-1).

In the mid-1950s Canada was on par with western European OECD countries. For most of the subsequent period European countries performed much better than Canada (Figure 1-1). There are two striking conclusions to be made as a result of these comparisons. The first is that many countries similar to Canada in economic structure have had rates of unemployment, even during the current recession, far below the rate of unemployment for Canada for at least the past decade. Secondly, Canada has been one of the worst performers in maintaining a low rate of unemployment of all OECD member countries.

Even these figures, striking as they are, do not tell the complete tale of unemployment. There are large numbers of unemployed left out of the official figures. For example, not included are the 427,000 people who, in the March 1983 survey of the labour force, reported that they were not in the labour force but wanted work and were available for work.[1] Nor do they include the over 400,000 people who are working part time but want full-time work. Adding these two groups

TABLE 1-1
Unemployment of OECD Countries, 1982

Rank	Country	Unemployment Rate
1	Switzerland	0.4
2	Iceland	0.7
3	Luxembourg	1.2
4	Japan	2.4
5	Norway	2.5
6	Sweden	3.1
7	Austria	3.5
8	New Zealand	5.3
9	Greece	5.8
10	Finland	6.2
11	Germany	6.8
12	Australia	7.1
13	Portugal	8.0
14	France	8.0
15	Italy	9.1
16	United States	9.7
17	Denmark	9.7
18	Netherlands	10.0
19	Iceland	10.7
20	CANADA	11.0
21	United Kingdom	11.2
22	Belgium	13.1
23	Turkey	14.4
24	Spain	15.9

Source: OECD, *Economic Outlook 33* (Paris, July 1983), p. 45.

to the current official estimate of 1.4 million means that in excess of 2 million people are unemployed and wanting work.

There is also evidence that this hidden unemployment effect has grown more serious over the past several years as the official rate goes up. Using a formula for measuring "real unemployment" developed by the U.S. Bureau of Labour Statistics, Richard Deaton has found that the differential between the official rate and the real rate, which includes discouraged workers and half of the involuntary part-time workers, was 1.4 per cent in 1976 when the official unemployment rate was 7.1 per cent, while in 1982 it was 15.5 per cent when the official unemployment rate was 11.0 per cent.[2] Unemployment is even more serious than we think!

Moreover, the experience of unemployment is not evenly distributed across all population groups. Unemployment is much more heavily concentrated among young people. The official youth unemployment rate for the year ending in August 1983 was 20.6 per cent, while a measure of discouragement and underemployment for that age group

FIGURE 1-1

**A Comparison of Unemployment in Canada, Western Europe
and the United States, 1955-82**

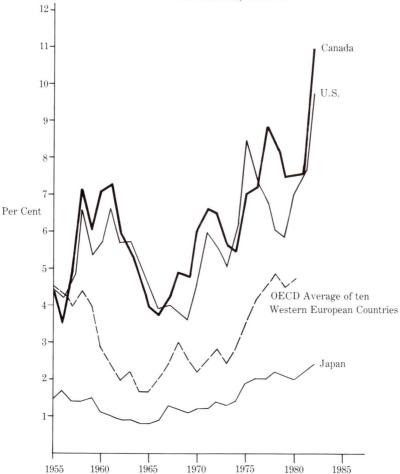

Source: OECD, *Labor Force Statistics* (Geneva: International Labour Office); adapted
from data compiled by Richard Deaton, Assistant Director of Research, CUPE.

requires that we acknowledge at least a 30 per cent unemployment
rate for young people in Canada.[3] In this age group the concentration
of unemployment is among those who have little education. In 1982
the rate of unemployment for Canadians aged fifteen to twenty-four
with less than grade 9 education averaged 31.9 per cent on an official
basis compared to 10.3 per cent for those with a university degree.[4]
Similarly, workers in the "blue collar" occupations have much higher
rates of unemployment than those in other occupations, as the loss of

employment has been concentrated in the manufacturing and primary resource sectors. The rates of unemployment for workers in materials handling, machinery, the construction trades, mining and quarrying, and forestry and logging were all in excess of 20 per cent on average throughout 1982.[5] Thus, unemployment is not just a problem of magnitude but it is also a problem of distribution. Certain groups are having to bear a much greater burden in their continuous inability to find work, their loss of income, the deterioration of their human capital, and their loss of status and self-esteem.

Our central objection to high unemployment is that it has devastating social consequences. We have been dismayed that the high levels of unemployment of the 1970s were frequently dismissed as not serious because of the extensiveness of existing social supports and because it was concentrated among young people and women.

For example, the unemployment insurance (UI) program was greatly expanded in the early 1970s as a measure of protection against the risk of unemployment. As unemployment steadily rose throughout the 1970s, there was considerable pressure put on the federal government to reduce UI eligibility and benefits. The federal government obliged. The consequence is that UI coverage is less now than it was before the major 1972 changes were introduced (Table 1-2).

The inevitable result of this erosion of UI protection is that the unemployed who are not eligible for UI or who have exhausted their

TABLE 1-2

Weeks of Unemployment Covered by
Unemployment Insurance Canada, 1970-81

Year	Person Weeks of Unemployment (000)	Regular Benefit Weeks Paid (000)	Regular Benefit Weeks Paid as a Percentage of Total Weeks of Unemployment
1970	25,740	19,817	77.0
1971	28,704	22,634	77.8
1972	29,224	N/A	N/A
1973	27,040	N/A	N/A
1974	27,092	25,803	95.2
1975	36,244	34,319	94.7
1976	38,272	32,329	84.5
1977	44,200	34,370	77.8
1978	47,372	36,575	77.2
1979	43,576	31,882	73.2
1980	45,084	31,262	69.3
1981	46,696	31,870	68.2

Source: Statistics Canada, *Statistical Report on the Operation of the Unemployment Insurance Act*, Cat. 73-001; idem, *Canadian Statistical Review*, Section 4 (various years).

benefits will have only welfare to fall back on. And it is apparent that welfare assistance plays a large and increasing role in supporting the unemployed as the unemployment insurance program is weakened. Welfare caseloads have risen dramatically because of unemployment all across Canada. In Metropolitan Toronto the welfare caseload related to unemployment more than doubled in the period of 1981 to 1983. The data indicate that there is a lag effect of about nine months in rises in unemployment and rises in welfare caseloads.

Moreover, the benefits paid to recipients of general welfare assistance in Ontario, and therefore to unemployment-related welfare recipients, is less than 50 per cent of the Statistics Canada poverty line for most family sizes. This condition has prevailed for at least the last two decades, and in Ontario these already inadequate levels have been allowed to deteriorate to the extent that the real purchasing power of a general welfare recipient has declined by as much as 20 per cent since 1975.[6] The majority of welfare recipients in Canada have suffered in this respect. Newfoundland, New Brunswick, Quebec and Ontario have all kept their welfare benefit increases significantly below the cost-of-living increase during the period 1974 to 1982.[7] The poor in Canada are getting poorer and unemployment is a major reason why this is occurring. Policies of restraint in income security are rationalized on the basis of the need to stimulate economic growth and reduce unemployment, but the experience has been that unemployment has risen consistently and the safety nets have eroded at the same time. This suggests to us that Canadians are not only having more difficulty finding jobs and therefore income, but when they can't find jobs, the income supports that they need are more difficult to find and less adequate than they have been in the past.

The Future: Unemployment or Full Employment?

It is our belief that the need for full employment has never been greater. Yet governments in Canada have abandoned any commitments they might have had in the past to keeping unemployment low. Admittedly the concept of full employment has defied precise measurement. In the 1960s the Economic Council of Canada considered 3 per cent unemployment to be full employment. Even this limited definition was dropped in the mid-1970s, as economists started claiming that 5 or 6 per cent unemployment was actually the best that the economy could do given the assumed trade-off against inflationary pressures.

Efforts to define away the unemployment problem by redefining the full-employment unemployment level have been elaborate. Throughout the 1970s and right up to 1981, claims were made that high unemployment was related to labour market supply factors such as the increase in youth and female labour force participation, the assumed work disincentive effects of unemployment insurance and structural mismatches in the supply and demand for labour. While the significance of these factors in altering labour market behaviour does have to be acknowledged, we believe that these arguments for public policy commitments to higher levels of unemployment represent not much more than rationalizations for the failures of neo-classical theories to adequately explain simultaneously rising unemployment and inflation. They represent the failure of public policy to create a sufficient number of jobs for all Canadians needing and wanting one.[8]

The prospects for employment opportunities for the future appear bleak. Despite the projected short recovery this year, most analysts see unemployment remaining above 10 to 11 per cent for at least the rest of the decade. The Conference Board of Canada forecasts a continuation of the same high levels of unemployment into 1988. *The Rocky Road to 1990*, a paper by the Ministry of State for Economic Development, points out that it will take two million extra jobs over the next decade to bring unemployment down below an "acceptable" 10 per cent. A document for the Department of Employment and Immigration fully expects a rate of unemployment for young people of 19.4 per cent in 1985.[9]

It is our belief that the goal of full employment is unassailable on both social and economic grounds. It is achievable but it will require a recognition of the real causes of unemployment and a commitment to social and economic policies with jobs and income security as their central objectives. Most of all it will require a different understanding of the nature of our economic problems.

The Costs of Adjustment

Between August 1981 and December 1982, Canada suffered a net loss of 608,000 jobs or 5.5 per cent of total employment.[10] There is little doubt where this most current economic decline is causing unemployment. Particularly severe cutbacks have been experienced in forestry production, metal mining and the manufacturing and trade sectors. Over 53 per cent of the total jobs lost during the worst part of the recession (August 1981 to December 1982) were in manufacturing, which lost 18.7 per cent of its total employment.

New job growth has occurred since 1982. There were 311,000 more jobs in August 1983 than in December 1982, including 55,000 more jobs in manufacturing and 34,000 more jobs in primary industries, not including agriculture. But this still leaves the total level of employment 262,000 less in August 1983 than it was in August 1981. Compared to August 1981, there are still 256,000 fewer manufacturing jobs, with large deficits also in the primary resource sector, construction, trade and transportation, communication, and utilities (Table 1-3). The only significant growth in the past two years has been in the services, which, along with public administration and agriculture, helped offset the declines in all other sectors.

TABLE 1-3

Employment by Industry, Canada

(seasonally adjusted August 1981/August 1983,
figures in thousands)

	August 1981	August 1983	No. Change	%
Agriculture	495	485	− 10	− 2.0
Other primary industries	324	283	− 41	− 12.7
Manufacturing	2,138	1,882	− 256	− 12.0
Construction	651	564	− 87	− 13.0
Trade	1,894	1,845	− 49	− 2.6
Transportation, communication and other utilities	901	860	− 32	− 3.5
Finance insurance and real estate	594	594	− 0	− 0
Services	3,229	3,414	+ 185	+ 5.7
Public administration	758	768	+ 10	+ 1.3
Total[1]	10,989	10,727	− 262	− 2.4
Full Time	9,521	9,047	− 474	− 5.0
Part Time	1,488	1,706	+ 218	+ 14.7

[1] Figures may not add up due to seasonal variations in specific industries and due to rounding.

Source: Statistics Canada, *The Labour Force*, Cat. 71-001, August 1981, August 1983.

Approximately half the job growth since December 1982 has been part-time employment. Since 1981, the number of full-time jobs lost in Canada amounts to close to half a million, while the growth of part-time jobs amounted to an extra 218,000 (Table 1-3).

The modest recovery since 1982 has been the result of a recovery in consumer spending and industrial production, but it appears short-lived. Projections by the Conference Board of Canada suggest that there will be slower growth in the years ahead compared to 1983....

Under current circumstances it is difficult for anyone to argue that the recent very high levels of unemployment are the product of insufficient demand for labour. There is no apparent willingness to acknowledge that unemployment of more than 10 per cent is related to weak economic performance. And there is a tendency to attribute the severity of the current recession to forces beyond our control. But there is evidence that the particular severity of Canada's experience reflects inherent problems in the Canadian economy which existed long before 1981. A recent analysis of the recession by Arthur Smith, former chairman of the Economic Council of Canada, and Barbara Smith claims: there has been a failure to realize fully the extent to which the severity and breadth of the recession were attributable to domestic economic dislocations and misjudgments in Canadian economic policy settings.[11]

TABLE 1-4

Gross Domestic Product per Capita, Rank Order

	1960	1963	1970	1975	1979
Switzerland	5	4	4	1	1
Denmark	10	9	5	3	2
Germany	11	10	7	7	3
Sweden	3	2	2	2	4
Luxembourg	4	5	6	11	5
Belgium	13	13	11	8	6
Norway	12	11	8	6	7
Iceland	6	6	12	12	8
Netherlands	8	7	9	9	9
France	9	8	10	10	10
United States	1	1	1	5	11
Canada	2	3	3	4	12
Japan	15	15	15	14	13
Finland	14	14	13	13	14
United Kingdom	7	12	14	15	15

Source: Adapted from OECD, *National Accounts* and *Main Economic Indicators.*

It is true that throughout the 1970s Canada had one of the highest rates of growth in employment and domestic product of any of the OECD countries.[12] But figures on real growth obscure the problems with Canada's economy and when they began. Part of the reason for the relatively strong growth rates in Canada's employment and domestic product was due to strong growth in population and labour force. When measured on a per capita basis, Canada's economy started to decline much earlier than 1981. Compared to other major OECD countries, Canada has slipped from one of the highest in per capita output to one of the lowest. In 1960 Canada's gross domestic product per capita ranked second only to the U.S. By 1975 Canada ranked fourth and by 1979 it had fallen to twelfth (Table 1-4).

Historical Weaknesses in the Economy

Historically Canada's wealth has come in large part from exploiting and exporting the natural resources with which we are well endowed. We have used the revenues gained from exporting staple products to offset a large imbalance of trade in manufactured goods. The end-products sector has always been relatively weak in Canada.

We import on a net basis approximately 25 per cent of all our manufactured goods in the country — a very high ratio compared to most other industrialized nations. Our largest trade imbalances in manufactured goods are in machinery for our primary industries, such as mining and oil, and heavy equipment for construction. This manufacturing trade imbalance signals a profound weakness in Canadian economic potential and the potential for generating employment opportunities. Manufacturing jobs tend to be more labour intensive than primary resource extraction jobs, and they have important multiplier effects by requiring extensive infrastructure development, such as education, transportation, and related services, as well as a network of feeder and support industries that also generate employment themselves.

Canada has also long been dependent upon foreign investment in its primary industries as well as in manufacturing. This dependence has been encouraged by all levels of government and has, during periods of growth, had important economic benefits. But such dependence has also had negative consequences, especially during periods of economic decline. These have been well documented by the Science Council of Canada.[13] Foreign-owned enterprises tend to purchase their production inputs from their home-based plants, and they do not have the same positive multiplier effects on employment that an industry has that uses locally produced inputs. Branch plants also have poorly developed research and development capacities, this work invariably being located in the country of ownership. The effect of a high level of foreign ownership is to limit the process of innovation and development in the Canadian economy, thus preventing the growth and expansion of new and innovative industries.

The foreign owners of branch plants also patriate profits and dividends from Canadian operations, and since 1971 this has contributed to problems in the current account of Canada's balance of payments. Increasingly large net exports of goods and services — selling more of Canada's national resources abroad — are required to finance this patriation of profits and dividends.

These structural weaknesses do tend to exaggerate the experience of recession because they mean that Canadian economic policy is constrained by fluctuations in international commodity markets and the decisions of foreign owners. These historical weaknesses are exacerbated by the problems of productivity in Canadian industry, by the process of industrial restructuring and by the new conditions of international capital mobility.

The Problem of Productivity

Canada's ability to produce efficiently has been in decline for at least the past decade. Low productivity growth has been a problem in most OECD countries since the early 1970s, but Canada's performance has been especially poor. Between 1973 and 1980 output per employed person actually declined by 0.2 per cent, while the U.S., the U.K., West Germany, France, Italy and Japan all increased their level of output per employee (Table 1-5).

TABLE 1-5

**Growth in Output per Person Employed,
Major OECD Countries, 1960-80**

	1960-73	1973-80
Canada	4.2	−0.2
United States	2.8	0.5
United Kingdom	3.6	1.7
West Germany	4.7	2.9
France	5.7	3.2
Italy	5.7	2.1
Japan	9.0	4.7

Source: OECD, *Economic Outlook* (Paris, December 1982), Table 17.

Most analysts agree that the slowdown in productivity is one important reason why Canada's overall economic performance has deteriorated relative to other countries. A slowdown in productivity growth means a slower growth in income for work (between 1975 and the end of 1983 the average take-home pay of a wage and salary earner declined by 2.3 per cent) and helps explain the problem of simultaneous inflation and stagnation.

The problem of productivity stagnation is not well understood by economists. It has recently been the subject of considerable attention by the Economic Council of Canada (ECC). Yet systematic efforts to determine the precise cause of our decline in productivity growth have not been entirely successful. Large residuals of unexplained productivity changes remain. The ECC claims that the largest single cause of the most recent decline in productivity growth since 1975 is the slowdown in economic activity. Since this was largely brought on by the contradictory policies of high interest rates on one hand and incentives to invest on the other, the culprit here can be directly linked to Canadian economic policy.

> In Canada... about 40 per cent of the slowdown since 1972 can be explained by factors other than the change in total factor productivity — mostly by the occurrence of a protracted recessionary period. The remaining 60 per cent is cessation of growth as yet unexplained, in total factor productivity.[14]

The remaining 60 per cent is attributed to unexplained residuals and constitutes the "productivity puzzle" plaguing the U.S. and other Western nations as well as Canada. The ECC identifies several possible areas of investigation to explain this rather large residual. They include technical change, economies of scale, internal organization, inflation and the weight of government.

One argument that attempts to explain productivity declines is that government is too large and is taking too great a proportion of the national product. But this explanation does not hold up under close scrutiny. There is no doubt that government activity in the economy has risen significantly since 1950. But the trend toward greater government spending relative to gross national product (GNP) is misleading. In order to understand the economic implications of greater government spending, we have to decompose the elements of government spending into direct spending and transfer payments to individuals. Since transfer payments to individuals represent the redistribution of private consumption, they cannot properly be regarded as government spending. Direct government spending as a proportion of GNP did rise steeply between 1950 and 1967, but this was in part explained by the incorporation of medical-care and hospital expenses into the public sector. When viewed in terms of the actual volume of government spending represented in deflated constant dollars, there has been an actual decline in government spending relative to GNP between 1967 and 1981.[15] This period corresponds to the period of greatest productivity decline in Canada.

The largest component of growth in Canadian government spending has been in the area of transfer payments. If the size of the public sector is not the problem in Canada's poor productivity record, perhaps Canada's "generous" transfer payments programs are contributing to work disincentives and therefore lowering productivity. A multicountry comparison of social welfare spending and productivity shows that there is in general a positive correlation between welfare spending and productivity (Figure 1-2). We have to look elsewhere for the cause of Canada's productivity problem.

Problems in the economies of scale of Canadian manufacturing have also been pointed to as the underlying reason for Canada's inability to develop a sound manufacturing base. The need to develop better economies of scale is also used to rationalize a commitment to free trade and greater access to foreign markets. But the problem of economies of scale in manufacturing has significance to forms of standardized mass production more common to the 1950s and 1960s. Increasingly, successful industry is dependent more on specialized production than long production runs. Moreover, new technologies of production are encouraging vertical disintegration of industries.[16] And the most recent Tokyo Round of the General Agreement on Tariffs and Trade (GATT) agreements has reduced the effective tariff barrier to and from Canada to a marginal per cent of the price of commodities, thus opening foreign markets to Canada, while also opening Canadian markets to foreign producers.

Conventional economic models used to explain productivity changes usually focus on the mechanical or technical inputs to the production process, including units of human labour distinguished only by skill

FIGURE 1-2

Government Spending and Productivity Growth

(international comparison of hourly output growth in manufacturing
and social-welfare spending as % of gross domestic product, 1960-79)

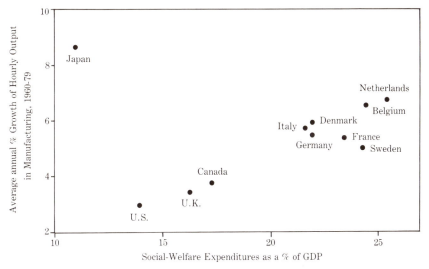

Source: Hourly output data from U.S. Bureau of Labor Statistics unpublished data,
1982; social-welfare expenditures include health, education, and income support
payments — from OECD, *National Accounts, 1982*, vol. 2, and unpublished
data. Figures on social spending are averages of levels in 1960 and 1979. From:
Bowles, Gordon and Weisskopf, *Beyond the Wasteland* (New York: Anchor
Press/Doubleday, 1983).

level. Much of the unexplained residual in productivity studies both in
Canada and the U.S. might be understood in an investigation of how
the social organization of production, and its impact on workers and
managers, affects productivity.

Labour productivity depends not only upon skill levels but also upon
work intensity. A worker's motivation to work will be conditioned by
a complex array of factors. Perhaps the most important element affecting work motivation will be conflict arising between labour and
management. There is a large body of literature bearing testimony to
the importance of work satisfaction to work intensity. Evidence suggests
that the conditions for greater work intensity will be diminished if
workers have little or no control over the production process, if they
are clearly distinguished from management by rigid and irrational layers
of authority and control, and if these divisions are reinforced by large
differentials in status and income.

There is also evidence that the wage/occupational structure in Canada
is highly segmented and inequitable.[17] We believe that conditions within

the workplace and divisions that are created between workers can lead to significant problems in productivity.

The conflictual nature of the Canadian industrial relations scene has been remarked upon by business, government and labour alike. The evidence of severe conflict between capital and labour is perhaps best illustrated by the Canadian record on strike activity. A recent study by the *Financial Post* found that in the period 1980 to 1982 Canada had the worst record in days lost per employed worker because of a strike.[18] Time lost during that period averaged 834 days per 1,000 workers per year compared to 752 for Italy. Canada's strike record has always been poor. Since 1973, it has averaged the second highest in days lost per employee among the major OECD partners (Table 1-6). The most striking conclusion reached by the *Financial Post* in its analysis of strike patterns is

> the remarkable correlation between the most strike prone industries and the accident rates of their employees. In fact strikes and accidents may have a common cause. Unions in four of the five most strike-ridden industries often do heavy physical work in remote locations typical of resource-related companies.[19]

In addition, the high degree of instability characteristic of the resource export industries which are subject to dramatic fluctuations in external demand and to levels of economic activity has been found to create an uncertain climate in labour relations, contributing to higher levels of strike activity and greater difficulties in resolving industrial disputes.[20]

There is, as the Economic Council of Canada reminds us, a very strong likelihood that productivity-growth declines that have affected most Western nations have common causes.[21] A recent investigation of productivity declines in the U.S. by Bowles, Gordon and Weisskopf confirms the belief that social factors have an important bearing on the

TABLE 1-6
Days Lost per Thousand Employees, 1973-83
(yearly average)

Italy	1,211
Canada	914
Australia	705
Britain	471
United States	396
France	192
Sweden	133
Japan	94
West Germany	40

Source: Strikes and Lockouts in Canada, 1973-82, Corporation and Labour Unions Returns Act, and U.S. Bureau of Labour Statistics, from the *Financial Post*, August 27, 1983.

productivity slowdown in the U.S.[22] A social model of productivity was employed and proxies were isolated to measure conflict between workers and management over issues such as the intensity of supervision, job satisfaction, work safety and income inequalities, and conflict between communities and corporations over issues such as pollution. Their empirical investigation of the productivity slowdown in the U.S. between 1966 and 1979 found that these social or institutional factors account for all of the productivity decline in the U.S. in the period 1966 to 1973 and two-thirds in the period 1973 to 1979. The remainder in the period 1973 to 1979 is accounted for by the lower level of economic activity in that period brought on by tight fiscal and monetary policies.

The Quality of New Investments

While the social factors we have identified may account for much of the poor performance of Canada's economy, there are other institutional factors which also act as impediments to productivity improvements. These problems are rooted in the structure of corporate behaviour, and they raise questions about the effectiveness of an economic recovery strategy that relies on the private sector for efficient investments and productivity growth.

The nature of corporate organization and the peculiarities of corporate behaviour have been investigated in a recent book by Harvard business analyst Robert Reich.[23] Reich argues that the organization of corporate life in America is at the root of economic decline. Reich shows how corporate management has undermined the American economy while it has restructured industry in the interests of short-term, largely "paper," profits. Corporate management is increasingly well schooled in intricate corporate accounting procedures and the legal intricacies of the tax code but knows all too little about factory techniques and the motivation of human beings. Reich argues that corporate management in America expends considerable energy on what he calls "paper entrepreneurialism" rather than real productive investment.

While it is difficult to generalize these conclusions to apply to Canadian corporate behaviour, there is evidence that similar conclusions can be drawn for Canadian business as well. In a recent statement, Thomas Maxwell, chief economist for the Conference Board of Canada, attributes Canada's poor productivity growth largely to the quality of Canadian management and its preoccupation with short-term profits.[24]

We are accustomed to believe that technological change always will increase productivity because it will increase the labour output ratio. But the effectiveness of new capital investments in Canada is questionable. A recent study by Uri Zohar for the Canadian Institute for Economic Policy found that at least part of the problem of productivity declines in Canada's manufacturing sector related to the poor quality and deterioration of capital stock in Canada....[25]

There have undoubtedly been significant improvements in productivity in certain sectors, such as in automobile manufacturing. But

Zohar's findings do suggest that Canada's industrial sector has suffered a deterioration in its capital stock. This raises questions about the effectiveness of an industrial strategy based on broad-based tax incentives to the private sector....

Capital Mobility

Industrial restructuring is inevitable — and can be desirable. There is evidence that the kind of industrial restructuring that we are experiencing in Canada is not all positive. There are basically three forms of industrial restructuring occurring in the economy. The first two are related to technological change. One form of restructuring occurs internally to existing industries by way of using new and better process technology to improve productivity in production. An example of this would be the use of robotics in automotive production or word processors in office work. The development of new technology also affects the structure of industry by way of opening up new opportunities for production. The demand for energy-saving devices leads to the development of biomass or solar technology, and there are a whole range of new consumer electronic products that have come on the market over the past ten years, such as video recorders and home computers. The third form of industrial restructuring may be the most important. It is the industrial restructuring that is the result of the global reorganization of industry.... In this sense the real problem of industrial restructuring is related to capital mobility and the emerging new international division of labour.

Plant closures and layoffs are not new to Canada. There is already evidence of rapid industrial change in Canada. The recent study by the Economic Council points out:

A surprising and little-known fact is that "birth rates" and "death rates" are very high. This is true in the average Canadian manufacturing industry but it is also true in other industries and in the United States.... An average industry had 88 firms in 1970. By 1979, no fewer than 38 deaths had occurred... with 32 of them being actual scrappings. At the same time, 25 births of new firms occurred... with 22 of these occurring through the construction of new plants. Bearing in mind that the picture is one of an extremely dynamic industrial structure with literally thousands of entries and exits over the decade, the turnover is enormous.[26]

The intensification of international industrial competition in the late 1960s and early 1970s required that Canadian industry attempt to reduce costs. Many corporations did so by way of reorganizing production internally, making new investments or reducing their work force. But many also decided that the most effective method of reducing costs and gaining greater flexibility in their production was to move. Capital mobility on a world scale has led to industrial restructuring that has had a severe impact upon Canada's economy and on our employment stability as well as the stability and integrity of many communities.

The conventional view is that layoffs and plant closures are the unfortunate by-product of an efficient and progressive economy. Labour, it is believed, cannot remain static, since firms must adjust to ever-changing circumstances if they are to remain competitive and profitable. Although it is recognized that layoffs result in hardship that must be borne by job losers, the benefits to society of industrial restructuring are supposed to outweigh the costs. Any undue hardship is expected to be compensated by unemployment insurance, and it is assumed new opportunities for workers will present themselves. This perspective provides an abstract if not idealistic rationale for industrial restructuring over the long run and it legitimates plant closures and layoffs as due to seemingly inexorable economic forces.

The reality, however, is quite different from the theory. As we have already pointed out, new job growth is not likely to occur in a manner that would replace the lost jobs with jobs of comparable wages. During periods of prolonged recession, workers are unlikely to be able to find new jobs, and as has been the case, unemployment insurance has not been adequate, as many people exhaust their entitlement to benefits and have no other recourse but welfare. But there is also evidence that this theory of the inevitability of industrial restructuring, plant closures and layoffs vastly overstates the need for unrestricted capital mobility.

The industrial restructuring that we have experienced is manifested in a global reorganization of production on a massive scale. There has been a dramatic shift in investment and production in steel, auto, shipbuilding, mining, electronics and textile industries to the "newly industrialized countries" (NICs). The condition under which this global reorganization is occurring cannot always be claimed to be favourable either to the Third World countries where new production facilities have been installed or to the "First World" which is losing its traditional productive base. For much of the Third World, these industries are export oriented and specifically geared to export to North America and Europe. The economic growth that is being experienced by these countries is more apparent than real, since the wage levels are so low that the indigenous population does not have the ability to consume the products of industrialization. This is particularly true in those parts of the world where assembly operations have been established in "free trade zones."

Economists Barry Bluestone and Bennett Harrison have identified the revolution in transportation and communications technology as the cause of increased capital mobility:

> The ability to move managers and key components at nearly the speed of sound by jet, and to move money and the information needed to coordinate production at nearly the speed of light enables capital,

as never before, to go anywhere in the world. As that technology continues to improve, as the costs of transportation and information decline, the ability of all forms of industry to move and to locate wherever they can get even the smallest cost advantage will become a primary factor in firms' location decisions. The competition for capital between communities in various parts of the country and between countries will be exacerbated. That is the greatest threat to working people from these technological advances, far more than the threat of robots on the assembly line.[27]

It is easy for us to regard this process of global restructuring with some inevitability. But the consequences for Canada can be devastating. It will intensify Canada's historical tendency to rely on staple export trade and will make it difficult for Canada to develop a domestic industrial strategy. The increasing competitiveness of the international economic order might also be understood as a process whereby corporations are seeking to bargain for a better business climate in North America by holding up the potential for super profits potentially earned elsewhere. These conditions jeopardize any local effort to stimulate investment growth and industrial innovation in Canada. Firms may take advantage of government assistance in the establishment of industry in Canada at its incubator stage, and when established, will find it easy to move to the Philippines or Brazil or elsewhere, where labour costs and labour conditions are viewed as more favourable.

Several recent examples of capital mobility in Canada serve to highlight the conflict between social and economic goals as a result of capital mobility. At the first glance, the closing of the Hamilton switch gear and control plant in 1979 by Westinghouse Canada seemed based on sound business analysis. The industry was faced with stiff international competition and unfavourable tariffs, and there was a need to rationalize operations in more-efficient facilities. However, the union involved contested this view, and a year later the Labour Relations Board confirmed the union's view that Westinghouse's management had decided many years previous that its long-term strategy for the plant was to run it down so that it could justify a closing to escape the union by moving to several non-union locations in southern Ontario. This procedure is sometimes referred to as "milking a cash cow." It involves a decision by a corporation, often many years previous to the closure, to not replace or repair old machinery or buildings, thus running them down and securing an accelerated cash flow from this activity to invest elsewhere.

A similar example here in Metropolitan Toronto was the Swedish multinational SKF. This historically efficient and profitable ball-bearing plant had been divested of its most profitable lines for several years, leaving it with a product line that could not be justified for continued production under market conditions in the early 1980s.

There are many other examples of corporate decision making which have similar questionable roots and have considerable social and economic costs that the corporation does not have to bear. These include Canadian General Electric's steam generator plant in Scarborough, Massey Ferguson's downtown Toronto plant and Canada Packers' meat-packing plant in Toronto.

We find it difficult to accept the claims of corporations that the decisions they make are always the best from a social point of view — it is also difficult for us to accept the notion that they are always economically rational as well. What is rational from the point of view of the corporation is not always rational and efficient from the point of view of society and the communities and workers involved. The social and economic effects of layoffs and plant closures can be significant, and corporations do not have to consider these costs in their decisions to lay off workers or close a plant. The corporate balance sheet does not have to account for externalities in assessing the cost of making a move. An economic structure that allowed for the full accounting of these costs might see considerably less capital mobility.

Implications for the Future

There is a clear and pressing need to address the structural and institutional weaknesses in the Canadian economy that are both creating the difficulties we now face and are undermining our future prospects. Canada's performance has been worse than most of the OECD countries, and there are lessons that we should be learning from our experiences.

The first lesson is that if we are to improve our chances at economic recovery and full employment then we must develop a sound and diverse economy. Our heavy reliance on imports in manufactured goods is not the basis for a healthy full-employment economy. Canada requires much greater attention to the growth prospects of manufacturing activities both for export and for domestic production.

The second lesson we should learn... is that the current policy framework which views the private sector as the "engine of economic growth and recovery" is misguided and probably will be unsuccessful even in the achievement of its own objective — economic recovery.

Industrial policy in Canada has been largely facilitated through the tax system. A series of generalized tax concessions to private industry has constituted the core of government efforts to direct and expand industry. These have included deductions from tax payable, accelerated depreciation allowances, tax holidays and tax credits.

Canada now has the most generous allowance for depreciation on fixed investments over the first seven years of an asset's lifetime, compared to the U.S., Japan, Germany, France and the United Kingdom.[28] These tax expenditures by the federal government have been estimated to amount to an average of $3.0 billion per year between 1974 and 1975.[29] And their cost has apparently outweighed their benefits in terms of new investment realized. The commitment to generalized tax concessions stems from the desire to reinforce the private sector's independence in making decisions about the magnitude, timing, type and distribution of capital investment rather than from a rational strategy for investment in new industries for the future.[30]

Our analysis suggests a need to look critically at our assumptions about private sector efficiency and market price signals as the basis for rational economic decision making. Other countries with a much better economic record than Canada's have recognized the need for public control of the investment process in a way that allows a country to strategically set out to achieve production and employment goals. We believe that for Canada to face the future with any degree of certainty we must develop alternative and more active policy instruments than those that attempt to passively support private sector activity.

The third lesson of importance is that poor labour-capital relations are part of the cause of our productivity problem. It is our belief that consideration of factors such as hierarchy in the occupational structure, repressive and unsafe work environments and the lack of democratic management structures is the best way to understand this conflict. Labour market policies for the future will have to address these issues and seek to find solutions to them.

Projections into the future are difficult to make. But we have identified at least two disturbing trends facing us in the years to come. The first is that technological change will result in substantial labour displacement that will not be adequately compensated by new job growth in other sectors. And the threat of a highly divided two-class society as a result of the current decline of traditional industries suggests potential for greater income inequalities in the future and considerable social tension. This tendency will be reinforced by efforts to cut back on social spending and income security programs.

Can Canada Compete?

UNITED AUTO WORKERS

With a membership of 110,000, the United Auto Workers (Canada) is one of Canada's most important industrial unions. Under the leadership of Robert White, it has chosen to be fully independent of its American counterpart.

In its appearance before the Macdonald Commission, the UAW spoke of finding for our society "an overall sense of justice and pride, of confidence and enthusiasm that the future can truly be called ours."

In this first excerpt from their December 1983 statement to the Macdonald Commission (see chapter 15 for another excerpt), the UAW deals with the changed economic climate facing Canadians. The union warns that "more of the same" in economic policy will likely prove disastrous. It argues that Canada can compete internationally by developing a flexible manufacturing sector, while continued reliance on restraint programs and resource exports is unlikely to produce a better life for Canadians.

In a part of their statement not reproduced in this volume, the UAW contends that reduced work time is one positive way of tackling the unemployment question. And the union also calls for a labour bill of rights to be embodied in our Constitution, on the grounds that our identity "is shaped and conditioned by our relationship to work."

Representing workers in Canada's major export industry, automobiles, the UAW is conscious of Canada's vulnerability to conditions in U.S. markets. It argues in favour of planning international trade, as opposed to adopting so-called free trade with the U.S.

The dominant economic fact of life for working people in the 1980s is the extent to which the world has changed. The postwar Canadian economy did include problems for working people, but it is fair to say that there was cautious optimism and high expectations, that progress — maybe not exactly the sort we'd like — would nevertheless continue to advance.

This mood no longer exists. It has been buried in a mud slide of unemployment and insecurity, attacks on past gains, and attacks on the trade union organizations that made such gains possible.

No longer do politicians and editorial writers proudly boast of our high standard of living; now they complain about "overpaid workers." No longer do parents assume their children will have it better; now they wonder where future jobs will come from. As the pessimism grows, so does the frustration.

Every day we hear lectures about the lack of productivity at the plant and office level, yet the incredible inefficiency of well over one million Canadians being denied the right to work is tolerated. In August 1983 the number of hourly workers employed in Canadian manufacturing was 1.2 million; that same month, 1.4 million working people — a greater number than those actually working for wages in manufacturing — were unemployed in our country.

Working people go on temporary strikes to defend what they have and they're slandered as destroying the economy. And, all too often, the force of the law is used to restrict workers further, to limit collective-bargaining rights and force workers back to work. Capital goes on strike, draining profits made in Canada permanently out of the economy, and no comparable furor erupts. In fact, the opposite happens: it's decided that the "investment climate" wasn't sufficiently favourable and we must give them *more* of our income and restrict them *less*.

Corporations devote an entire collective-bargaining presentation to a never-ending list of takeaways and then conclude with the need for a new spirit of cooperation. Just as finance ministers devote a budget speech to policies which totally contradict everything labour has been advocating, then piously conclude with an invitation to greater consultation....

The Changing International Economy

The most important economic development in the postwar period has been the erosion of the undisputed dominance of the U.S. in the world economy. The U.S. does, of course, remain the most powerful capitalist economy; the key point, however, is that in the immediate postwar period the U.S. had virtually no challengers, while today the challengers are there and their challenges are growing. Because of Canada's heavy dependence on, and integration with, the U.S. economy, these developments are fundamental to discussing Canada's economic future.

In the postwar period, potential challengers to the U.S., and therefore Canada, were limited by a number of factors:

• Europe and Japan were devastated by the war and were in the process of rebuilding.

- The high standard of living in the U.S. had created a large market for durable consumer goods; such goods had only a limited market in other countries because of their lower standard of living. This meant that overseas markets did not have the domestic base to develop the capacity to compete in the U.S. market. The U.S. market was therefore protected.
- High transportation costs, inadequate communication facilities, gaps in international finance, trade barriers such as tariffs, all combined to limit competition and protect U.S. producers.
- Third World countries had the further disadvantages of a lack of skills and poor domestic infrastructure (internal transportation, utilities, suppliers).
- The U.S. monopoly on technology was overwhelming.

The critical development of the past few decades was that all of the above "barriers" to competition were eroded. Europe and Japan, with massive U.S. aid, were reconstructed; international finance expanded rapidly; technological advances lowered transportation and communication costs; international agreements lowered tariff barriers; consumer tastes became more standardized internationally; infrastructures were improved in the Third World; and technology was disseminated on a wider base.

A primary vehicle for creating these changes was the multinational manufacturing company. It was in this period that the multinationals really came into their own and rapidly came to dominate international production. In their drive to internationalize production, they not only laid the basis for supplementary developments in transportation, communications, international banking and elsewhere, they also affected tastes and international technology.

As they sought new markets, these multinational corporations standardized consumer tastes, and "American" goods became increasingly common throughout the world. This did increase the possibility of more exports from North America, but it also allowed foreign corporations to use their growing domestic base to export to an increasingly similar market in North America.

And as the U.S.-based multinationals sought cheaper locations for their own subsidiaries, or cheaper outside suppliers wherever they could find them, they effectively spread some of their technology to these other areas. In many cases, these new corporations emerged only with government help, because the American invasion (what was dubbed "The American Challenge") was threatening domestic economies and a national response seemed essential.

In essence, these U.S.-based multinationals were laying the groundwork for new competitors — new competitors in the form of other multinationals who would challenge the U.S. corporations, and new competitors in the form of other countries who could compete with

North America for jobs (as often as not directly via the U.S. multinationals).

The dramatic intensification in international competition has meant a widespread and massive restructuring of the world economy. Three dimensions of this restructuring stand out:

- Because this restructuring is not planned but evolves through competition in the marketplace, it is *uneven*. Competition, by definition, means winners and losers: some companies grow, while others collapse; some industries expand, while others decline; some countries prosper, while other stagnate.

  This unevenness means that even if the global economy were to end up more efficient overall, particular workers, sectors and countries may not participate in this potential. In fact, they could be left worse off.

  Serious questions, especially at the national level, consequently emerge to challenge this road to "progress."

- A vital aspect of this competition and restructuring is the technological revolution. As scientific breakthroughs are integrated, at an accelerating pace, with manufacturing operations, every workplace — whether it's one of the losers or winners — is radically transformed. While this raises a number of important questions, a predominant question has been the *labour-displacement* implications of the new technology.

- This industrial restructuring has been taking place in the context of not only the recent recession, but a consensus of expectations that *slow growth* will be a long-term characteristic of our economies. This slow growth means that competition for markets will be even more intense and that alternative job opportunities will be even more scarce.

To varying degrees these developments represent threats to working people everywhere. Canada is, however, particularly vulnerable: we are linked to the U.S. economy, an economy that has lost much of its historical competitive edge; we face this competitive future with a relatively weak manufacturing base (we have the highest per capita manufacturing deficit in the world); we are especially weak in those manufacturing sectors that are the key to future strength — the machinery sector and the high-tech sector; and we do relatively little research and development, depending on the U.S. parents of subsidiaries in Canada for much of our technology.

Resource Dependency, High Tech and the Strategy of Export Orientation

The Canadian response to this new environment has, essentially, been "more of the same." As in the past, the development and export of our resources is seen as the key to our prosperity. As in the past, it is hoped that the spin-offs from the export sector will support at least a moderate manufacturing base and the manufacturing base can further be strengthened by focusing on export markets. And, as in the past, the key to such export success has been seen as a "favourable invest-ment climate," which, in turn, has meant wage restraint and a deter-mination to be labour cost-competitive. This strategy will fail.

Let's start with the priority given to the resource sector. To some people there is nothing wrong with Canada's overwhelming focus on resources. If, to use the jargon of academic economists, we have a "competitive advantage" here, why should we not exploit this advantage?

The first point to note is the extreme difference in labour intensity between the resource and manufacturing sectors. If we have a positive balance of trade, but one achieved by exporting resources and import-ing manufactured goods, we're still essentially importing the equiva-lent of three to four jobs for each job produced by exports, because there is a much lower labour component in our exports than in our imports.

More important, the "comparative advantage" argument misses the essential difference between resource dependence and manufacturing dependence: the flexibility that a country has with a strong manufac-turing base. If a resource becomes depleted or becomes obsolete because of replacements, there is little scope for adjustment and a response. If, on the other hand, a country has a strong manufacturing base, so it can build tools and machinery and develop new products, then it has the flexibility to respond to change and new challenges.

With a strong manufacturing base, a country has a measure of auton-omy because it has the skills, equipment and facilities to increase its self-sufficiency. It doesn't have to shudder helplessly at the prospect of the shutting down of one-resource towns, since other options exist. It can adjust to the decline of certain products and the phaseout of certain technology. It can survive a world that is rapidly changing.

These are not abstract points. The warnings are there when we look at communities like Sudbury and Schefferville. And the dangers of an overdependence on resources emerged out of two very important pres-entations before this commission: representatives of two of our most important resource sectors — forestry products and minerals — stated bluntly that the depletion of low-cost resources, the increase in foreign competition, and productivity growth would erode job prospects in the resource sector. According to the *Financial Post:*

It is not a happy story that the Macdonald Commission on Canada's future heard.... The message given the Royal Commission [by repre-sentatives of the Canadian pulp and paper and mining industries] ...

was that mining and forest-product industries clearly won't provide as much support for the Canadian economy as in the past.[1]

It is important to emphasize that this issue is not simply a regional one pitting the East against central Canada or northern Ontario against southern Ontario. It is the resource-dependent communities and regions that must be the most concerned with the need to diversify into manufacturing: to build on the resource base and increase Canadian content by doing more of the processing of the resources into manufactured goods, and by producing more of the machinery that cuts the trees and mines the minerals.

The issue is not whether Canada should stop exporting its resources; given the resources we have relative to our population, it's clear that Canada will continue to emphasize this natural wealth. Rather, the issue is that we must correct the existing imbalance and put a greater priority and emphasis on our manufacturing base.

At the other extreme, at least on the surface, is the emphasis on letting "losers" go and supporting "winners" — particularly ... high tech. There are no detailed Canadian studies, as far as we know, of the possible job impact of high tech. But a U.S. study indicates the illusions lying behind such a strategy. According to a Bureau of Labour Statistics analysis of job increases through 1990, the high-technology jobs of computer programmers, computer systems analysts, computer operators and data-processing machine machanics will indeed grow very fast. But because they're starting from such a low base, they will represent *less than 3 per cent* of the overall increase in jobs! Because Canada's relative potential in this sector lags behind that of the U.S., this conclusion would be even more true in our case. The numbers, in terms of potential jobs, are simply not there.

Furthermore, there is a lack of appreciation of the links between high tech and the rest of manufacturing. High tech does not occur in isolation; it is integrated into other sectors of manufacturing. This means that if we don't maintain our manufacturing base, we lose a potential base for applying high tech. It also means that the definition of which industries are "high tech" is misleading. Auto, for example, is often presented as a declining industry and is contrasted to high tech. But, in fact, auto is a major *user* of high tech: more than half the robots used in manufacturing and a high proportion of computer-aided design and manufacturing are, and will be, used in auto. Auto is, in a very real sense, "high tech."

It is interesting to note that one of the rationales for emphasizing high tech is that the market has already condemned other sectors to an inevitable decline. But if the criterion is the market, then the market has, just as clearly, also excluded Canada from high tech. In fact, a comparative analysis will show that our relative international competitiveness in the so-called declining smokestack industries is *stronger* than in high tech!

To enter the high-tech sweepstakes we not only have to make up for the fact that we're already far behind the major high-tech countries — Japan, the U.S., France, West Germany — but we also have to address the threat of emerging low-cost competitors from the Third World: Taiwan, Hong Kong, Singapore and South Korea.

Even if we simply confine ourselves to North America, the number of communities and jurisdictions that are determined that they will be the new "Silicon Valley" shows the futility of this strategy at the national level. Making Ottawa into a Silicon Valley does not solve the problem of unemployment in Saint John, Trois Rivières, St. Catharines or Vancouver.

And even within the Silicon Valley, the problems of lowering wages to meet the competition, and ongoing insecurity, re-emerge as the Ataris of the corporate world move to the Far East. Said one industry spokesman: "It's the only way to stay in business."[2] And, according to *Business Week:*

> New England is often held up as a region that has successfully transformed its economic base with services and high-tech industries replacing mills and shoe factories.... But according to MIT economist Bennett Harrison, the reality is far bleaker....
>
> The same interregional and international dispersal of production that sent the mills abroad is also at work in the high-tech field. Local minicomputer companies, for example, are spinning off production of basic components to low-wage areas outside New England.[3]

What both the resource-dependency and high-tech supporters have in common is that they're part of a strategy that is dominated by an export orientation and the god of becoming "internationally competitive." The essence of such an export-oriented strategy is its basic acceptance of the free market and the unilateral power of private corporations over our lives. Government involvement is not excluded, but it is viewed as either temporary, or an instrument to supplement the market, or a force to limit challenges to the market (such as worker resistance to market logic).

The labour movement does not question the importance of productivity gains, but this is different than accepting the rules of international competitiveness. Productivity improvements are essential to improvements in the standard of living, but in a market economy, they are not enough: in a market economy, one can become more productive but still lose out to others whose productivity is growing even faster. In the international market economy, it is *relative* competitiveness — and not productivity per se — that determines the standard of living.

Once a country accepts the priority of becoming internationally competitive, particularly in the intensely competitive world that is emerging, all progressive proposals come up against the challenge that they will make us "less competitive":

- Workers face this daily as corporations use this argument, backed by a real threat, to restrain and roll back not only wages, but basic shopfloor rights gained over decades of struggle: seniority, health and safety, working conditions, limits on arbitrary management rights.
- A positive use of legislation, or an expansion of the public sector, comes up against similar arguments: we can't significantly increase minimum wages or impose plant closure legislation because it will damage the "investment climate." We can't increase pensions, extend unemployment insurance (UI) or improve day-care services because a larger public sector that provides social services and benefits threatens the investment climate.
- Regional inequities confront the same dilemma. We can't have manufacturing plants in the Maritimes because it's not "competitive"; we can't build machinery in the West because we can buy it cheaper elsewhere.
- Attempts to affect market-corporate decisions can't be direct, because that would hurt the investment climate. So democratically elected governments are reduced to bribing corporations to invest here — bribing them with our money and bribing them with the promise that they'll keep labour in its place.

Playing this game of "international competitiveness" therefore undermines Canada's autonomy to carry out a national program to improve our society, although elected, even well-meaning governments find that the real decision makers are the amorphous market and the multinational corporations who control production. At issue is a meaningful democracy and the collective ability to really — rather than just formally — shape our lives.

As Eric Kierans stated so eloquently in the 1983 Massey Lectures, a country that tells people rooted in one region that they must migrate out of their communities to have any hope of gainful employment, a country that denies economic justice and increases economic inequality in the name of "economic reality," a country that reduces its land and labour to being only commodities and factors of production, a country that subordinates its culture and politics to becoming "internationally competitive," soon ceases to be a nation with a common purpose and a basis for unity — it is reduced, instead, to being one economic factory in a global economic rat race.

One standard reply to this is that these sacrifices and the acquiescence to international competitiveness are "investments." If we play the game, we will ultimately win; progress and security will ultimately be achieved.

No convincing argument for this position has been presented. In the early 1970s, the investment climate was apparently excellent, but the profit boom we witnessed led to no new manufacturing base. In the mid-1970s, wage controls were sold as providing the breathing room for establishing structural changes. Again labour made (involuntary) sacrifices, but all that resulted was the highest unemployment rates since the Depression and more calls for restraint.

Canada will not achieve security for its citizens by playing the game of international competition. There are too many players now who have a manufacturing and technological base superior to our branch-plant economy. There are too many governments that are determined to play the same game and too many countries that will invite in multinationals to combine the most advanced technology with Third World wages.

We can cut our standard of living in order to compete, but so can other countries. And, in many cases, we could not realistically cut it enough. Consider, for example, wage comparisons since 1960. In 1960 Japan's manufacturing hourly costs were about 10 per cent of ours and Europe's were 30 to 40 per cent. Today Japan has reached about half our level, and most European countries are very close to our levels. This would, according to those who emphasize labour costs, suggest that our competitive position must be strongly improved today. But it isn't.

There are two reasons for this apparent anomaly. First, the technological and productivity advances of Europe and Japan were much more important than the labour costs; in spite of extremely rapid growth in labour costs relative to Canada, their competitive strength is greater today than it was in 1960.

Second, even though our labour-cost disparity with the advanced countries has narrowed, new competitors have emerged with labour costs that are 80 to 90 per cent below ours. And, more important, they have emerged in an international context characterized, as we explained earlier, by a breakdown in the barriers to competition which had existed in all past periods of history.

These points can be illustrated if we look at labour costs in the Canadian auto, aerospace and agricultural implements industries.[4] In each case, average hourly compensation is significantly below that of the U.S. And industry analysts agree that our productivity in these sectors also compares very favourably. So it would seem that we should enjoy the job and security benefits of a better "competitive" position.

But we don't. And the reasons for this should help us understand why we can't win playing this game:

- Labour costs and productivity are only one factor determining the location of production. Other factors include the historical location of related facilities (auto), political factors (aerospace), distance to markets (agricultural implements) and local-content requirements.[5]
- Even in terms of labour costs, we may be cost-competitive relative to *average* U.S. costs but not to the lower-wage U.S. South.
- Similarly, the competition is increasing with lower-cost countries outside the U.S. In auto, for example, the Canada-U.S. share of the home market is now under 80 per cent and projected to fall to the 60 to 65 per cent range if nothing is done. And of the market that remains with the U.S.-based multinationals, more of the content is projected to be sourced overseas.
- There will always be someplace, somewhere, that can do it cheaper. This point was made particularly clearly in a report describing the concern of Hong Kong and South Korea that the "cheap-labour countries" are undercutting them. While wages in Hong Kong and South Korea are $1.15 per hour and $1.40 per hour respectively, wages in Indonesia are 40 cents per hour.[6]

As a General Motors (GM) plant chairman told the *Wall Street Journal*, "...how can all the plants be Number One? It's an unattainable goal, but the competition is never-ending."[7]

Planning Our International Trade

Debating trade issues in terms of free trade versus protectionism can be very misleading. All countries have some sort of industrial policy — some policy that attempts to gain jobs domestically at the expense of the jobs being located elsewhere. Free traders do not oppose this general policy of getting jobs at the expense of others; what they oppose is doing it by means of tariffs, quotas, content rules and other so-called trade barriers.

But if it isn't done by these means, it's done by other means: concessions from workers to attract investments, cutbacks in social services to allow grants, subsidies or low taxes to corporations, looser environment standards, etc. In other words, free traders argue that domestic jobs should be increased not by forcing the corporations to act in a particular way but by bribing them.

The first problem with free trade is, therefore, that it is socially expensive in the context of international competition. Free traders expound on the costs of protectionism but they ignore the costs of "buying" jobs.

The second problem is that as each country reacts to the policies of another, the bidding gets more expensive. Even those who play the game, and make concessions to the multinationals, simply pay more with no guarantee that it will be enough. In fact, as each country refuses to stimulate its economy, on grounds that this will drive up its own costs and therefore leave it less competitive, the international recession drags on. And the short-term domestic strategy whereby the recession allegedly improves competitiveness by "cutting the fat" in the economy, threatens to result in long-term damage. As the recession continues, not only weak firms but some stronger firms get into difficulties; uncertainty limits investment and the industrial base is permanently damaged.

The third problem is that the results are so unequal. Where economic relations between countries remain unequal over long periods of time, the breakdown of these relations becomes a serious likelihood. Economic relations can only be viable in the long term if they include a measure of equity.

Fourth, the problem with encouraging the internationalization of production is that it increasingly limits the autonomy of a particular nation. In Canada's case, where internationalization means increased integration with the U.S., the issue is not just limits on our sovereignty, but our survival as a political entity. We already face severe regional tensions; to the extent that Alberta sees its economic future tied to a North-South flow of resources and goods, or Quebec defines its economic sovereignty in terms of attracting investment from the U.S. and gaining more access to the markets of the American East, or British Columbia looks more and more to the Pacific Rim, what happens to the economic rationale for keeping the nation together? And what subsequently happens to the cultural and political rationale?

Canada cannot win playing this game. We have never had a strong manufacturing base. We did not have one thirty years ago, and we will not be able to develop one magically now — especially when the level of international competition today is so much greater than it was then.

In making these kinds of arguments, we will be accused of lacking confidence in Canada's potential. The opposite is true. Those who argue that we should play the game of international competitiveness are, in spite of the macho rhetoric, subordinating Canada's potential to the dictates of international markets and the unilateral power of multinational corporations. We, on the other hand, are arguing that we must and can find an alternative that gives society real control over its future — control to build a society that doesn't have to write off full employment, security, equality as "unrealistic."

This does not mean that we cut ourselves off from international trade; we do not dispute the benefits of international economic relations. It does mean that:

• We oppose the strategy of increasing our trade dependence. Rather than hoping to get more jobs by increasing our exports of manufactured goods (an illusion), we focus more seriously on import replacement: producing more of the goods and machinery we ourselves use.

- Changing the way we relate to the international economy; increasing the role of government in planning trade. Some examples of various degrees of such planned trade are:

  — Bilateral deals with Third World countries, such as the oil deal between government-owned Petro-Canada and Mexico.

  — Our grain deals with the USSR: government-to-government deals of mutual benefit.

  — Discussions on the Airbus are at government-to-government levels (more than two governments) and the outcome will include a planned division of research and jobs between the countries (some limited competition for jobs will still exist).

  — "Voluntary" restraints on auto exports from Japan, the Auto Pact, and the content proposal of the Automotive Task Force are various kinds of arrangements that allow for domestic safeguards in place of the unplanned vulnerability to the market.

A public debate on this issue will soon raise a host of questions: Can modest government involvement achieve "planned trade"? How far would we have to go in terms of the government's direct role? In which sectors can we "reasonably" increase our self-sufficiency? What might we expect in the way of retaliation? Can trade be planned without planning the domestic economy? What kind of domestic policy would be necessary to offset regional concerns?

We don't underestimate these questions. We appreciate that a country as internationally dependent as Canada has become over the past decade would face serious transitional difficulties in even slowing down the trend to increased internationalization.

But the present direction we're heading in is a dead-end street. We suffer through "short-term pain" only to learn it will be long-term pain. We believe that the alternative holds out the hope that we can eventually build something, that the transitional pain will be worth it. We must stop limiting our questions to "How can we become more competitive?" and begin asking whether this is in fact the game we want to play....

The starting point must be our private and social needs — labour rights, a national sense of equality and community. Starting with the priority of "international competitiveness" is a way of more firmly consolidating the status quo and reducing politics — our collective ability to change the world — to an adjunct of "economic reality." We must begin to assert our confidence in making economic structures truly subordinate to our social goals.

3

The Waste Economy

MANITOBA POLITICAL ECONOMY GROUP

The authors of this submission to the Macdonald Commission believe that it is possible to develop a political economy that is at the service of people. Yet, they contend, most analysis obscures the fundamental character of the economic system: the authoritarian and demeaning character of the workplace; the economic waste and human misery associated with unemployment and underemployment; and the squandering of resources for the benefit of the few.

While most orthodox accounts take the efficiency of the economy as to be self-evident, given the proliferation of goods and services available for private consumption, these political economists disagree. A belief in market efficiency, which is deemed to depend on the outcome of profit-maximizing behaviour of private enterprise, in fact leads to the wrongheaded conclusion that increased profits are equivalent to increased human economic welfare.

In what follows, the Manitoba Political Economy Group demonstrates that Canadians are forced to suffer human injury and economic losses in order to sustain the institutional arrangements that characterize our political economy. Though very much a polemic, many of their arguments are echoed by other groups represented in this volume, including the Canadian Institute for Economic Policy.

The group is composed of nine individuals. Errol Black and Ted Winslow are professors of economics at the University of Brandon. Robert Chernomas and Cy Gonick are professors of economics at the University of Manitoba. Fletcher Barager, Stephen Gelb, Michael Janzen, Jim Hirichishen and Ken Waldhauser are graduate students in economics at the University of Manitoba. This excerpt is drawn from their twenty-five-page brief entitled "Whose Economy Is It Anyway? A Program for Economic Democracy and Recovery in Canada."

The proponents of pro-business economic strategies assume that a profit-based private enterprise economy is more efficient than any other alternative. We see it as being enormously wasteful. What other conclusion can be reached when over the past several years a million to a million and a half workers have been rendered unproductive by forced idleness; when over a third of our productive capacity is sitting unused; when billions of dollars of our savings are squandered to finance corporate takeovers and mergers, and investment abroad, all of which add nothing to our capacity to produce; when 2 per cent of our gross national product (GNP) regularly goes to advertising, which contributes nothing to our knowledge about the quality of goods we buy; when an enormous amount of worker energy is devoted to fighting their bosses and disrupting production; and when an equal amount of energy and supervisory manpower is devoted to policing, monitoring and spying on a resistant and alienated work force — do we really need nearly a million managers and supervisors to keep our economy going?

Wasted Labour

We obviously waste labour if we do not use it when it is available to us. Statistics Canada has developed a measure of "underemployment" in terms of hours lost (1) through measured unemployment, (2) through part-time workers wanting full-time jobs but unable to find them, (3) through working short time. This is termed the unutilized component of the available labour supply. It amounted to 15.3 per cent in 1982. Using 3 per cent unemployment as our definition of full employment, we calculate a 12 per cent loss of output due to unemployment.

The obvious cost of wasted labour is the goods and services which do not get produced. But there is another cost which is often ignored or downplayed in discussions of the consequences of underemployment. The results of research done for the American economy by Professor M. Harvey Brenner of Johns Hopkins University revealed

... that a one percent increase in the aggregate unemployment rate sustained over a period of six years was associated with:
- 37,000 deaths (including 20,000 cardiovascular deaths);
- 900 suicides;
- 650 homicides;
- 4,000 state mental hospital admissions; and
- 3,300 state prison admissions.

While the numbers, and perhaps the incidences for at least some of these variables, for example, homicides, are lower, it is probably safe to say that the "social trauma" resulting from unemployment manifests itself in the same ways in Canada. Moreover, there are many other

manifestations of social trauma which are not included in this list —
wife battering, child abuse, alcoholism, a host of physical and mental
disorders (ulcers, hypertension, severe headaches) and so on — which
do not result in death or admission to mental hospitals, etc.

The costs of these consequences of unemployment assume two forms.
First, the capacity of people to participate in production is severely
damaged; indeed, in many cases they are permanently incapacitated.
And second, society has to deal with these problems, which means that
resources must be diverted from some activities, such as preventive
health care, education and house building, to the care, maintenance
and control of the victims of unemployment, to the staffing of mental
hospitals and prisons, to urban police forces and so on.

Wasted Supervision and Wasted Worker Effort

A second major source of waste in the Canadian economy stems from
the authoritarian character of the workplace. Despite all kinds of
evidence to the contrary, the entrenched political economy continues
to insist that work is solely instrumental — a source of income, pres-
tige, etc. — and has no merit in its own right; in other words, jobs are
treated as "bads" — things that people would not do if they had alternative sources of income. This idea is a perversion, for it denies the
possibility that individuals can, through their work, develop their creative capacities and derive satisfaction from contributing to activities
that enhance society.

Such a concept of work has profound consequences. In particular, it
provides the justification for the creation of workplaces that are mini-
ature replicas of the police state, complete with psychological testing,
constant spying (one-way mirrors, electronic eyes, etc.), close supervision and an elaborate system of punishment and reward which
discourages innovation and creativity.

Not surprisingly, the realities of the workplace create the results on
which the received concept of work is predicated. Workers learn to
have jobs, and channel their energies and creative potentials, that find
no outlet in their work, into figuring out ways to "do the bosses" who
have created the conditions they have to contend with on the job. The
manifestations of worker resistance to the objective conditions of their
jobs are legion — soldiering, absenteeism, sabotage, wildcat strikes
and fiddles of every description.

The maintenance of the authoritarian workplace results in incredible
losses in social productivity which take the forms of wasted supervision
and wasted worker effort.

- *Wasted supervision:* Nearly 7 per cent of the Canadian labour force
  is engaged in managing and supervising workers. This is a much

higher proportion compared to some other advanced economies whose economic performance is superior to ours. In Germany and Sweden, for example, the proportions are 3.0 and 2.4 per cent, respectively. Clearly, the implication is that if we had more democratic workplaces in Canada, where workers were actively involved in shop and office floor decision making, we could eliminate many unproductive supervisory jobs. Overstaffing in lower and middle management is widely acknowledged by many business executives as a major cause of their high cost of production. By eliminating, say, a third of these supervisory jobs and shifting these employees to productive tasks, we could add an additional 3 to 4 per cent to productive employment.

- *Wasted worker effort:* There have been numerous studies of the effects of greater worker involvement in decision making, job rotation and cooperative systems in coordination on worker productivity. Almost without exception, these studies show that increased democracy in the workplace pays off in higher productivity. By a democratic workplace we do not mean suggestion boxes and advisory councils, but substantive worker control over the organization and content of work and involvement in the formulation of company policy. There are roughly 1,000 firms in North America with some form of worker ownership and/or control, many of which have been in existence for a decade or more. While most of them are fairly small, their experience is not without significance. They have enjoyed a productivity advantage over conventionally owned and managed companies in the range of 15 to 30 per cent. What this signifies is that by maintaining undemocratic production systems we waste 15 to 30 per cent of our potential output. Using the lower figure for purposes of measuring the waste burden, we could increase hourly output by at least 15 per cent without pushing workers harder or exposing them to more hazardous work conditions.

Wasted Capital

Fiscal restrictiveness, harsh monetary restraint and inordinately high interest rates have put a virtual freeze on new investment and idled 30 per cent or more of plant capacity. These policies were introduced to combat inflation and to produce enough slack in the economy to tame an increasingly restrictive and demanding work force. The policies have succeeded for now — but at what cost? If the "cold bath" had not chilled investment, our capital stock would be considerably larger today than it is, and hourly output would be much higher as a result. We estimate the loss in output attributable to the depressing effect of economic policies on investment spending to be on the order of 2.5 to 3.0 per cent. Low capacity utilization costs an additional 1.5 to 2.0 per cent in output. Summing these, the cost of the capital waste due to restrictive government economic policies comes to 4 to 5 per cent in lost output.

An additional 4 to 5 per cent of potential output per year was lost because of the fact that an average of nearly $9 billion a year of investable capital was used in totally unproductive corporate takeovers between 1975 and 1981, rather than being used for investment in new production. Over the same period an average of nearly $3 billion was invested by Canadian capitalists abroad in the form of direct investment capital. If this capital had been invested in Canada, it would have added 1 to 2 per cent to output.

The total lost output due to unused, unproductively used and exported capital adds up to 9 to 11 per cent. But there is still one other major source of waste related to capital expenditure. Compared to other advanced industrial economies, Canada devotes an inordinate proportion of its capital investment to resources and related infrastructures. In relative terms, next to Ireland, we have the smallest manufacturing sector of all advanced industrial countries. Less than a third of our exports is composed of finished products, compared to an average of nearly 60 per cent among other industrial countries. Even this figure is an exaggeration of the extent of our industrialization, because much of our exports of end products arises from the Auto Pact. The overall effect of the Auto Pact has been negative, insofar as Canada has a large and growing deficit in the intrafirm exchange of vehicles. Excluding Auto Pact exchanges, the proportion of Canada's exports accounted for by finished manufactures falls to 22 per cent — which leaves us in the company of countries like Brazil and India.

Most manufacturing in Canada is done either by the subsidiaries of foreign-owned firms or under licence from foreign countries. Either arrangement restricts Canadian production to the domestic market. But even so, a massive proportion of the finished products sold in Canada are imported. During the 1970s our trade deficit in fully manufactured end products totalled $88 billion. In the first two years of this decade, our end-product deficit totalled nearly $40 billion. These imports were paid for by the export of raw materials. It is a poor exchange. The resource sector is highly capital intensive compared to manufacturing. This means that we sacrifice many potential jobs by emphasizing resource extraction rather than manufacturing. It also means that we sacrifice considerable output. If only one-fifth of capital investment were shifted from resources to manufacturing we would gain an extra 2 per cent of output.

Adding up all these components of wasted capital leads to the conclusion that we produced 11 to 12 per cent less output than would have been possible had we: fully utilized existing capital; maintained investment spending levels at the historical norms; used savings for new plants and equipment rather than for takeovers of existing facilities; ensured that investment took place in Canada rather than abroad; and shifted some of our investment from resource extraction to the production of manufactured goods.

Wasted Spending

It would be possible to list a variety of goods and services whose contribution to the general welfare is nil, close to nil or even negative. By tranferring resources from the production of some relatively useless commodities to the production of more-useful goods and services, we would enhance our collective and individual well-being. But this is a sensitive issue which should be decided democratically through the ballot box and, in a more egalitarian society, through personal choice.

There are some items, however, where judgments can be more easily made. Take defence spending. As many Canadians would agree, there is no security in the age of nuclear warfare. Canada could make a much greater contribution to world peace by disarming unilaterally and extricating itself from alliances such as NATO and NORAD. We could likely cut our defence budget in half without loss of security and with a sufficient budget to maintain our contribution to United Nations peace-keeping forces and other functions, such as policing our fisheries.

Currently, Canada spends $7 billion on defence. The amount is expected to rise to $10 billion by 1985. A large part of the military hardware we use is imported — mainly from the United States. More generally, the defence budget is very capital intensive. It absorbs enormous amounts of capital while creating relatively few jobs. The U.S. Bureau of Labour Statistics shows that every billion dollars spent on defence produces directly and indirectly some 76,000 jobs. The same billion dollars spent for health services would create 139,000 jobs, for education services, 187,000 jobs, and in machinery production, 86,000 jobs. Resources used for military purposes represent resources that are not available for the production of socially useful goods and services. Freeing up half the current defence budget for other purposes would allow us to add 1.5 per cent to our output of socially useful goods and services, and achieve a net gain of 0.5 per cent in total output.

Advertising is another expenditure of dubious value to society. The resources devoted to producing ads for McDonald's, Burger King and Wendy's alone would be enough to build a few badly needed hospitals. It seems reasonable to assume that we could easily survive with about half the advertising currently produced. This would save about $3 billion or 1 per cent of GNP, which would then be available for more urgently required and useful purposes.

The Waste Burden

Our estimates of the waste burden of the Canadian economy are summarized in Table 3-1. In brief, we calculate that a more democratically organized economy that made full productive use of its capital and labour and redirected some of its expenditures and investment,

TABLE 3-1

The Waste Burden of Canada's Economy, 1982

	Amount ($ billions)	Per cent of GNP (%)
Wasted labour	39	12
Wasted worker effort	49	15
Wasted supervision	10	3
Wasted capital	36	11
Wasted spending	7	2
Total	141	43

could increase the total amount of useful output by $141 billion over what was actually produced in 1982 — 40 per cent more than we produced in 1982. Over a period of just two and a half years we could have doubled our living standard!...

We make no claim to numerical accuracy. Given the range of waste revealed in our analysis, we always chose the lower figure. Moreover, we could have added substantially to our list of wasted expenditures by including the excessive money spent on marketing foods associated with the oligopolistic structure of the production and distribution systems and the hidden costs of unemployment, such as crime control, etc....

Our numbers are obviously ball-park figures. Even if they are too large by half, they reveal the enormous sacrifice of potential output we make in order to maintain the prevailing economic system. Nor do we argue that it would necessarily be in society's best interests to take all the gains that could be realized in the form of an addition to living standards — as conventionally measured. Translated from output to hours, we could have enjoyed 1982 living standards with much more leisure time. The lifting of the waste burden in 1982 would have allowed a reduction in the average full-time work week from thirty-eight hours to twenty-eight hours with no loss of consumption!

Scapegoating the Public Sector

CANADIAN UNION OF PUBLIC EMPLOYEES

With approximately 300,000 members, the Canadian Union of Public Employees (CUPE) is Canada's largest union. CUPE members come from diverse backgrounds and live in every region of Canada. They work for municipalities, day-care centres, electrical utilities, social service agencies, schools, libraries, community colleges, hospitals, universities, nursing homes and a wide range of other public sector organizations. Members also work in the private sector in nursing homes, voluntary agencies and related services. Within its membership there are numerous occupational groups, including school custodians, librarians, social workers, tradespeople, nursing assistants, cooks, secretaries, technicians, broadcasters and many more.

CUPE's sixty-page brief to the Macdonald Commission pointed out that the Canadian economy fails the basic test of meeting human needs. In this excerpt (see chapter 19 for a second excerpt) CUPE argues that a revitalized public sector is indispensable for economic recovery. It destroys the various myths that have arisen as business groups argue simultaneously for less government and more government handouts. CUPE proposes public planning, public ownership and the expansion of the public sector to resolve our present economic crisis.

As a union which represents public sector workers, we have some specific observations to make on the economy arising from the experience of our members in providing a wide range of services to the public. The commission is aware that the public sector has been the brunt of a good deal of criticism in recent years. Governments have been blamed for a wide range of economic and social evils, ranging from skyrocketing inflation to a decline in the moral fabric of society. Similarly, public sector workers have been maligned for alleged featherbedding, earning excessive incomes, engaging in irresponsible strike activities and, in general, being a burden and a parasite on society.

The public sector has become the most common scapegoat for the economic problems of Canada.

Moreover, cutting the public sector has been the most widely propounded solution to our economic woes. Slashing government spending, cutting social programs and reducing the influence of government in the economy are widely held as the panaceas for restoring our economy to health.

We are not uncritical of the way many public services are administered. Our members see mismanagement and incompetence in many areas of the public sector. We also witness needless waste of public resources and the implementation of policies which do not result in improved and more efficient services to the public.

At the same time, we believe that there are a number of misconceptions about the source of the problems of government and therefore the kinds of solutions which are ultimately required to resolve these problems.

Perhaps the most basic misconception concerns the role of the public sector in society. Although there has been a good deal of talk in recent years about how government is gobbling up the economy and placing an excessive burden on the private sector, the reality has been very different. If there is one criticism that ought to be made about the role of government in the economy it is that it has been, and remains, far too subordinate to the interests of the corporate sector. Instead of reflecting the interests of ordinary Canadians, government policies have been excessively concerned with placating the demands of business.

This is not to suggest that governments do nothing for ordinary citizens. As we are well aware, governments provide a wide range of vital social and public services. Yet the extent to which governments have assisted the business community is too little understood. And it is through an understanding of this function of government that a more balanced appraisal of public policy can be made.

There are a number of ways in which the public sector supports or subsidizes the private. Government establishes the economic infrastructure required to allow business firms to operate profitably. It provides a large market for the products and services of the private sector.

Government absorbs the costs of educating and training the labour force. It provides a wide range of financial services to assist the corporate sector, such as business advice bureaus and export loan guarantees. Government also subsidizes many corporations directly and indirectly through literally hundreds of different assistance programs. The public sector frequently provides venture capital for private firms, through agencies like the Federal Business Development Bank, thus absorbing the risks associated with new products or industries, while permitting the private sector to make profits if they succeed.

Government pays for various employee benefits and related services, such as health care, which would otherwise have to be paid by employers. It provides a wide range of police, fire and other security services which protect the assets of the private sector. The public sector provides a framework of legislation which regulates industrial relations and assists employers in managing their work forces.

Another form of support for the private sector occurs through the contracting out of a wide range of government services. From the provision of garbage collection to security services, private firms have been given the opportunity to make profits by carrying out public sector services or activities.

And, lastly, government manages the economy in a manner which is designed to foster the growth and profitability of the private sector. Creating a "favourable investment climate" has long been a central objective of government policy.

A second myth that has been widely promoted is that the public sector is not productive while the private sector is. This view only makes sense if the definition of productivity is one which equates it in a simplistic fashion with profitability.

Whether an activity is seen as productive or nonproductive has nothing to do with whether it is public or private. Rather it has to do with how we define productive activities. A maintenance engineer in Air Canada who does the same work as a maintenance engineer in CP Air is not "unproductive" simply because his or her employer is in the public domain. A service worker in a privately owned nursing home is no more "productive" than one in a public nursing home simply because his or her employer is a private firm.

Similarly, there is nothing inherently unproductive about the jobs of hospital workers, garbage collectors, hydroelectric utility workers, school secretaries and other public sector workers. The work they perform in providing needed services to society is neither more nor less "productive" than that provided by the private sector. Moreover, there is a strong case to be made that if we define productive·work in terms of social needs, far more work in the private sector could be defined as "unproductive" than in the public.

A third myth is that the public and private sectors are basically separate and therefore that figures on the share of the public sector in the economy reflect, in some objective way, the extent of the public sector burden on the productive private sector. Aside from the point made earlier that the public sector has remained largely subordinate to the private, the reality is that the public and private sectors are intertwined in such a way that it is exceedingly difficult to evaluate their respective roles in the economy. This point has been well illustrated by the Australian economist Hugh Stretton.

For example, a private firm mines public coal or oil, and sends it by private ships using public docks and navigational aids, or by public pipelines or freight railways, to a private gasworks or a public power generator. There it is transformed and sent through public wires or publicly franchised private pipes to (say) a private brickworks where it mixes with private clay to produce bricks, which go by private truck over public roads to (say) a Housing Commission building site. There a private contractor puts the bricks into a house which a public agent then sells to a private buyer, who pays for it (and for all the foregoing processes) from income earned from either the public or the private sector. It would be possible to find other countries in which the same process happens in the same way but with most of the public-private relations reversed.

Another example: public money funds university research in solid-state physics. Private journals publish it. Private firms which live chiefly on public defence contracts use the research to develop cheaper and better circuits which enable public and private telecommunications companies to commission the development of better machinery from private manufacturers. Users of the machinery improve the efficiency of a large number of private and public activities.

These are not special cases. Most of our processes of production and distribution have the same character — from raw material to finished product or service, the stuff typically passes from private to public hands and back again a dozen times before delivery to its final use.

...So it is not sensible for our national economic managers to obsess themselves with "the size of the public sector," meaning by that everything which public bodies happen to do or own, as if our public and private sectors were separate and independent, each autonomously producing a different basket of goods. But some of our masters do talk like that and act as if they believe the sectors have that sort of independence. When politicians say "we must restrain the growth of the public sector to allow recovery of the private sector," what does that really imply? It implies that more private gas is to produce less public power. Less public power is to produce more private bricks. More private bricks are to produce less public housing. Less public housing is to shelter more private buyers. Less public research is to produce more private industrial innovation and development. More private transistors are to produce fewer public telephone channels which are to carry more private communications. Less public education is to generate more private skills, and fewer public orders for educational materials are somehow to generate more private supplies of educational materials.[1]

The preceding discussion illustrates the complex pattern of interdependence between public and private sectors. It also shows the many ways in which the public sector can *and does* contribute to the profitability of the private sector. Many of the problems we see in the public sector stem directly from this subordination to the private. For example, a wide range of public services are contracted out or privatized so that private firms can make profits. Yet the quality of service received by the public is almost invariably inferior to that provided when the public sector does the job itself.

In other cases, management practices, borrowed from the private sector, are introduced which bear little or no relation to the fact that a human service is being provided. The employees affected become alienated from the work they perform and the citizens who depend on the service become frustrated about the insensitive manner in which it is administered.

In a larger sense, the policy of cuts which has been so vigorously promoted by the private sector has resulted in declining standards and growing dissatisfaction among citizens who quite rightly feel that their tax dollars are producing less and less in the way of real services. This is, of course, true: what their taxes are paying for are more and more corporate subsidies and handouts.

The subordination of the public sector to the private is also reflected in the shift in the burden of taxation from corporations to ordinary citizens which has occurred in the past three decades. In 1950 direct taxes on persons (principally income tax) amounted to 19.7 per cent of total government revenue. Corporation taxes in the same year represented 21.4 per cent of government revenues, a larger share than that paid by individuals. By 1982, after many years of business lobbying, taxes on individuals had risen to $57.8 billion or 39.2 per cent of government revenues. In contrast, taxes on corporations had risen to $9.1 billion and the share of revenues paid by corporate taxes had fallen to only 6.4 per cent.

Thus, in the past three decades, corporate taxes, which once substantially exceeded those imposed on individuals, have fallen to one-sixth of what individuals pay. Table 4-1 provides data on the taxes paid by each group from 1950 to 1982.

Many corporations have witnessed a major reduction in their effective tax rates, despite growing profits. This is demonstrated most clearly in the case of the banks, whose profits have risen from $556 million in 1971 to $1,630 million in 1982, while taxes on these profits have fallen from $277.7 million or 49.9 per cent to $104.8 million or 6.4 per cent. Table 4-2 gives the pre- and post-tax profits of the banks from 1971 to 1982.

The point we wish to make from this discussion of the role of the public sector in our economy is that the limitations on public programs stem not from any inherent characteristics of government in the abstract, but rather from the kinds of governments we have had administering the public sector and the priorities of those governments. These priorities have not been primarily ones of providing high-quality public

TABLE 4-1

Corporate and Personal Taxes as a Percentage of Total
Government Revenues

(excluding intergovernmental transfers)

Year	Corporate Taxes ($ billion)	Corporate Taxes as a Percentage of Total Revenue	Personal Taxes ($ billion)	Personal Taxes as a Percentage of Total Revenue
1950	.99	21.4	.91	19.7
1960	1.56	14.5	2.79	26.1
1970	3.07	9.6	11.55	36.1
1980	12.2	11.0	42.2	36.5
1982	9.06	6.4	57.77	39.2

Source: Statistics Canada, *National Income and Expenditure Accounts*, Cat. no. 13-001.

TABLE 4-2

Profits and Tax Rates of
Canadian Chartered Banks, 1971-82

Years Ended October 31	Pre-Tax Profits ($ million)	Taxes ($ million)	After-Tax Profits ($ million)	Effective Tax Rate (%)
1971	556.0	277.7	278.3	49.9
1972	668.8	313.4	355.4	46.9
1973	778.5	376.5	402.0	48.4
1974	874.6	433.6	440.9	49.6
1975	1,234.3	591.0	663.3	44.7
1976	1,199.6	536.3	663.3	44.7
1977	1,243.0	512.4	730.6	41.2
1978	1,495.4	518.4	977.0	34.7
1979	1,346.5	227.2	1,119.2	16.9
1980	1,452.1	209.6	1,242.5	14.4
1981	2,178.8	458.8	1,720.0	21.2
1982	1,630.2	104.2	1,525.4	6.4

Source: Bank profits reported by the Parliamentary Standing Committee on Finance, Trade and Economic Affairs, July 30, 1982, p. 112; Bank of Canada (1982 figures).

services to ordinary citizens. True, as a result of popular pressure in the period following the Second World War, they did expand public and social services significantly. But in the last decade this process was stopped and then put into reverse. Instead governments have been working to dismantle many of these services because they want to shift resources to the private sector.

The fact that current government policies are less and less concerned with satisfying the social needs of Canadians does not mean that government cannot be used to implement the kinds of policies needed to resolve our basic social and economic problems. The adoption of fundamentally different policies which do reflect the concerns of ordinary Canadians is perfectly feasible and workable.

Indeed, when we look at specific programs of government, we find that there is widespread popular support for many of them. For example, numerous opinion polls have confirmed that Canadians support medicare and do not want to return to private medicine. The popularity of Petro-Canada was, ironically, a major factor in the downfall of the Clark government. There is no lack of public support for better day-care or more extensive nursing home facilities. There is no lack of support for a better school system or improved municipal services.

The problem that we face is, quite simply, that governments have not had the political will to press for the kinds of improvements needed in the public sector.

Equality — Still a Canadian Principle?

5

The Rise and Fall
of the Welfare State

SOCIAL PLANNING COUNCIL
OF METROPOLITAN TORONTO

In this second excerpt from the Social Planning Council brief (see chapter 1) the nature and purpose of social spending and the welfare state are clarified, arguments in favour of restraint are examined and found wanting, and it is shown that economic efficiency and social equity are not at all incompatible.

The post-Second World War national consensus that gave rise to social policy developments in the 1950s and 1960s emerged out of the necessity, on social and political grounds, of preventing the recurrence of the social disruption of the 1930s. The new Keynesian framework provided the economic justification for increased social spending on income security, health, education and housing. For economists this spending served a dual purpose of meeting social needs and of lending stability to the economy by sustaining demand. The feasibility of expanding social programs was founded upon the notion that it was essential to achieve, if not "full employment," then at least high levels of employment and steadily rising incomes. The political compromise of this new framework was that income and services would be increasingly socialized, but investment was to remain private. The role of government was to create a stable market for investment.

The development of social policy in Canada was slow at first, particularly since the strong economic growth and relatively low levels of unemployment resulted in reduced political pressure for new social programs. Complex political negotiations between the federal and provincial governments on appropriate responsibilities and the sharing of tax revenues further dragged out its development. The strong tradition in Canada of commitment to residual or needs-related programs put further barriers in the way of the development of social policy.

Prior to the Second World War the only national welfare program in Canada was the means-tested old age pension. Each province had its own workmen's compensation plan, and most provided welfare benefits to single or deserted mothers.

By the early 1970s, an "institutional" welfare state existed in Canada. Government spending on income security and social services was tied to the level of unemployment, the aging of the population, the educational requirements of the young, and the medical needs of an industrial society. A vast array of nondiscretionary universal social programs was an accepted part of Canadian life. Total government spending increased from 16.5 per cent of gross national product (GNP) in 1950 to 31.4 per cent of GNP in 1974.

While these social policy achievements do represent real social progress, it is important to remember that poverty, inequality and social need were not alleviated. Significant levels of poverty remained, while the growth of the tax and transfer system did not result in a more equitable distribution of income over the thirty-year period. Social programs were tainted by their stigmatizing elements, and the welfare state was perceived as bureaucratic, inflexible and unresponsive to community needs. A large unfinished agenda remained, including income support and supplementation, pension reform, sickness and disability insurance, and a range of social and community-based services. Nor was full employment ever achieved, and efforts to extend collective-bargaining rights, social entitlements and rights for women, racial minorities, Native groups, and the handicapped were fiercely resisted.

The Fall of Social Policy

No sooner had this limited welfare system been established in Canada than we began to see it dismantled. By 1975 there was considerable pressure to curtail the development of new programs, and the wisdom of existing spending levels was called into question. Escalating inflation, rising unemployment, productivity declines, balance-of-payment problems, declining real-tax revenues and the rising public debt led government and business to back out of the agreement that allowed for expanding social programs. The validity of the Keynesian solution was now suspect, as the levers of demand management could apparently no longer reconcile economic growth with social progress. If the postwar consensus saw social policy growth and economic growth as mutually supportive, the post-1975 belief was that it was precisely government spending on social programs that was at the root of our emerging economic problems. Canadians had come to "expect too much from government" and the social security provided to Canadians was "undermining market discipline." Certainly social programs were expensive and we could no longer afford them at the level we had come to expect.

Both federal and provincial governments have embarked upon significant social-spending cutbacks. Combined federal-provincial spending on social programs declined from 20.1 per cent of GNP in 1975 to 19.4 per cent in 1981. The federal government has taken the lead in cutbacks.

Social program spending by the federal government declined from 9.7 per cent of GNP in 1975 to 8 per cent in 1981.

Transfer payments to individuals have been the main target. The most serious of these were the reductions in unemployment insurance as a result of changes that reduced both eligibility and benefits [see chapter 1 and Table 1-1 for evidence on this point — Ed.]. Direct federal contributions to the unemployed declined from $2.5 billion in 1975 to less than $1 billion in 1981, while total program costs climbed in that period because of rising unemployment.[1]

The indexation of family allowances has been undercut several times, so that benefits paid out in 1983 are already 30 per cent less than they would have been had indexation been maintained.[2]

Federal and provincial income maintenance programs have declined from 18.9 per cent of GNP in 1978 to 18.2 per cent in 1981 — the only period of decline in the postwar period.[3]

More recently, federal efforts have been directed to reducing transfer payments to the provinces, principally for health and postsecondary education. The federal share of five major provincial social programs was 48 per cent in 1975 and had been reduced to 41 per cent by 1981. It is projected to decrease to 38 per cent by 1987 without any further changes. Real spending on social programs administered directly by the federal government, including health and social services research, numerous housing programs, manpower training, environmental health programs, meat and drug inspection, and social and health services for Native People, declined by 15 per cent between 1975 and 1981.

The Reasons for Restraint

Several key factors in the 1970s precipitated the dramatic shift away from the dual goals of maintaining high levels of employment and expanding social programs and social security. The first was a steady deterioration of the competitiveness of Canadian industry. Canada suffered large and growing deficits on its balance of international payments. The second important factor was the increase in the federal deficit, which reached a record $4.8 billion in 1975. The deficits on the balance of payments and the public account were thought to have one single cause — inflation. Nor could the Keynesian framework account for or deal with simultaneously rising inflation and unemployment. The problem of inflation was seen as leading to the ruin of the Canadian economy. This prompted a re-evaluation of policy directions and set the stage for a dramatic reversal of previous spending commitments.

In 1975 three important policy decisions signalled the departure from past practices: the imposition of wage and price controls; the Bank of Canada decision to curb the growth of the money supply; and a decision by the minister of finance to limit future contributions to health care.

Monetarist and supply-side economic doctrines replaced much of the policy framework of the Keynesian era. The monetarist influence focused on high interest rates and money supply limitations, and the supply-side influence focused on putting additional funds into the hands of private investors and entrepreneurs. This policy framework has remained more or less intact since the mid-1970s and provides the rationale for current government behaviour.

Real interest rates remain high by historical standards; wage controls are in place in the public sector; governments have made significant reductions in their social program commitments; and tax policy has been fashioned to reinforce the private sector as the "engine of economic recovery."

Increased international competition, the deterioration of Canada's manufacturing base, high unemployment and capital mobility demonstrated to us the harsh new economic realities: that new, more-effective levels of capital accumulation need to occur in order to improve our economic efficiency, and that governments face a fiscal crisis. The fiscal crisis is the main reason espoused for the erosion of social programs or an inability to expand them. But it is not the only reason. Other arguments have been made that see government inefficiency as inherent to state activity, public programs and government enterprise as inherently nonproductive, taxes as confiscation of private entitlements, income security as undermining work incentives, and government as supplementing the family. As such, opposition to government spending and social programs emerges as opposition to protection from market forces.

There is some truth in this assertion. Adequate income security does make it less necessary for individuals to rely on their performance in the market and more on collective provision. Otherwise it wouldn't be worth much to us. But the extent to which it has undermined the market in Canada is vastly overstated. Moreover, it is not clear that equity objectives are incompatible with efforts to improve our economic efficiency. Indeed they may be essential.

The Role of Social Policy

Some clarification of the nature and purpose of the welfare state and social spending is required here. The idea of a welfare state is often associated with high levels of government spending and the transfer of income and services to the poor. But an advanced welfare state is not necessarily based on high government spending or more redistribution to the poor. The proper conception of an advanced welfare state is in its commitment to the idea of "social citizenship" for all members of society. This means that individual welfare should not depend on how one performs in the marketplace, within the family or with private resources. "A state is a welfare state when it guarantees a decent standard of living to all, as a citizen's right."[4]

Thus, principles of the welfare state include: that all people be guaranteed basic economic security independent of their relationship to the marketplace, that beyond minimum economic security that distributive justice and substantive equality exist and that there be a commitment to "social solidarity."[5] Social solidarity means that a society is made up of individuals who are mutually dependent on each other. It is the opposite of the belief that in a society each person is responsible for his or her own happiness and welfare.

It should be clear that the commitment to this ideal form of welfare state has never been achieved in Canada. Despite the number of universal social programs in Canada, our welfare system is still dominated by the notion of welfare as residualism. Social assistance and even unemployment insurance are heavily stigmatizing, and adequate income in sickness, disability and retirement still depends on a person's ability to purchase private insurance, which in turn depends on his or her performance in the labour market. And there is considerable pressure, within the context of the current commitment to restraint, to depart from the principle of universalism in a number of areas. The most obvious of these is the erosion of medicare, but a reduction in eligibility for unemployment insurance and the pressure on programs such as family allowances and old age security are other examples of a belief in the notion that universalism is "too expensive." Proposals for universal income security are treated as naive and unattainable.

The problem is that anything but a commitment to universalism in social policy is likely to jeopardize even further the future of social policy in this country. Nor are commitments to selective income security based on the principle of more efficient targeting always well founded on the basis of their redistributive impact. The commitment to restraint, and therefore selectivity on the grounds of unaffordability, is not justified purely on economic grounds. Finally and perhaps most disturbing is that a selective welfare state will leave us unprepared to deal with emerging social and economic realities.

The Importance of Universality

Social policy as it has developed in Canada has never evoked mass political support for all its elements. There is considerable support for medicare and family allowances, but it is not clear that the same support exists for unemployment insurance, social assistance and most of our social services funded under the Canada Assistance Plan. This might help explain the lack of opposition to the erosion of these latter programs compared to the considerable opposition to those that affect the middle class, such as medicare and family allowances. The importance of universalism is precisely in the universal support it evokes for state spending. The more people that receive high-quality services and protection from market forces, the more likely they will provide political support for high levels of state spending. This broad-based political support for social policies in turn helps foster the basic sense of social solidarity and shared responsibility that forms the basis of an advanced welfare state. The future of social policy will be put in further jeopardy if it is seen as public policy that deals only with a minority of the population yet costs taxpayers of the middle class. Thus, there is a real danger that efforts to be more "efficient" in the delivery of social programs will sow the seeds of destruction for those very same social programs.

Is Selectivity More Efficient?

Advocates of increased selectivity in social programs often argue that under the current system payments or services are provided to people who do not need them and that a more selective approach would allow for a more efficient targeting of benefits to appropriate recipients while allowing for an overall reduction in benefits. There are two arguments here and they are often confused in the public mind. The first is the issue of progressivity; the other is the issue of the magnitude of government spending.

The progressivity of demogrants such as family allowances, to use one example, cannot only be judged on the basis of the distribution of benefits paid. The tax system used to finance universal payments also has redistributive implications. What is important and often ignored in the attack on demogrants is an assessment of the distributive impact of *net benefits*, that is, benefits net of the transfer and tax implications. It is less evident that family allowances are regressive and inefficient using such a framework.[6] Indeed, the evidence is that the family allowance program is reasonably progressive within the existing distribution of income. Any effort to target payments on the lowest-income groups may provide higher payments to these groups, but the implications of a net benefit analysis suggest that when the tax implications are considered, those who would benefit the most would be both the needy and the well-off at the expense of the middle class.[7] If redistribution is the issue in a consideration of selectivity over universality, then advocates of selective payments had better look elsewhere for mechanisms to redistribute income.

Is Restraint Necessary?

Arguments against universality are similar to those that deny the possibility of expanding state spending and taxation in difficult economic times. These arguments assume that there is some optimal level of income distribution, government spending and taxation. None of these are true.

The need-for-restraint argument often focuses in on the level of the federal deficit. In 1975 the federal deficit had reached a record $4.8 billion. This level of deficit remained throughout the 1970s until the onslaught of the 1981 recession forced federal spending into a deficit of $10 billion in that year and to over $25 billion for 1982. Projected deficits for coming years are in excess of $30 billion [the deficit for 1983 was $29.6 billion and for the first eleven months of 1984 was $31 billion — Ed.].

The most recent dramatic increase in the federal debt has been the result of the particularly severe recession in Canada which we have argued in "Economic Decline in Canada" (chapter 1) is the result of the failure of public policy in developing a diverse and resilient economy. But the need for restraint was argued long before 1981. It was being made at the same time that the general government financial balances were not high in Canada compared to other Organization for Economic Cooperation and Development (OECD) countries (Table 5-1). Canada's net government deficit was lower than the average for the major OECD countries up to 1981. The main reason for the federal

TABLE 5-1
General Government Financial Balances
(surplus [+] or deficit [−] as percentage of nominal GNP/GDP)

	1979	1980	1981	1982	1983
United State	+0.6	−1.3	−1.0	−3.8	−4.4
Japan	−4.8	−4.5	−4.0	−4.1	−3.4
Germany	−2.7	−3.2	−4.0	−3.9	−3.7
France	−0.7	+0.3	−1.9	−2.6	−3.4
United Kingdom	−3.2	−3.3	−2.5	−2.0	−2.5
Italy	−9.5	−8.0	−11.7	−12.0	−11.6
Canada	−1.9	−2.1	−1.2	−5.3	−6.5
Total of above larger countries	−1.8	−2.5	−2.6	−4.1	−4.4
Australia	−1.5	−1.0	−0.1	+0.4	−4.4
Austria	−2.5	−2.0	−1.8	−2.5	−3.5
Belgium	−6.9	−9.3	−13.1	−12.2	−11.3
Denmark	−1.6	−3.2	−7.1	−9.1	−9.3
Netherlands	−3.7	−3.9	−4.8	−6.4	−6.9
Norway	+1.9	+5.7	+4.8	+4.4	+2.1
Sweden	−3.0	−4.0	−5.3	−6.9	−8.0
Total of above smaller countries	−2.8	−3.0	−4.1	−4.8	−6.2
Total of above countries	−1.9	−2.6	−2.7	−4.1	−4.6

Source: OECD, *Economic Outlook* (Paris, July 1983).

deficit over the 1970s rests in the revenue restraint policies the federal government pursued in order to provide more incentives for private investment.

The largest reduction in government revenues is contained in what have become known as "tax expenditures." These are a series of tax policies — income exemptions, deductions and special credits or allowances — that reduce the effective tax paid by individuals and by corporations. In 1979 the federal minister of finance estimated that tax expenditures then stood at a level of $32 billion. Over $16 billion was from new exemptions and deductions enacted in the 1970s.

Tax expenditures mainly benefit the rich and affluent. In his November 1981 budget the federal minister of finance estimated that 29,000 tax filers with gross incomes over $100,000 received tax expenditures nearly equal to 20 per cent of their incomes, an average of $40,000 annually per tax filer.[8] Those with average incomes received tax expenditures equal to only 4 per cent of their incomes, about $700.

Effective corporate tax rates declined during the 1970s from 38 to 29 per cent, resulting in an annual loss of over $4 billion in revenues. These tax expenditures policies to stimulate corporate investment have been judged to be not cost-effective.[9]

The April 1983 federal budget liberalized rules governing the investment tax credit, broadened the range of construction equipment items eligible for that investment tax credit, converted some investment tax credits to cash refunds, established a number of special recovery programs for business, and put into effect special tax incentives for research and development, at a total cost of over $2.5 billion. People of modest and ordinary means saw their taxes increase as a result of the elimination of the $200 federal tax reduction and the $100 automatic standard deduction for charitable donations, and a net revenue increase of $585 million from changes in the child-benefit system.

Revenue restraint is at the root of our inability to generate sufficient tax income to pay for adequate social spending. A removal of the inequitable and apparently ineffective tax-expenditure provisions of the past decade would reduce significantly the current federal deficit. A full-employment policy would reduce it even further.

Can we afford to raise taxes in order to finance social programs? International comparisons again show that the tax burden upon individual Canadians is not large when compared to other countries in the OECD. In a twenty-one-country OECD comparison Canada ranks one of the lowest in the percentage of gross earnings taken by income tax and social security. The average one-earner, four-person family in Ontario has an overall tax burden of just over 15 per cent, while for the U.S. it is over 20 per cent, and for Germany and the U.K. it is over 25 per cent. For Sweden and Denmark it is approximately 35 per cent (Figure 5-1).

Opposition to an expansion of social spending is often opposition to redistribution. The perception underlying this position is that Canadian social spending has been overgenerous in redistributing income and has undermined economic efficiency. While there is no optimal distribution of income in economic theory, the belief that redistribution has occurred is belied by the reality. The fact is that the incredible growth in government spending in the period 1950 to 1975 did little to redistribute income in Canada. Evidence suggests that the total package of welfare programs, including the effects of taxes and transfers, left the distribution of income constant throughout that period (Table 5-2).

Nor has the growth of social programs eliminated poverty. The incidence of poverty in Canada declined steadily over the 1960s and 1970s. But poverty among the elderly, especially women, is exceedingly high, and there has been a dramatic increase in the number of people in poverty between 1980 and 1982.

Opposition to social spending in Canada may be rationalized by reference to the high level of the government deficit or even a perception of excessive levels of spending. But this is not the real reason for opposition to social spending. Opposition to provision of adequate social security and a more equal distribution of income rests in the belief that more social equity undermines market efficiency.

Are Efficiency and Equity Compatible?

The relationship between efficiency and equality in market economies has never been effectively resolved in economic theory. There is certainly no apparent optimum distribution of income in theory, although an extreme degree of equality or inequality would likely impede economic performance. But the current framework operates on the assumption that more equality and more social security are inimical to more efficiency. Equity has to be traded off against growth and efficiency.

This view is simply not true. Greater equity can be achieved in the pursuit of more efficiency. Indeed, it may be that more equity and more security of income are the essential prerequisites to sound economic performance. A recent study of the relationship between growth and equity policies in a number of Western nations found that "the very best performers seem to have two characteristics in common. They enjoy more egalitarian income distribution... and they are far more successful at converting savings to productive investment."[10]

The achievement of growth and improved productivity does not require increasing profit levels in the private sector or augmenting the private savings of high-income individuals. It requires that we consume less than we produce, that we convert our savings into investments in

FIGURE 5-1

Income Tax and Employees' Social Security, 1976-81

(contributions as a percentage of gross earnings[1])

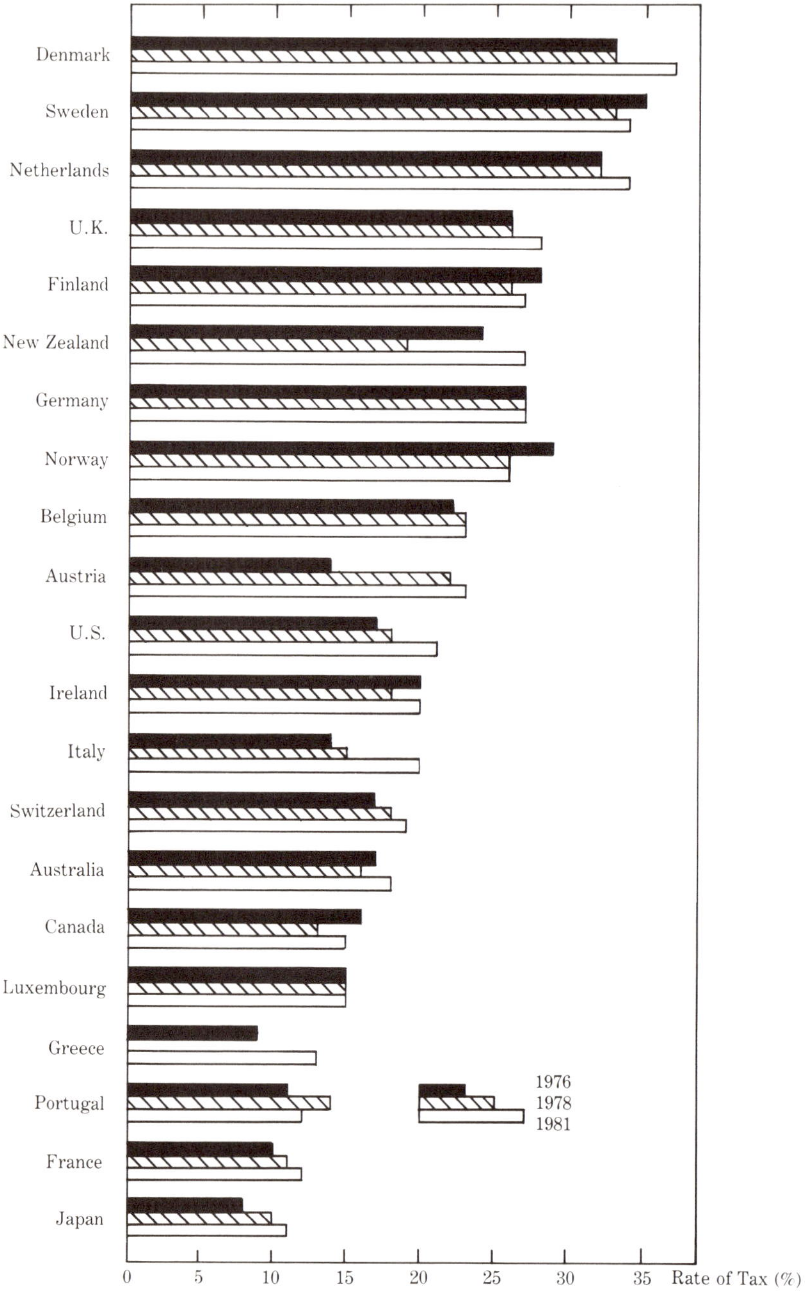

Denmark
Sweden
Netherlands
U.K.
Finland
New Zealand
Germany
Norway
Belgium
Austria
U.S.
Ireland
Italy
Switzerland
Australia
Canada
Luxembourg
Greece
Portugal
France
Japan

1976
1978
1981

0   5   10   15   20   25   30   35   Rate of Tax (%)

[1] Countries are ranked by the 1981 figures.

Source: OECD, *The Tax/Benefit Position of a Typical Worker in OECD Member Countries*, (Paris, 1983).

TABLE 5-2

**Percentage Composition of Income of Families and
Unattached Individuals by Income Quintiles, 1951-78**

Year	Bottom Quintile	Second Quintile	Middle Quintile	Fourth Quintile	Top Quintile	Total
1951	4.4	11.2	18.3	23.3	42.8	100.0
1954	4.4	12.0	17.8	24.0	41.8	100.0
1957	4.2	11.9	18.0	24.5	41.4	100.0
1959	4.4	11.9	18.0	24.1	41.6	100.0
1961	4.2	11.9	18.3	24.5	41.4	100.0
1965	4.4	11.8	18.0	24.5	41.4	100.0
1967	4.2	11.4	17.8	24.6	42.0	100.0
1969	4.3	11.0	17.6	24.5	42.6	100.0
1971	3.6	10.6	17.6	24.9	43.3	100.0
1972	3.8	10.6	17.8	25.0	42.9	100.0
1973	3.9	10.7	17.6	25.1	42.7	100.0
1974	4.0	10.9	17.7	24.9	42.5	100.0
1975	4.0	10.6	17.6	25.1	42.6	100.0
1976	4.3	10.7	17.4	24.7	42.9	100.0
1977	3.8	10.7	17.9	25.6	42.0	100.0
1978	3.9	10.4	17.7	25.5	42.5	100.0

Source: David Ross, *Income Distribution* (Ottawa: Canadian Council on Social Development, 1980).

productive activity and that we manage those investments efficiently and rationally. For reasons we have outlined in "Economic Decline in Canada" (chapter 1), this is not occurring. It is not likely to occur without a substantially different framework for economic decision making.

It may be that the dynamics of the labour market are interfered with by a generous unemployment insurance program when unemployment is low; private saving is reduced if security in retirement and protection against sickness and disability is guaranteed; levels of taxation on the wealthy and on corporations that are required to fund high-quality social security and services will cut into private profits, and under current market conditions will discourage investment. Under these circumstances, equity can be considered to be in opposition to market efficiency. But the alternatives appear both unrealistic and unworkable. If individuals have their sense of security removed from them, they will be far more likely to resist industrial restructuring and innovation, a need that in Canada is universally agreed upon. As state spending on income security and services decreases, levels of consumer spending and employment will decrease, thus reinforcing the downward spiral. Efforts to shift responsibility away from the public sector back to the private sector or the family are proving disastrous. Private profit-making nursing homes, for example, have notoriously low stand-ards, and the contemporary family is not capable of taking on more responsibility for its members, since they are increasingly alone and increasingly in the labour market. The theory that informs the current public-sector-restraint/private-sector-growth policy is plagued with these contradictions.

6

Fighting Poverty: The Effect of Government Policy

NATIONAL COUNCIL OF WELFARE

The National Council of Welfare submitted to the Macdonald Commission, in January 1984, a 186-page report entitled Poverty and Public Policy *that is probably the most complete single statement on poverty in Canada available today. Prepared by Ken Battle, director of the council, the report presents a wealth of statistical material and analysis. It provides an in-depth profile of poverty, examining short-term and long-term trends as well as the social conditions of poverty. It points out the paradox that while social spending by governments represents an important percentage of income for the poor, the poor don't receive a high percentage of social spending. Moreover, some social spending, such as welfare payments, is being cut, though it is universally recognized that recipients remain far below the poverty line — for example, single persons receive only about 44 per cent of what is necessary to meet minimum standards.*

In this excerpt the council shows how government policies have failed to deal with the income inadequacies and inequalities that prevent millions of Canadians from fully participating in the life of society.

What influence has public policy on poverty in Canada?

Surprisingly little is known about this crucial question. The reasons for the lack of detailed knowledge on the relationship between public policy and poverty are themselves worth separate investigation. But as we shall see, the "data gap" on poverty and social programs, the conceptual and methodological complexities of the issue, and the inadequacy of resources directed to the study of poverty in Canada all contribute to our ignorance.

What follows is an attempt to explore this question — more precisely, to identify the factors that influence poverty and the role of public policy in tackling the problem.

Major Trends

The risk of poverty has declined considerably for Canadian families, but much less so for unattached individuals. The proportion of families with incomes below the poverty line went from 20.8 per cent in 1969 to 13.9 per cent in 1982 — a substantial 33 per cent decline. However, the poverty rate for unattached individuals fell by only 11 per cent, from 42.8 per cent in 1969 to 38.2. Unattached Canadians face more than two-and-a-half times the risk of poverty as those living in families.

We also find a striking difference in progress against poverty between families headed by men and those led by women. The poverty rate for the former has been cut in half, from 19.1 per cent in 1969 to 10.0 per cent in 1982. By contrast, the number of the latter living in poverty was little different in 1982 (45.4 per cent) than in 1969 (46.9 per cent). Moreover, women now head up more than one-third (36.0 per cent) of poor families — double their share in 1969 (16.6 per cent).

The influence of age on poverty also demands explanation. Our analysis showed that families headed by middle-aged and older persons have enjoyed a considerable reduction in poverty over the years, but that those headed by Canadians thirty-four and under (in particular persons under twenty-five) have not, and now face a higher risk of poverty than other families. Among individuals, however, only those sixty-five and older have experienced a significant reduction in their poverty rate (16 per cent between 1969 and 1982), and in any case still face a very high (57.7 per cent) risk of poverty.

While the long-term trends show improvement for some groups, the recent picture is less promising. Generally, the decline in the poverty rate appears to have halted and, in some cases, reversed. The poverty rate for families declined from 13.1 per cent in 1979 to 12.2 per cent in 1980, was virtually unchanged for 1981, and rose to an estimated 13.9 per cent in 1982. The proportion of individuals living under the low-income line levelled off at about 38 per cent for 1981 and 1982. The total number of Canadians living in low-income households increased from 3.5 million in 1981 to around 4.0 million in 1982.

We also see a recent large increase in the poverty rate for families headed by women (38.1 per cent were low income in 1981, 45.4 per cent in 1982) and for persons under twenty-five (from 22.7 per cent in 1981 to 29.7 per cent in 1982). Families with children also experienced a significant increase in poverty recently. The risk of poverty rose for young single Canadians as well (38.4 per cent in 1981, 43.6 per cent in 1982) and for single men in general (24.5 per cent in 1981 to 29.7 per cent in 1982).

Behind the Trends

The factors that influence poverty can be divided into two broad classes. There are developments in the economy and society that raise or lower various groups' susceptibility to poverty. There is also the impact of government programs and policies.

Working Wives

The increase in the labour force participation of wives — from 3.5 per cent in 1931 to 50.5 per cent in 1981 — is a major social and economic development.

Wives' contribution to family income is undoubtedly a key factor in the substantial 26 per cent increase in real income from 1971 to 1981. Less often recognized, however, is the important role that the rise in the proportion of working wives has played in the decline in the risk of family poverty.

What would be the extent of poverty among couples if wives' earnings were excluded from family income? In 1981, 9 per cent of Canadian couples were poor. Without the wife's financial contribution, the poverty rate among couples would have been 14 per cent. The number of low-income couples would have been 772,000 instead of 481,000 — 61 per cent more. Among the regions, Ontario would experience the largest increase in the number of low-income couples if wives did not work in the paid labour force: there would be 78 per cent more poor couples, and the poverty rate among couples would have been 12 per cent instead of the actual 7 per cent in 1981.

A wife's contribution to family income comes not only from earnings, but also from unemployment insurance should she become unemployed. If her husband is out of work, her earnings help cushion the shock to family income.

The poverty statistics support our hypothesis of the influence of working wives on the family poverty rate. In Canada the proportion of families with more than one worker increased from 41 per cent in 1961 to 60 per cent in 1981. Almost half of non-poor families had two earners in 1981 and another 18 per cent counted three or more, whereas only 17 per cent of poor families had two earners and a mere 4 per cent three or more.

Marriage Breakdown

Since 1968, the divorce rate has gone up by 500 per cent. Four in ten Canadian marriages now end in divorce. These statistics are familiar enough, and Canadians need only look around them to gain first-hand evidence of the epidemic of marriage breakdowns.

The impact of separation and divorce on the changing face of Canadian poverty is borne out by the statistics presented earlier. The poverty rate among female-headed families has not improved over the years. Of course, not all women who break up with their husbands become heads of families. Those without children or other dependents become what Statistics Canada terms "unattached individuals" — a category which includes those who are commonly described as single people. The poverty rate for these women is still very high — in 1981, 42.8 per cent were poor, compared to 32.5 per cent of unattached men. Women comprise 62.3 per cent of all such single Canadians below the poverty line.

Why women who separate or divorce are so prone to poverty is examined in detail in the National Council of Welfare's 1979 report *Women and Poverty*, which argued that the large majority of women are obliged at some point in their lives to take charge of their own economic needs because of divorce, separation or widowhood. Though more and more women are joining the labour force and making substantial contributions to family income, sex-typed socialization and continued discrimination in the job market (including pay, opportunities for advancement, adequacy of pensions and other benefits) combine to place women at a considerable disadvantage in the labour force. When they find themselves on their own, most women are unable to replace the income they enjoyed as part of a two-spouse household, even if they have or take a job in the paid work force. Other sources of income — alimony and child support payments, welfare, survivor's pensions and public pensions, savings and insurance from a deceased husband — are generally inadequate. Women who live alone, whether they work or not, are likely to receive a low or inadequate income; women who, having lived on a two-spouse income, suddenly find themselves on their own must contend with a drastic reduction in their standard of living.

The Aging of the Population

In a report released in 1984, the National Council of Welfare examined the economic situation of elderly Canadians, and past and projected growth in their numbers. The demographic statistics are startling.

At the turn of the century, one Canadian in twenty was sixty-five or older. Today one in ten is aged. Fifty years from now, one person in five will be elderly.

In 1901, 48.8 per cent of aged Canadians were women. In 1981 women represented 57.2 per cent of the elderly. By 2001, six in ten senior citizens will be women....

The aged traditionally have been a high-risk group in terms of poverty. However, improvements to the retirement income system have substantially reduced the rate of poverty for families headed by elderly men and, to a lesser extent, for the unattached elderly (who nonetheless still face very high odds of being poor, especially the majority, who are women).

Thus, the falling rate of poverty for families led by elderly men has contributed to the decline in the family poverty rate overall, while the continued high risk of poverty for unattached aged Canadians (who make up a very high 41.4 per cent of all the unattached poor) helps account for the relatively high and only modestly improved poverty rate among unattached Canadians....

Unemployment

While there is abundant statistical evidence to corroborate the inverse relationship between poverty and strength of labour force attachment, there is no iron law of determinism tying changes in the general unemployment rate with changes in the general poverty rate. When the jobless rate was only 4.4 per cent in 1969, the poverty rate was 20.8 per cent for families and 42.8 per cent among unattached Canadians. Ten years later, the overall unemployment rate had risen to 7.5 per cent (a substantial 70 per cent increase over the 1969 rate), but the incidence of poverty was lower among both families (13 per cent instead of 21 per cent) and unattached individuals (40 per cent in 1979 as opposed to 43 per cent in 1969). Clearly there are factors other than the labour force which affect the size of the low-income population.

There is no question that worsening unemployment in the past few years has increased the ranks of Canada's poor, and helps explain the rise in the incidence of poverty between 1981 and 1982.

The latest figures from Statistics Canada show that 28.1 per cent of the labour force was out of work at some point in 1982, compared to 22.1 per cent in 1980 and only 19.1 per cent in 1977. Canadians are out of work longer now than in years past; the average duration of unemployment rose from 14.8 weeks in 1980 to 15.2 weeks in 1981 and 17.3 weeks in 1982. Moreover, the average bout of unemployment is longer for older workers; in 1982, unemployed workers under twenty-five faced an average of 15.4 weeks out of work compared to 18.1 weeks for prime-age workers (twenty-five to forty-five) and 20.5 weeks for those forty-five and older. Unemployed men tend to be out of a job longer than women.

The "official" unemployment rate is quite restrictive in definition, basically covering only jobless persons who actively looked for work and were available for work during the past four weeks. If we expand the definition of unemployment to include the so-called "hidden unemployed" (those who have become discouraged and are no longer actively looking for work), a "real" jobless rate can be computed. Table 6-1 shows the official and real jobless rates for Canada and each province in 1981 and 1982.

Another disquieting fact is that the jobless rate among the full-time labour force (defined as persons employed full time, involuntary part-time workers and unemployed persons looking for full-time work) now exceeds the unemployment rate for the part-time work force (that is, persons voluntarily working part time or the unemployed seeking a part-time job). In 1982, 12.7 per cent of the full-time labour force was out of work, compared to 11.6 per cent of part-time workers. The full-time jobless rate rose by 48 per cent between 1981 (when it was only

TABLE 6-1

**Official and Real Unemployment Rates,
Canada and the Provinces, 1981 and 1982**

(per cent)

	1981		1982	
	Official Rates	Real Rates	Official Rates	Real Rates
Newfoundland	14.1	23.4	16.9	35.7
Prince Edward Island	11.4	18.5	13.1	25.9
Nova Scotia	10.2	16.1	13.2	22.2
New Brunswick	11.7	19.3	14.2	28.6
Quebec	10.4	17.1	13.8	23.0
Ontario	6.6	9.9	9.8	14.1
Manitoba	6.0	8.7	8.5	13.6
Saskatchewan	4.6	6.6	6.2	10.8
Alberta	3.8	5.4	7.5	11.1
British Columbia	6.7	10.0	12.1	18.3
CANADA	7.6	12.4	11.0	17.4

8.6 per cent) and 1982 (12.7 per cent), whereas the 1982 part-time unemployment rate (11.6 per cent) rose only 18 per cent over its 1981 level (9.8 per cent).

Families headed by women traditionally experience a higher risk of unemployment than those led by men. In 1982 the jobless rate among women who head families was 12.2 per cent, compared to 7.4 per cent for male family heads. This fact is reflected in the higher poverty rate for families led by women. However, it is worth pointing out that the jobless rate among men who head families increased more from 1981 to 1982 (by 72 per cent) than among female family heads (whose unemployment rate rose from 8.9 per cent in 1981 to 12.2 per cent, a 37 per cent increase).

In contrast to families, unattached men are more likely to be out of work than unattached women. The jobless rate for unattached men went from 8.3 per cent in 1981 to 12.9 per cent in 1982 — a sizeable 55 per cent hike — while the unemployment rate among unattached women was lower (7.6 per cent in 1982) and increased less over 1981 (by 32 per cent). Significantly, unattached men experienced a 14 per cent increase in their poverty rate, while unattached women in fact were slightly less likely to be poor in 1982 (42.8 per cent were low-income) than in 1981 (45.0 per cent).

Youth unemployment is a major economic and social problem and directly affects the number of young Canadians with incomes under the poverty line. The official unemployment rate for persons under twenty-five was 18.8 per cent in 1982, while their real jobless rate was 28.2 per cent; each of these figures was substantially less in 1981 (13.3 per cent and 20.4 per cent, respectively). The other age groups have lower official and real jobless rates.

Again, it is important to remember that unemployment can place a family or individual below the poverty line not only because of lost earnings. The unemployed must turn to government income programs which, in turn, may or may not provide enough replacement income to keep them out of poverty.

The first line of defence is unemployment insurance (UI), which pays 60 per cent of a claimant's average weekly insurable earnings up to a maximum of $231 (for 1983) and fifty weeks' worth of benefits. Since the poverty line for one person works out to about $182 a week for a metropolitan centre (less for smaller communities), many unemployed single people have a reasonable chance of remaining out of poverty.

However, this statement must be tempered by the fact that some single workers cannot qualify for unemployment insurance benefits because they have not worked long enough. The qualifying period ranges from ten to fourteen weeks during the last year and varies according to the regional unemployment rate. Moreover, the qualifying period is longer for claimants who have collected benefits in the last year and for persons who were working at their first job or who came back to work after being out of the labour force for more than a year. In addition, a recipient with fewer weeks of insurable employment receives benefits for a shorter period (the regulations are too complex to explain here). Young workers are more apt to fall into those categories and, of course, will receive lower benefits, since their earnings are on average lower, so the inability of unemployment insurance to protect their incomes is reflected in the substantial increase in the poverty rate from 1981 to 1982 for unattached individuals under age twenty-five.

Unfortunately, unemployment insurance is less capable of replacing sufficient earnings for a one-earner family to keep it above the poverty line. A single parent with one child, for instance, needs $240 a week just to clear the poverty line in a metropolitan centre such as Vancouver, Toronto or Montreal; yet the most he or (more likely) she could get from unemployment insurance is $231 a week; few single mothers would qualify for the maximum benefit anyway because their insurable earnings are likely to be substantially below $20,000 a year. A one-earner couple with one child needs $302 a week to keep out of poverty, a figure in excess of the maximum unemployment insurance benefit of $231 a week....

The final resort for the unemployed is provincial social assistance ("welfare" as it is commonly known). Those who do not qualify for unemployment insurance, or who are awaiting or have run out of benefits, must turn to welfare if they cannot find a job. Welfare benefits guarantee an income far below the poverty line. Therefore, inflating the welfare rolls is another way that unemployment increases poverty.

The Role of Government

We have just argued that a major government program, unemployment insurance, helps some single unemployed Canadians avoid poverty but leaves one-earner families with unemployed breadwinners under the poverty line. We can apply the same yardstick — the poverty line, or whatever measure of adequacy one wants — to test the adequacy of other income programs as well. Thus, the benefits paid by the old age security and guaranteed income supplement (OAS/GIS) programs ensure some (but not all) elderly couples an income above the poverty line, but leave many other couples and all single persons sixty-five and over who rely on OAS/GIS for most or all of their income far below the poverty line. Social assistance ("welfare") payments are low in every province and guarantee a poverty income.

Such an approach is straightforward enough, but it is hardly a sufficient measure in itself of the capacity of government to tackle poverty. Income schemes such as family allowances and the child tax credit and provincial income supplements and tax credits improve their recipients' income, even if they are not generous enough to make a large dent on the poverty statistics. A poor family with two children will receive $1,370 worth of federal family allowances and the child tax credit in 1983; its total income is still below the poverty line, but $1,370 less than if federal family benefits did not exist. Similarly, without the OAS/GIS, the low-income population would be swollen enormously by destitute elderly persons.

Nor is Canada's social security system comprised only of programs which supplement or replace income. There is a wide variety of social services, provided largely by the provincial governments, which provide in-kind benefits for low-income (and other) families and individuals. The impact of "non-income" social programs on poverty may be less visible and more indirect, but no less important.

For example, visiting nurses, homeowners benefits and "meals-on-wheels" enable many modest-income elderly Canadians to remain in their homes or apartments rather than move to an institution. They may remain poor in cash terms, but the services provided improve the quality of their life and allow them to live relatively independently. They also may live in subsidized housing. The aged are more likely than younger persons to require some form of health care; national health insurance provides doctors' and hospital services at far less direct and indirect cost to the elderly than the mixture of private health insurance and charitable medicine which existed before medicare. Indeed, before medicare, serious or prolonged illness plunged many Canadian families into poverty, so national health insurance is in this sense a vital income security as well as health program.

There is another dimension entirely of public policy — fiscal and monetary policy, employment and regional development policy, indeed almost all aspects of economic policy — which has an influence on poverty.

Canada's social security system is financed through a mixture of general revenues and contributions — for example, employee and employer contributions to the Canada and Quebec Pension Plans (CPP/ QPP). Policies that stimulate economic growth increase the tax base which supports social programs and (in theory, at least) improve prospects for new social spending; they also reduce demands on the social security system, since fewer people need unemployment insurance, welfare and other programs. The other side of the coin entails a double bind: in tough economic times, the social security system must contend with increasing demands for assistance, while at the same time facing budget cuts because of government restraint.

Economic policies which reduce unemployment help fight poverty, but they cannot "solve" the poverty problem in and of themselves. Some of the traditional groups in the poverty population — persons with severe physical or mental handicaps and the aged — cannot be expected to work for most of their income. In realistic terms, a "full employment" economy (even one where 4 or 5 per cent unemployment is considered acceptable) appears to be an unrealizable goal. Much of the poverty in Atlantic Canada and in economically disadvantaged communities (including Indian reserves) stems from chronic unemployment that appears firmly resistant to economic development and employment measures.....

The Working Poor

As shown earlier, a large proportion of the low-income population — 44 per cent of non-aged families and unattached individuals below the poverty line — obtains most of its income from work. Many workers, even those who are employed full time and year round, do not earn enough to keep above the poverty line, especially if they have dependents. The wage ladder is a prominent and seemingly immutable feature of all economies.

Minimum wages are not high enough to provide an income above the poverty line for family heads and, in some provinces, single persons. In any case, many single workers who earn the minimum wage work only part time or part year and so number among the working poor.

The only practical alternative appears to be some form of income supplement for the working poor. The federal-provincial Social Security Review in the mid-Seventies failed to bring such a program into effect, and Canada's working poor remain a largely ignored segment of the low-income population. Only Saskatchewan and Quebec provide some form of income assistance directed to the working poor specifically....

Families

Families with children have enjoyed a significant enrichment in federal child benefits. The family allowance program, established in 1945, extended its age limit from sixteen to eighteen and fully indexed benefits to the cost of living starting in 1974; in addition, benefits were boosted substantially in 1973 and 1974. In 1979 the federal government added a new child benefit program, the refundable child tax credit, which uses the income tax system to deliver benefits to low- and middle-income parents....

Federal child-related benefits have been enriched sufficiently to have an impact on the family poverty rate. Again, however, while most poor families have incomes so far below the low-income line that even the substantial boost in federal family benefits cannot fully close the poverty gap, any increase in income is welcome and eases their financial plight. Current (1983) benefits — $342 in family allowances and a maximum child tax credit of $343 for each child — are worth a great deal in proportionate terms to lower-income families; for instance, they add 19 per cent to the income of a single mother earning Ontario's minimum wage and supporting two children.

The Aged

The elderly, particularly men who head families, have benefitted greatly from improvements in public programs over the past two decades. While there is still a long way to go in reducing the risk of poverty, particularly among the single aged (most of them women), no better example can be found of the power of public policy to reduce poverty.

Federal income security programs for the aged — old age security and the guaranteed income supplement — assure single Canadians aged sixty-five or over an income of $522.07 a month (October through December, 1983). Couples with at least one member aged sixty-five or over are guaranteed an income of $924.34 a month, provided the other member is at least sixty years old. Moreover, a few widows and widowers aged between sixty and sixty-five — but by no means all — are assured an income of $462.17 a month from the spouse's allowance.

Table 6-2 shows the combined maximum benefits in 1983 from the federal programs plus the various provincial supplements. (The table

TABLE 6-2

**Maximum Benefits from Federal Programs
for the Aged[1] and Provincial Supplements, 1983**

	Single Persons			Couples		
	Federal Programs	Provincial Supplements	Total	Federal Programs	Provincial Supplements	Total
Newfoundland	$6,147	—	$6,147	$10,883	—	$10,883
Prince Edward Island	6,147	—	6,147	10,883	—	10,883
Nova Scotia	6,147	$ 219	6,366	10,883	$ 438	11,321
New Brunswick	6,147	—	6,147	10,883	—	10,883
Quebec	6,147	—	6,147	10,883	—	10,883
Ontario	6,147	587	6,734	10,883	1,915	12,798
Manitoba	6,147	188	6,335	10,883	405	11,288
Saskatchewan	6,147	300	6,457	10,883	540	11,423
Alberta	6,147	1,140	7,287	10,883	2,280	13,163
British Columbia	6,147	467	6,614	10,883	1,196	12,079
Yukon	6,147	1,200	7,347	10,883	2,400	13,283
Northwest Territories	6,147	900	7,047	10,883	1,800	12,683

[1] Old age security and guaranteed income supplement.

does not include provincial refundable tax credits to which the aged might be entitled....)

The immediate reason for the high rates of poverty among Canada's aged becomes evident when the benefits from the federal and provincial programs are compared with the poverty line. The figures are shown in Table 6-3.

While current benefits are not sufficient to bring all the aged up to the low-income line, improvements to federal income security programs have played a vital role in improving the income of the elderly. Starting in 1966, the age of eligibility for old age security was lowered by one year each year until it reached the current sixty-five in 1970. The federal government made two important changes to the program in 1973. The monthly payment was increased by 20 per cent in April and, beginning in October, benefits were fully indexed to the cost of living on a quarterly basis.

The guaranteed income supplement came into effect in January of 1967. Like old age security, the guaranteed income supplement was fully indexed to the cost of living starting in October 1973. In addition, Ottawa has substantially boosted benefits four times since the guaranteed income supplement began.

These changes have raised the value of old age security and guaranteed income supplement benefits to elderly Canadians over the

TABLE 6-3

**Difference Between the Minimum Income
Guaranteed to the Aged and the Poverty Line, 1983**

	Single Persons	Couples
St. John's	− $2,827	− $ 949
Charlottetown	− 1,636	640
Halifax	− 2,608	− 511
Saint John	− 2,827	− 949
Montreal	− 3,302	− 1,584
Toronto	− 2,715	331
Winnipeg	− 3,114	− 1,179
Regina	− 2,527	− 409
Edmonton	− 2,162	696
Vancouver	− 2,835	− 388

years.... The fact that benefits are fully indexed to the cost of living is crucial; without this protection, the incomes of most elderly Canadians would have been seriously eroded during the period 1974 to 1982 when inflation averaged 10 per cent a year.

Social Spending and the Poor

Canadians at all income levels depend on government programs for an increasing share of their income. Federal, provincial and, in some cases, municipal governments offer a complex array of programs which replace, supplement or substitute for earnings from work. At some point in our lives all of us benefit from family allowances, public pension and income security plans for the aged (provided we live long enough) along with various tax credits, exemptions and deductions, and to a varying extent substantial segments of the population receive income from programs such as unemployment insurance, workers' compensation and social assistance.

There is clear statistical evidence to show the growing importance of government payments to Canadians' incomes over time. In 1969 public transfers represented an average 6.0 per cent of the income of all families and 10.7 per cent for unattached individuals. By 1981 these shares had risen to 8.1 per cent for families and 14.2 per cent for individuals.

As one would expect, government income sources are more important to lower-income than higher-income families. In 1969 families in the lowest income quintile relied upon government sources for 38.4 per cent of their income. The figures decline steadily as income rises, to the point where families in the highest income quintile counted government transfers as only 1.9 per cent of their income. The pattern is the same for unattached individuals, except that those in the lower- and middle-income groups rely more heavily on government than do families.

By 1981 the proportion of income from government had risen substantially from 6.0 per cent to 8.1 per cent for families (a 35 per cent increase) and from 10.7 per cent to 14.2 per cent for unattached individuals (a 33 per cent rise). Table 6-4 shows that families and unattached individuals in the middle range increased their share from government most between 1969 and 1981.

The improvement in social benefits, coupled with the increase in the population (especially among the elderly), has substantially increased social spending in Canada.... In 1968 government programs such as family allowances, old age security, unemployment insurance, workers' compensation and welfare paid out $5.5 billion in benefits to Canadians. By 1982 payments to individuals from income security and social insurance programs totalled $43.4 billion — a real (that is, after-inflation) increase of 172 per cent. Transfer payments rose from 19.6 per cent of total government spending in 1968 to 21.8 per cent in 1982. As a proportion of the gross national product, government transfers increased from 7.5 per cent in 1968 to 12.2 per cent in 1982.

TABLE 6-4
Government Transfers as a Proportion of
Income, Families and Unattached Individuals,
by Income Quintile, 1969 and 1981

(per cent)

	1969	1981	1969/81
Families			
Quintile			
lowest	38.4	46.9	22
second	10.6	14.0	32
middle	4.9	7.1	45
fourth	2.8	4.3	54
highest	1.9	2.5	32
total	6.0	8.1	35
Unattached			
Individuals			
Quintile			
lowest	63.4	66.7	6
second	55.0	60.3	10
middle	13.2	18.1	37
tourth	3.5	5.2	49
highest	1.7	2.1	24
total	10.7	14.2	33

Federal transfers to the provinces for health insurance, social services and welfare programs increased markedly. Ottawa transferred $875 million to the provinces in 1968 and $6.7 billion in 1982 — a real increase of 160 per cent. For most of the period since 1968, federal transfers to the provinces for health and social programs constituted about 10 per cent of all federal expenditures; the proportion dropped to 7.9 per cent in 1982.

For many, the obvious question is why such enormous sums of money have not had a greater impact on poverty. After all, $43.4 billion worth of transfer payments works out to about $10,860 for every low-income man, woman and child.

There are reasons why increased social spending does not cut the poverty rate as much as one might expect. Welfare, a major income security program for the poor, sets its rates at levels far below the poverty line. Other programs, such as family allowances and the child tax credit, are not generous enough to have a major impact on the poverty rate, even though they provide a badly needed income supplement for poor and modest-income parents. Not all social spending goes on income programs; social services provide benefits in kind that are not reflected in the income and poverty statistics.

The other major reason why social spending has not drastically reduced the poverty population is that not all, or even most, of the money is directed to the poor. Canada's social security system is built on a foundation of universal programs (such as old age security, the Canada and Quebec Pension Plans, family allowances, unemployment insurance and workers' compensation), upon which rest programs such as provincial social assistance, tax credits, income supplements and the like which are generally targeted on lower-income Canadians. The two largest federal direct transfer programs pay out enormous amounts to large segments of the population — for 1983-84, an estimated $7.8 billion in old age security cheques to all 2.5 million elderly Canadians, and another $2.3 billion in family allowances to all families with children.

Table 6-5 shows the share of major social program benefits among family units according to income quintile. The data, from an Economic Council of Canada study, are for 1975, but the pattern is probably much the same today.

Family allowances go to all families regardless of their income. Family units in the top income group received the largest share of family allowances. The low figure for the lowest income category (5.7 per cent) stems in part from the fact that many elderly families (without eligible children) and unattached individuals fall in the bottom income quintile.

Unemployment insurance payments are distributed more or less proportionately, except that the lowest category again received relatively little because so many low-income Canadians are not in the work force and thus not eligible for unemployment insurance. However, the Canada/Quebec Pension Plan, old age security and guaranteed income

TABLE 6-5

**Distribution of Before-Tax Benefits,
Major Social Programs, Family Units
by Income Quintile, 1975**

(per cent)

Quintile	Family Allowances	UIC	C/QPP	OAS	GIS
Bottom	5.7	8.1	26.8	38.0	47.4
Second	12.6	22.0	30.8	31.3	33.1
Middle	22.1	25.0	18.4	13.6	7.1
Fourth	28.8	22.6	12.7	8.2	5.6
Highest	31.6	22.3	11.3	8.9	6.8
Total	100.0	100.0	100.0	100.0	100.0

supplement show a progressive pattern of benefits because they serve the aged, who figure disproportionately in the lower quintiles; the GIS is also income-tested.

The Tax System and Inequality

The income tax has a much smaller effect on the unequal distribution of income than is popularly believed. Table 6-6 shows the share of money income going to the different income groups before and after taxation.

The income tax system only mildly reduces the extreme inequality of income in Canada. Income taxes modestly reduce the share of income held by higher-income families and unattached individuals, thereby increasing the proportion for middle- and lower-income family units. However, the amount of redistribution is relatively small, and the after-tax distribution of income remains heavily skewed in favour of the affluent minority of Canadians.

Tax expenditures — exemptions and deductions which allow portions of income to be exempted from taxation or to be taxed at reduced rates — are regressive in their distributional impact: they benefit high-income taxpayers the most, pay smaller amounts to middle-income tax filers, and benefit lower-income Canadians least and, in some cases, not at all. Familiar tax expenditures in the personal income tax system include: exemptions from taxable income of contributions to registered retirement savings plans (RRSPs), registered pension plans (RPPs), and registered home ownership savings plans (RHOSPs); exemptions for dependent children; the deduction of $1,000 of interest income (from savings accounts, bonds, mortgages and so on) from taxable income; the child-care deduction; the married or equivalent exemption; and the

TABLE 6-6

**Distribution of Income, Families and
Unattached Individuals, Before and After Tax, 1980**

(per cent)

	Total Money Income	Income After Tax
Families		
Quintile		
Bottom	6.0	6.9
Second	12.8	13.7
Middle	18.3	18.6
Fourth	24.1	23.9
Top	38.6	36.9
Unattached Individuals		
Quintile		
Bottom	4.5	5.2
Second	9.4	10.8
Middle	15.4	16.5
Fourth	25.7	25.6
Top	45.0	41.6

aged exemption. The corporate tax system also has many tax expenditures.

Tax expenditures are expensive, largely hidden from public view, and are increasing faster than direct spending on visible government programs. The growing cost of tax expenditures and the addition of new tax breaks during the 1970s reduced the progressivity of the personal income tax (the only form of taxation which is progressive as opposed to proportional or regressive).

Personal tax expenditures grew from $1.4 billion in 1971 to $6.2 billion in 1977, representing a substantial 29 per cent annual average rate of increase. Corporate tax expenditures in 1975 have been estimated at $4 billion, so it is probable that the $6.2 billion worth of personal tax expenditures in 1977 represented only half of all government revenue lost due to personal and corporate tax expenditures.

Tax expenditures have risen faster than direct expenditures. Between 1975 and 1976, for example, federal direct spending rose by 10.4 per cent, but the revenue loss from twenty personal tax exemptions increased by 17.9 per cent. Some tax expenditure items went up by very large jumps — tax savings resulting from the deductibility of RRSP contributions rose by 40 per cent between 1975 and 1976. Looking just at the costs to the federal treasury, the deductibility of contributions to registered pension plans and RRSPs together cost $1.65 million in 1978, $2 million in 1979 and $2.6 million in 1980 — a rate of increase of 21 per cent from 1978 to 1979 and 30 per cent between 1979 and 1980.

Because of marginal tax rates and larger disposable income, higher-income tax filers derive far greater benefits from tax expenditures than lower-income tax filers (those too poor to pay tax benefit only from refundable tax credits such as the child tax credit). In 1976, 53 per cent of an estimated $7.1 billion worth of personal tax expenditures went to the highest-income 20 per cent of tax filers, while only 1 per cent went to those in the bottom 20 per cent. While a median-income tax filer saved $400 in 1976 from tax expenditures, the highest-income 5 per cent of tax filers averaged savings of $2,662 — more than six times as much.

In our view the federal government should take a long, hard look at each tax expenditure as a potential candidate for abolition or reduction. Corporate as well as personal tax expenditures should be scrutinized carefully.

Economists have seriously questioned the effectiveness and cost-efficiency of corporate tax expenditures intended to encourage investment. The cost of such concessions is enormous. To take just two types of corporate tax expenditures, in 1980 over half a billion dollars in corporate taxes were foregone as a result of various investment tax credits, and $600 million because of lower corporate income tax rates on manufacturing and processing profits.

Personal income tax concessions are also costly, and most benefit tax filers in the higher tax brackets. In 1980 over $4 billion worth of tax revenue was lost to just five personal tax expenditures — deductibility of CPP/QPP contributions ($540 million), UI contributions ($250 million for employees), RHOSP contributions ($95 million), contributions to RPPs and RRSPs ($2.6 billion) and the child tax exemption ($655 million). We are not saying that all such tax measures be abolished; rather, they should be evaluated one by one to determine if they are worth the cost and whether or not there are alternative ways of accomplishing their stated objectives.

In the current period of financial restraint, improvements in social programs are difficult to finance. Governments must look to reallocation of existing spending in order to pay for benefit increases. Tax expenditures overwhelmingly benefit affluent Canadians. Social welfare programs, inadequate though they may be, help the poor. Logic and a sense of equity would indicate that cuts should be made in tax expenditures, not social spending.

7

Economic Policy and Well-Being

CANADIAN MENTAL HEALTH ASSOCIATION

The Canadian Mental Health Association has a long-standing concern with the human impact of unemployment. Their aim that mental health problems be prevented through sound economic and social development policies was elaborated as early as 1955 in the association's brief to the Royal Commission on Canada's Economic Prospects headed by Walter Gordon. A 1983 resolution of the association recognizes that unemployment is not, in the majority of cases, the fault of the individual and that it can be eradicated only if changes are made to the economic system. The association's brief to the Macdonald Commission demonstrates the dynamics through which economic policies affect Canadian's health, sense of security, sense of community, freedom and self-respect. A somewhat shortened version of its presentation is reprinted here.

Economic policy is potentially destructive: policy decisions can lead to unemployment, poverty and other economic causes of deprivation. These erode the individual's and society's mental and physical well-being. They eat away at the individual's and at society's pocketbook. The individual is exposed to chronic stress associated with deprivation (it is estimated that 16 to 28 per cent of Canadians live below the poverty line); he or she is exposed to loss of self-respect, frustration and anguish. Society staggers under the burden (in 1982, socioeconomic costs of unemployment alone were estimated at $50 billion); as a nation we suffer from the correlates of poverty and chronic stress. We live in the shadow of widening gaps between the haves and have-nots....

Economic policy is not dictated simply by economic conditions. As a society, we *choose* our economic policies. Whether choices are good or bad depends not only on how well the constraints and possibilities of reality have been taken into account, but also on the values which shape these choices. Therefore, values that guide policymaking are a central issue.

In the realm of policymaking, even among the best-intentioned, the issue of human well-being is easily relegated to the back bench. Paradoxes can slip in where none are intended. For example, in the Macdonald Commission's terms of reference and preamble, Canada's commitment to "economic and social progress of its people" is referred to and instructions are given and instruct us to examine arrangements needed "to promote the liberty and well-being of individual Canadians." On the other hand, the commission's discussion in the section entitled "What goals? What policies and programs?" is wholly in economic terms. It is our intention to arouse awareness of such paradoxical attitudes. Through increased awareness we can strive to eliminate them.

The following essential elements of well-being for individuals have critical relevance to economic policymaking: health, sense of basic security, sense of community, sense of freedom, and self-respect....

Health

Good health is fundamental to well-being. Furthermore, productivity and efficiency depend on a healthy work force. Our association's study clearly demonstrates the deleterious effects on health of unemployment and poverty. Countless studies have demonstrated the positive correlation between increases in the rate of unemployment and increases in the rates of alcoholism, malnutrition, ulcers, heart disease, lung disease, weight loss and obesity, hard drug abuse, infant mortality, and suicide. Clearly both unemployment and poverty result in a decreased ability to purchase goods and services necessary for the upkeep of physical health (for example, adequate housing, food, clothing, dental care and so on). Both place Canadians in a state of chronic stress — stress in turn, contributes to the onset of a number of diseases (for example, heart disease) and to behaviours that increase the likelihood of becoming ill (for example, substance abuse). Unemployment and poverty are direct outcomes of economic policies and of the economic structures that these policies promote. Furthermore, ill health is costly to our nation. Preventing ill health means preventing unemployment, poverty and their attendant stress.

Sense of Basic Security

This element is essential to well-being because insecurity about the requirements of a decent standard of living and a productive social role undermines people's enjoyment of life and, moreover, makes them fearful about change and new initiatives. Such insecurity is greatly affected by the threat of unemployment and by a lack of effective assistance in finding new employment and in acquiring the skills for it. The possibility of losing one's job has a much more profound impact on one's well-being and that of one's family than the risks that investors incur as a matter of course; it is a threat to the kind of life one has built for oneself. In the case of the self-employed, unstable prices, unanticipated high interest rates and unstable community spending power are sources of insecurity — much more so than rising prices in themselves. Farmers in particular had to worry about the sharp increase in interest rates a few years ago, as had many homeowners. Even when these families did not lose their homes or farms, the very threat of losing them undermined their well-being. Fixed-income earners, too, are exposed to uncertainty, although of a more gradual kind, if their income is not inflation-indexed.

While we acknowledge that a degree of uncertainty is part of life and thus inescapable, we must differentiate between the uncertainty that derives from "the human condition" and that which is induced by an economic system. Such structural insecurity is avoidable. When economic policy confines itself to crisis management rather than to economic planning that stabilizes conditions for individuals, families and communities, then it serves to reinforce the instabilities to which our economic system is structurally prone.

Sense of Community

A sense of community is important both for what it gives to the individual and for the commitment to the community that it induces in the individual. To the individual it gives a sense of group identity, a social network providing mutual aid and a set of relationships for sharing interests, aspirations and feelings. In turn, an individual with a sense of community will help others meet these needs. In the context of economic policymaking, the communities that are particularly important are the workplace, the neighbourhood and the town or city as a whole.

Footloose industries and plant shutdowns are probably the most serious threat to a sense of community. While victims of shutdowns may initially band together in response to their common plight, the community itself will disintegrate if people are forced to move in search of jobs. Hopelessness, apathy and depression can quickly displace a sense of community. Unemployment can destroy an entire community.

On the other hand, economic policy could promote a sense of cohesion by facilitating more participatory structures in the decision making of enterprises. This includes participation of workers in the plant and the participation of local political representatives. Clearly our choice is between policies that encourage decision making which is responsible to the community as a whole and those that emphasize profits and corporate power.

Sense of Freedom

The sense of freedom from oppression and restriction comes not only, nor even primarily, from freedom from government restrictions. It requires freedom of opportunity, not only in the sense of having no governmental barriers to reasonable aspirations, but of being able to avail oneself of opportunities. A person boxed in by debilitating circumstances will not be free, even if the government does not intervene. In fact, that person will be unfree because of government inaction. Other external agents have the power to constrain freedom — for example, a corporation that chooses to relocate workers from their jobs and perhaps ultimately from their community, thus depriving them of the option of continuing their established pattern of living and community commitments.

Self-Respect

One of unemployment's most devastating effects is its erosion of self-respect. This is a nearly universal phenomenon. It not only darkens the unemployed individual's image of life, but also puts great stress on the quality of family relations.

Our association's studies have cited numerous investigations that indicate a strong positive correlation between increased rates of unemployment and various manifestations of loss of self-respect, such as increases in depression, anxiety, self-deprecation, fatalism, anger, spouse abuse, child abuse, mental hospital admissions, homicides, rape, property crimes, racism, youth alienation, children's problems in school, and divorce. Almost every painful social consequence known to humankind is related to unemployment. Just as a physically unhealthy society is costly, so too is one that is socially and psychologically destructive.

Self-respect is also undermined by poverty and the condition of being trapped in a low-status job. Being excluded from participating in the pursuit of those activities and aspirations that characterize the mainstream of society, makes the individual feel that he or she is of less worth than most other citizens.

Unemployment, poverty, inadequate skills, and labour market conditions that hold certain groups in obviously inferior conditions are clearly the outcomes of economic policies.

Conventional Economic Goals

Economic goals, as conventionally articulated, concern themselves more with means than with ends, even though they are used in the policy-making process as though they were ends in themselves. Well-being goals do not appear to be incorporated into conventional goals.

The following general pattern emerges as the effective ultimate aims of conventional economic policy:

- *The promotion of the growth of overall prosperity:* This refers to the prosperity of the population as a whole, irrespective of the distribution of prosperity. The promotion of investment, employment, and productivity growth all serve this aim. It is also what underlies the cost-benefit analysis of government projects. What counts is whether there is a net gain in material prosperity, even if it is to the detriment of certain groups.

- *Economic freedom:* Individuals are to have certain freedoms as to how to earn their money and how to dispose of it. Investor freedom is deemed particularly important in this context.
- *Price stability and avoidance of declines in the value of the Canadian dollar:* Inflation has been treated as a major evil for whose prevention we are willing to pay in unemployment and the misery that our study has shown to result from it.
- *Employment:* Although the goal of full employment seems to have been jettisoned by governments, unemployment certainly is of concern. The real question is how important it is relative to other goals.
- *Limits on economic uncertainty:* Although the fundamental commitment to an open, competitive economy builds uncertainty into the very structure of the economic system, policy will at times try to offset it by compensatory intervention, such as to stabilize prices, assist jeopardized enterprises and provide insurance benefits to the unemployed.
- *The avoidance of politically unacceptable inequalities between regions and socioeconomic groups:* This is less a pursuit of the minimization of major inequalities in general than of those inequalities that affect groups which have some leverage on the political process.

As far as the priorities among these goals are concerned, the emphasis in economic policymaking has been on overall prosperity, on economic freedom and on containing inflation and holding up the value of the Canadian dollar. The avoidance of economic uncertainty and of inequalities have at best been secondary goals. The minimization of unemployment seems to have been emphasized more in policy discussion than in policy action.

In terms of well-being, the human wastage is immeasureable. Just as an example, we know that approximately 250,000 Canadian children are dependent on parents who are on unemployment or welfare rolls; the Canadian Teachers' Federation laments the increasing number of children who come to school dirty, underclothed, depressed and, perhaps worst of all, hungry. The evidence is chilling. Repercussions on well-being must not be ignored. They must not be seen in isolation from economic policy decisions.

Economic Goals in the Service of Human Well-Being

It is not economic aggregates such as the gross national product (GNP) or a price index or even the national unemployment rate which should be the ultimate concern of economic policy. These concerns should simply *serve* the aim of human well-being. Economic policy must be designed *directly* to advance this aim, rather than to pursue economic goals that merely, on average, promote well-being in the lives of individuals. Our current approach makes social policy very much a residual field. Its purpose is to bandage those wounds inflicted by our economic policy. A more rational approach is the integration of economic *and* social policy, resulting in one set of goals geared toward human well-being.

This would put the economic aim of maximizing the growth of material prosperity in a new light. Instead of treating it as an end in itself, it would be pursued to the extent and in the form that well-being is promoted, that is, such that the impairment of health, sense of security, community and freedom, and of self-respect resulting from poverty, unemployment, discrimination, dehumanizing work conditions and economic instability is minimized. To the extent that economic growth is injurious, it must be rejected. Merely to maintain a high standing in international GNP-league tables is not the same as advancing the quality of life.

This is not to say that economic growth is bad; in fact, the recent poor growth performance of the Canadian economy has been a serious source of suffering. What it does mean is that the manner in which growth is pursued should be guided by its implication for well-being. Thus, to cut back on social services and those forms of public investment that have important consequences for improving people's lives in the short term or the long term appears to be very much an anti-well-being policy strategy. Quite apart from the likelihood that this impairs growth as a whole, it tilts economic development away from the *kind* of growth that would improve people's lives.

In those policy choices where we are faced by a trade-off between overall economic growth and a less unequal distribution of income and life chances, the goal of human well-being again is an important guide. Certainly it is more crucial that people now living in misery be able to enhance their spending power and their opportunities to be productive, and to overcome economic dependency, than it is for the affluent to make additional expenditures on luxuries.

In the trade-off between inflation and unemployment, a well-being perspective requires us to look at the human benefits and costs of choosing any particular strategy. The containment of inflation, while clearly desirable, is not to be purchased with the suffering that unemployment causes. As long as we do not insist on keeping fixed-income earners vulnerable to inflation and instead adopt indexation, inflation is a minor problem in terms of well-being. But unemployment is destructive of its victims. This applies not only to those who have built their lives around their employment, but also to young people unable to find jobs at the outset and thus often in despair of finding a useful role in society.

Unemployment might initially make its victims angry, but eventually hopelessness engenders depression and apathy, so that the unemployed, contrary to what one might expect, are not a spontaneous political force with a voice of their own.

The Protection of Communities

The stewardship of our country's productive resources must not tear asunder the human networks that form communities; in fact, the stewards (entrepreneurs and managers) must strive to strengthen those bonds, particularly in areas dependent on only a small number of employers.

Capital can not take precedence over human life. Workers and their families invest in their communities by buying houses, developing friendships and integrating their lives into the community. To ignore this investment is to put the interests of profit-making institutions before the quality of life of individuals who are directly affected by decisions, such as shifts in production operations. It is true that considerations of efficiency may be involved, but the *appropriate* efficiency calculation is the maximization of well-being, not the maximization of profits.

Technological Change, Social Polarization and Economic Planning

Although this submission is devoted to the discussion of those policy goals that should hold even when economic circumstances change, a brief reference to a current structural development will help to highlight some imminent issues for well-being and economic policy. Such a development is the current computer revolution and its promises and dangers. Its promises are sharp increases in productivity, the liberation of workers from dangerous and monotonous kinds of work, the creation of new and more challenging kinds of employment opportunities and greatly improved information available both to organizations and to households. The dangers, however, are that it both intensifies unemployment and polarizes Canada's labour force between those who benefit in terms of employment and earnings and those who are pushed into the low-wage service sector.

Such polarization is destructive not only of those who are left behind in the disadvantaged sectors of the economy, but it is also a threat to everyone if it results in social strife, as well it may. Even if such polarization were merely the result of a structural transition, in our society a transitional upheaval comparable to that of the Industrial Revolution surely will not be accepted without serious challenges to the prevailing order.

The emerging technological revolution will make the distribution of employment and income increasingly critical issues in the political arena.

This underscores a point we have made before, namely, that in the pursuit of economic growth distribution must not be neglected or treated as a secondary concern. Distribution may in fact become more important as a political issue than growth, and so it should, given their respective implications for human well-being.

Given these dangers ahead of us, far-sighted economic planning is needed. To limit economic policymaking to crisis management is a prescription for disaster. In particular, planning has to be done now in order to deal with the distribution consequences of basic structural changes. This applies not just to employment provisions relating to work hours, educational leaves, etc., but also to an incomes distribution policy, which integrates a labour-market strategy for shaping the pattern of earnings in industry with a social security strategy. If some of the more utopian predictions concerning automation are realized, it may well become necessary to develop a system of income distribution that is to a considerable extent independent of employment. Moreover, technological planning is necessary if we want to make sure that we benefit from technological changes rather than become their victims. We must stop treating technology as an idol by first creating it and then treating it as something that controls us. We must instead learn to control technology for our benefit.

Technological planning should be concerned not merely with the allocation of resources for industrial research and development, but also with the application of technology in industry in the light of its consequence for human well-being. Emphasizing technology that helps to prevent or overcome serious forms of deprivation, such as that of the physically handicapped or that of people in hazardous work environments, should be part of the planning in this area.

The current approach in business circles of advocating a reduced role for government in the economy does not make sense in light of these impending issues. To the extent that businesses cannot reasonably be expected to promote the public interest at the expense of markets and profits, it is the responsibility of government to provide them with incentives and constraints that will ensure that their actions also serve the public's well-being. When this is not possible, government has to perform these functions itself. That includes making public investments when private investments are insufficient to keep the economy at a high employment level.

Government must assume responsibility for long-term planning, not only for the level of economic activity, but also for the development and utilization of technology and for the distribution of employment and income. Private enterprise must also respond to the challenge facing the society in which it operates. It has an opportunity to adapt profit-oriented planning to future needs, in the interest of protecting our public, and to provide institutions that would enhance the well-being of people.

The Exclusion of Women from Economic Planning

WOMEN AGAINST THE BUDGET

Women Against the Budget is a large coalition of women's groups, women trade unionists and individuals who came together in response to the unprecedented attack on human rights and the public sector launched by the government of British Columbia in a budget and legislative package of twenty-six bills presented on July 7, 1983. While the coalition was conceived as a part of the fight against Social Credit legislation, it was determined to broaden the debate to include discussion of the overall situation of women in the Canadian economy. Its appearance before the Macdonald Commission reflects the coalition's resolve that inaction on key issues affecting women be addressed in any forum where economic decisions affecting women's lives are discussed. The coalition's statement, reprinted here largely in its entirety, presents an analysis of how the Canadian economy has functioned and how women have been excluded from economic planning. The brief was prepared in cooperation with the Women's Research Centre in Vancouver by Megan Ellis and Esther Shannon of Women Against the Budget and by Jan Barnsley, Diana Ellis and Jean McIntosh of the Women's Research Centre.

There is no doubt that economic development — the creation or expansion of the economy, of a community, region or country — is the core of nation building. Economic development defines settlement patterns, reaches daily into the marketplace and factory, and determines our standard of living. Historically, the nation builders have been recorded as men. Etched on the front of schools and dotted across the map of Canada are the names we learned in social studies class — Champlain, Galt, Laurier, McGee, Tupper, Fraser. Future textbooks will likely describe the nation-building efforts of Blair, Trudeau, Irving, McMahon and Smallwood.

From the early fur-trading days to present energy explorations, the relationship between nation builders — those who develop and those who govern — has been close and mutually beneficial. The men and companies shaping Canada's economic development play an intensive role in government policy decisions. For example, Harold Innis points out that "it is no mere accident that the present Dominion coincides roughly with the fur trading areas of northern America...the Northwest Company was the forerunner of the present confederation."[1] Furthermore, the very political act of constructing the Canadian Pacific Railway was intended to hasten settlement of western Canada and thus prohibit its annexation to the United States. It also brought the wheat economy to the prairies and a pattern of settlement and urban development that remains inextricably linked to the rail line.

Continued development of northern Canada's oil and gas has included enactment of federal policies to ensure Canadian sovereignty in the high Arctic; formation of a government-owned resource company — Petrocan; construction of instant, isolated resource-based settlements and, despite regulatory delays, the intricate agreement between local, provincial, federal and international government and industry to construct pipelines and coal development projects and so on.

For those of us who are governed — who are outside the corporate and government world — the benefits of developing the economy in this way are not so obvious. With the singular exception of Justice Berger's inquiry into the Mackenzie Valley Pipeline, people's concerns about economic development have been given short shrift. What is important to development planners as they assess socioeconomic impact are narrow interpretations of factors of production such as labour (how many workers are needed), transportation (how do we get the resource out), and environment (where can we dump the tailings). Community concerns and the concerns of women and families are seldom, if ever, seriously taken into account.

The Exclusion of Women

The historical exclusion of *women* from the public worlds of business, finance, economics and politics means even less is known about how women live and work, and the resulting invisibility is reflected in public policies and legislation. The world of women — the private world of the home, the family, community, and limited areas of the labour force — if seen at all, is seen as peripheral to those who plot Canada's economic future.

However, the contribution of women to the economic development of this country has been, and continues to be, an enormous contribution of time, self, energy and ability. These contributions have been shaped not only by particular environmental conditions and economic organization but also by varying conceptions of femininity, sex roles, and female status vis-à-vis male status. The work that women do — household and subsistence production, child care, labour force participation, employment, and income generation — has a pervasive influence on the general quality of life that they are able to maintain, their capacity for personal fulfilment, and the survival and well-being of their families and communities.

Yet, in the majority of cases where this development characterizes the economic structure and organization of the country, women are excluded from all states of the process, from planning, to execution, to completion. Many recent studies that specifically address the concerns of women in relation to development note that accounts of women's work are rarely found. Women's working situations, and descriptions or analyses of the work itself, are poorly or minimally articulated into general accounts of economic development. Beneria makes the following statement in an article written in 1980:

> Available estimates of the world's working population grossly under-estimate women's participation in economic activities and cannot tell us much about what types of tasks women perform in terms of the existing gender-related division of labour. Yet we have reached a period in history in which the most basic tenets and assumptions influencing relationships between men and women in society have been called into question, and these include the existing division of labour.[2]

Although the question of the role and value of women's work has been raised many times and in many different parts of the world, the problem continues to exist. Women's interests and spheres of activity continue to be seen as at best marginal to and at worst irrelevant to economic development. Women *may* become visible if they work in the paid labour force, that is, outside the home in what is often called the public world. But even in this regard provision is rarely made for their participation, and again their interests are seen as secondary at best.

Exclusion can therefore be understood to mean the following:

- A failure to see the sexual division of labour as significant to the process of economic development, with the result that only "men's work" is defined as relevant. Family, household and the domestic sphere are defined as marginal, and the work of the domestic domain and the character of the domestic economy remain invisible, unexplored and unconsidered.
- A failure to raise any questions that specifically concern women in the process of development, based on the lack of recognition that these issues are of crucial concern to women. Women are seen as being definitionally irrelevant to the process.

The traditional view of women in economic development has been, at best, to consider them as manipulable members of the paid or unpaid labour force. For example, the vice president of AMAX of Canada in 1980 described the proposed work force for the northwest B.C. molybdenum mine at Kitsault and said, "We're hoping to encourage mine workers with families to come here... the ideal would be 60 per cent married workers and 40 per cent single people. That makes for more stability in the work place."[3] These comments illustrate how women are seen as providers of service to husbands, children and the community. However, this work is not considered real work and women's needs, in order to carry out this work, were not taken into consideration in the socioeconomic assessment planning for Kitsault or other similar communities.

In some cases women's economic development concerns are assumed to focus on affirmative action and employment. Even when this limited view is acknowledged, it is not necessarily planned with women's interests in mind. A B.C. coal town planning study investigating the possibility of nontraditional work for women stated: "The effect of increasing the proportion of females in the direct labour force is to reduce the projected town population...the potential reduction in service and housing requirements may be considered important in policy analysis."[4] It is clear that these planners have absolutely no understanding of women's work inside and outside the home and the needs that arise from that work, not the least of which is adequate child-care and family-support services. The most horrifying revelation of their scenario, however, is the way the living needs of women and children are being *bartered* for supposedly decreased infrastructure costs.

Beyond this view of women and family as exploitable human units available to meet industrial and governmental economic development labour strategies, the actual lives, needs and concerns of women are invisible. The existing separation between the public world of development and the private world of home and family enforces and encourages women's continued invisibility.

An Economic Framework That Includes Women

An account that fully includes women is one to which the analysis of the sexual division of labour and the domestic economy is integral, not marginal, and one that seeks to explain the character of the relationship between the domestic domain and the wider society other than in terms of, for example, "women's role in the family"[5]....

It is essential that an analysis begin with the household and/or family, the basic unit of membership in our society, and with the definition of this unit as an *economic* unit, with the recognition that the work of the household is work. It is predominantly women who do the work of the domestic domain. Any analysis must also proceed with their contribution in these terms. This analysis includes women directly in the focus of the investigation. Women's concerns with economic development would be one of the issues; women's participation in the process another. Women must not be seen as passive recipients, but as members of the household, the community and the society, with active interests and concerns based on active participation. This would be the case whether they worked in the household only, or in the household and the labour force. In considering economic development in these terms, the household/domestic economy thus becomes an integral part of the overall analysis of development and change.[6]

Canada's Economic Decision Making

In addition to the need for this new framework, further changes are needed in economic planning and decision making.

We are speaking as women residents of British Columbia. In B.C., we have had a wealth of experience with federal, provincial and international economic initiatives — particularly with regard to resource development projects. From this experience, we have learned a great deal about the economy, about how economic decisions are made in this country and about the impacts of these decisions on women's lives.

We have seen clearly that the modus operandi of Canadian economic decision making is expediency. In spite of the long history of energy/resource development in Canada and in B.C. specifically, Canada has still not developed a comprehensive policy or approach to energy/resource development. Further, Canada's approach to socioeconomic assessment of megaprojects has been one of ad hoc responses (as Andrew Thompson, commissioner of the West Coast Oil Ports Inquiry, pointed out in his report in 1978). For example, discussions about transporting Alaskan gas and oil south through Canada had been going on for more than a decade when this government's impact exercises finally began in northeastern British Columbia. This was *after* approval had been given for the largest capital project undertaken by private industry in Canada's history, the Alaska Highway Gas Pipeline, *after* agreements had been signed with the U.S., and *after* dates had been set to begin pipeline construction.

We've seen economic expediency manipulate even such a widely supported Canadian value as the institution of the family — as evidenced by the stages of development of single-industry towns in B.C. During the resource extraction process, when an "independent" work force is seen as preferable, unmarried workers or workers who will leave their families behind are given priority for jobs. At stages when a longer-term work commitment is required, it is then expedient for workers with families to be hired and to bring their families to the town, for the "stability" the families provide. Of course, it is an exceptional single-industry town that provides the adequate housing, social services, transportation, recreation and health care that those "stabilizing" families need to survive.

And we know that some provincial or territorial governments in this country will even be so crass and obvious in their attempts to control the energy development work force that they will subsidize alcohol but ignore the problems of the high costs and unavailability of fresh produce in resource communities.

It is also clear, from watching economic initiatives in this country, that Canada does not have an industrial strategy: economic decisions are not based on the needs of the people of Canada but rather they are based on what benefits the multinational apparatus, which is largely American dominated. Operating in the absence of an industrial strategy, with ad hoc responses based on expediency, has proved to be profitable for *some* Canadians. The vested interests of corporations and, in turn, of governments are served well by these practices. It is those of us who are governed — who are outside the corporate and government worlds — who suffer. It is community concerns and the concerns of women and families that are seen as exogenous factors and are seldom taken into account in economic decision making.

We are the targets of myths and manipulation. When new economic initiatives are in the works, governments sell them to us by promising that they will mean more jobs. We know that in northern B.C. those jobs have rarely materialized but go instead to international teams of resource extraction/development workers. The "northern vision" attitude from the 1950s has contributed to the myth that any economic development — even "boom and bust" development — is good, but we know that the consequences are most often degradation of the land and disruption of social communities. We know the impact of an economy dominated by corporate strategy that requires periods of high unemployment. In such periods we are expected to buy the myth of restraint — to accept that governments simply can't afford social services and medicare and even human rights — at least that's what the government of B.C. would have us believe. And all the while corporate profits rise until profit margins reach the level that is considered appropriate for new investment. It is ironic that in "good" economic times governments tell us the social services that our tax dollars pay for are basic human rights, but in "bad" economic times they are the first programs to be cut — with the result that when we need them most, they're gone. As an example, witness the attacks on medicare which, if successful, will require user fees from people whose livelihood is threatened by unemployment and rising prices.

In B.C. and other parts of Canada the microtechnology revolution is quickly replacing resource development as our saviour. If we oppose it, we are derided for being "anti-progress." As women, our criticism of "progress" and "technological development" is frequently caricatured as a biological fear of science and machinery. In fact, anyone who has the audacity to criticize the corporate strategy of megaprojects and boom-bust development is characterized as being anti-progress. We are neither anti-progress nor anti-change. But we *are* catagorically opposed to technological and resource development at the expense of the economic, physical and emotional health of those people whose labour is seconded to build it.

It is time to cut through the myths and manipulation that have produced widespread cynicism and alienation. Governments and the corporate sector have to start telling the truth! Their economic practices have not produced the classless society North America is supposed to be nor the "chicken in every pot" we were all promised after the last Great Depression. And ours is not an economy out of control. There are decisions being made by governments and corporations: decisions to put hundreds of millions of dollars into highways and stadiums rather than social programs or health care; decisions to delay new investment until profit margins grow still higher. Different decisions can and must be made based on different priorities.

The Public Commission on Social and Community Service Cutbacks has reported: "Everywhere in this province, one of the richest in Canada, residents expressed uncertainty, often approaching despair, about the future...they saw the way of life in their communities 'deteriorating, and could only imagine worse for the future.' "[7] On a macrolevel, the people of Ocean Falls and Tasu in the Queen Charlotte Islands, who saw their communities die, and, on an individual level, the Community Incentive Program workers who are in danger of losing their $50-a-month supplement know first hand the despair the Public Commission referred to.

The cost in human terms and in economic terms is too great to continue on the path of corporate expediency and ad hoc economic responses.

The cost is especially high for women.

The Impact of the Economy on Women

When the Women's Research Centre did a socioeconomic impact study related to proposed construction of the Alaska Highway Gas Pipeline, our researchers found that:

> The women, on the whole, seemed to feel that if this pipeline was an economically viable project, it would be built, despite people's concerns. They saw themselves as those who must cope with whatever the governments and big business did to their town, their world, when major development took place.[8]

That is what women's role has been traditionally: we are expected to cope, to adjust, to pick up the pieces. Whenever our husbands go off to work camps and resource towns, when major development takes place, *or* when the bust follows the boom — as it inevitably does — women are expected to provide the social services and other assistance that governments say they can't afford to provide.

We see it happening now in B.C. The government, using the myth of restraint as the only option, is cutting programs for handicapped children and the elderly; they are freezing welfare rates; they are threatening services for the disabled, day care, legal aid, and crisis and preventive services for women and children who are victims of violence. Women in the North have told us that they are appalled at the effect of the education cutbacks on their children. One community's school bus service has been cut back, so that the children now arrive at school an hour and a half before school starts. Of course further staff and maintenance cuts mean the school doors don't open until 9:00 and there is no supervision of the children as they play and wait outside for that hour and a half. When services are cut back, the burden of filling the gap falls on women. For most women, in these times of recession, that burden is being added to an already dangerously over-extended workload — that of a job in the labour force and the tasks of raising a family — on less money with fewer support services. Women are already providing more than should be expected of them. We have a right to say "enough"!

In recession-hit communities in northern B.C., the loss of work for the major breadwinner in a family plays itself out in various scenarios:

- Many families simply stay where they are, knowing there is no work in other parts of the province either. So far they have been managing on unemployment insurance and by bartering for services, rather than paying cash.
- Many families use their savings to live on, thus losing that security they were raised to respect. When these savings finally run out, which of course happens at different times for different families, there is *always* a crisis.
- In one northern resource town the mine has closed — first temporarily, now permanently. The crisis-centre worker noted an escalation of marriage breakups after the unemployment benefits ended.
- Some families decide that while the woman stays in the community with the children, who are in school, the man will travel to other parts of the province or country to try to locate work. The women sometimes go on welfare, although we do know of some instances where women could not get welfare in these situations unless they presented a court order stating they had charged their husband with desertion. Other women manage to find part-time work through a government job-creation grant or by working as a waitress or clerk. Women are expected to manage — to bear the responsibility of keeping the family together.

- Some men leave the family, ostensibly to find work, and do not return.

The choice for governments when they decide to cut social services is to "pay now or pay later." For women there is no choice: we and our children pay now in the strain of carrying unbearable burdens and we pay for years to come as we suffer the costs in long-term damage both to our families' physical, emotional and mental health, and to our economic status.

To say all of this is unfair is an understatement. It is also wrong-headed in economic terms.

Perhaps pushing women back into the home worked in earlier times — it has certainly been done before — but times have changed. After the Second World War, women, who had been encouraged during the war to join the work force, were sent home. They were subjected to an emotional and cruel campaign that said that if they stayed in the work force they were taking jobs away from the men returning from the war, the men who deserved jobs. Similarly, today we know that women in B.C. are caught in a vicious Catch-22 situation: if they are on welfare they are castigated as welfare bums; if they work outside the home they are accused of taking jobs away from men — even though the jobs available to women are in the low-paying female job ghettos and are jobs which most men refuse to consider.

Many of us have grown up with the romantic notion of how our mothers baked their own bread, canned fruit and vegetables and made their children's clothes to contribute to the economy of their families, to help make ends meet.

But to repeat, times have changed and we can't go home again — it doesn't make sense, because it isn't cost-effective. In simple terms, it costs more to bake your own bread than it does, in this technological age, to buy processed bread. And more to the point, statistics show that most families need two salaries to survive. Sixty-one per cent more families in B.C. would be poor without that second income.[9] Whether they stay at home or not, an incredible 68 per cent of female-headed families live below the poverty line. And for those 10 per cent or more of Canadian women who are battered women, economic independence is critical — a matter, often, of life or death.

So the strategy of pushing women back into the home doesn't work.

But what we are seeing in this country and in this province are attempts to hold down wages in the public sector and thereby, by a "happy" accident, force wages in the private sector to drop. Working women, who already earn appreciably less than working men, will suffer most. In addition, education cutbacks will mean that women will never move out of traditional job ghettos. Increases in course costs, decreases in funding, strict control of university and college programs, all combine to limit women's educational possibilities.

And, as microtechnology becomes our new economic saviour, we can see what the effects on women will be. As the B.C. Federation of Labour has stated:

> While micro-technology will affect the employment of all workers to some degree, it will be women who are affected disproportionately. Most studies agree it will be the workers in the clerical, bank, retail and service sectors who will bear the brunt from micro-technology.[10]

Conclusion

The picture we've presented of how the economy impacts on women is drawn from years of documenting women's situations, from working with women in rape crisis centres, in transition houses, in unions, in educational institutions and in the home. What we've learned is that an economy based on corporate expediency and ad hoc responses does not work for us.

Changes are needed in economic decision making. It is essential to include women's perspective and to recognize their work in the home and outside, in the work force, as the valuable contribution it is to our economy and to the quality of life. Decisions can and must be made that take into account and consider the impact of economic development on women.

Governments must make choices and decisions based on a commitment to the greater good, a commitment, if you will, to a "just society": a society that moves beyond the profit-margin mentality and its illusions of "success" to a vision that encompasses the needs of its citizens to work, to grow and to achieve their full potential as individuals and as members of a community.

9

The Persistence of Inequality

NATIONAL ACTION COMMITTEE ON THE STATUS OF WOMEN

The National Action Committee on the Status of Women, referred to as NAC, is a voluntary feminist organization working to improve the position of women in Canada. NAC consists of almost 300 nongovernmental organizations — some regional, others Canada-wide. NAC grew out of the Committee for the Equality of Women, which worked to establish the Royal Commission on the Status of Women. Called the most powerful lobby for women in Canada, NAC promotes reform in laws and public policies, sensitizes public opinion to women's concerns and fosters cooperation among women's organizations. In its twenty-eight-page brief to the Macdonald Commission, "Future Employment Initiatives," NAC argues that business and government solutions to the economic crisis will act to the detriment of women. This excerpt deals with governmental policies that are undermining the economic independence of women.

Women are poor, by comparison to men, both nationally and internationally. Canadian women who worked outside the home in 1981 earned an average of $9,383, compared to $18,519 for male workers. One-quarter of all men earned $25,000 or more, while only 5 per cent of women workers earned that salary. Women comprised 67 per cent of single low-income earners, and were the heads of more than one-third of low-income families.

While working outside the home for low wages, these same women, and others who did not enter the paid labour force, continued to perform domestic work estimated, by the Quebec Advisory Council on the Status of Women, to equal 50 per cent of the gross national product (GNP). The value of this work is, strangely, not included in the calculation of the GNP.

Internationally, the United Nations reported in 1983 that women do two-thirds of the world's work, receive only 10 per cent of earnings paid and own only 1 per cent of its property.

In Canada, as in many other countries, women's paid work is limited to a few sectors, is poorly paid and lacks benefits and job security relative to that of most male workers.

It is our intention to review recent governmental policies which have prevented or failed to advance the attempts by women to gain economic equality with men. We will outline current disturbing trends in employment developments and will argue that the current governmental reliance on "the business environment" to solve the economic crisis will act to the detriment of women.

Wage Control Programs

The wage control programs in Canada have had a profoundly negative impact on women.

At the federal level, one cannot avoid the conclusion that the program arose partly because women workers were struggling for needed employment rights. The clerical (CR) group of the public service, employing about 39,000 women, had struck successfully in 1980 for a substantial increase, and the Canadian Union of Professional and Technical Employees and the Canadian Union of Postal Workers had conducted successful strikes leading to attainment of paid maternity leave.

Progress in such areas has been arrested by the Public Sector Compensation Restraint Act (PSCRA) and its 6 and 5 policy. First, by limiting wage increases to a uniform percentage, it has increased the wage gap between men and women in the public service, as percentage increases on higher salaries are greater than on lower salaries. Seventy per cent of women, compared to 28 per cent of men, employed in the federal public service, earn less than $20,000 per year. Only 5 per cent of women earn over $30,000, compared with 27 per cent of male workers.[1] The act even rolled back previously won increases for women, such as the 12.25 per cent the clerks were to receive in December 1982.

Secondly, the act effectively eliminates collective bargaining, since collective agreements can only be changed by agreement of the parties, and Treasury Board is agreeing to very few changes. Women have therefore no effective means to continue to bargain on the issues affecting them, including effects of technological change, health and safety, and sexual discrimination and harassment.

At the provincial level, the impact of these programs on the working poor is evident in the examples of nursing aides and assistants, employees in nursing homes in Ontario.

- River Glen Haven union members interviewed by the *Star* are depressed, scared for their jobs and mad all at the same time. Only

Phillips, whose husband makes a decent wage, dares speak for the record.

> The girls (nurses' aides and registered nursing assistants) signed union cards 16 months ago for the simplest reason of all. Until this summer they were making $4.32 an hour. Under the province's compulsory arbitration system in the health care sector, they stood to jump into the $7 to $8 dollar-an-hour bracket with most other unionized homes.
>
> Beaverton's just 10 miles down the road. They do the same work and get twice what we do. And we hadn't had a raise for two years. I told lots of the girls "Don't quit, don't take another job, our award is coming." Now I wish I hadn't.

The controls limit the Sutton workers to a top wage of $4.95 an hour next summer. But with arbitration suspended by law, it's not clear how they'd get even that!

Meanwhile, the employers all get the same provincial per bed subsidy whether they're paying the work force $4 an hour or $8. "Management must love it," said Phillips. "It's great for profits. But how can they dare control our wages when groceries and gas and everything else is going up like mad?"

- Employees of the Ark Eden home for retarded and severely malformed children in Barrie joined the Christian Labour Association of Canada last fall. They hoped for a big boost in wages ranging from $3.57 to $4.29 an hour. Union spokesman Hank Kuntz says arbitration would undoubtedly have lifted wages to the $7 range in a two-year deal.

  Now he says the controls program freezes those forty-three union members in poverty. "It's a tremendous windfall for the employer, because he's getting the same grant as everyone else. But it's totally unjust. These are the poor and they're keeping them down," Kuntz said.[2]

At the federal level, the saving of $250 million of the estimated payroll in 1982 is a pittance relative to the amount of the deficit arising from dealings with the corporate sector:

- *Tax changes:* The budget injects several billion dollars into the business sector, in part through the increase in the deficit and in part through a transfer of income from people to business by means of changes in taxation.

  Most of the increase of $9 billion is due to government's dealings with the corporate sector. Half of the increase ($4.3 billion) comes about through a fall in corporate and energy tax receipts; some of this is due to the recession, but $1 billion is due to the abandonment of business tax increases in the November budget ($450 million) and to the recent tax relief for the energy sector ($500 million).

A further $1 billion of the deficit is on account of subsidies to the energy sector.[3]

Parental Rights

Paid maternity leave and access to quality, reasonably priced day care are essential to women workers.

Paid Maternity Leave

Paid maternity leave is an inexpensive benefit, estimated by the Federal Reserve Bank of Boston to cost 0.1 per cent when spread over total staff, for fourteen to sixteen weeks at 70 per cent of full pay, or two cents per hour per employee in the case of the Canadian Union of Postal Workers demand of twenty weeks paid maternity leave.[4]

Canada is a signatory of the United Nations Convention on the Elimination of All Forms of Discrimination Against Women, which contains this provision:

> In order to prevent discrimination against women on the grounds of marriage or maternity and to ensure their effective right to work, States Parties shall take appropriate measures: to introduce maternity leave with pay or with comparable social benefits.[5]

An opinion poll conducted in January 1982 asked this question: "A suggestion has been made that all female workers in Canada be eligible for paid maternity leave, similar to that granted recently to postal workers. In your opinion should paid maternity leave be available to all female workers or not?" Sixty-one per cent of Canadians answered yes (34 per cent said no, and 5 per cent had no opinion). There was little difference in the attitudes of men and women.[6]

Yet Canada's legislated rights on this issue, namely, fifteen weeks of unemployment insurance benefits to a maximum not exceeding 60 per cent of the woman's wages, or if less, 60 per cent of the maximum insurable amount, compares very poorly with most European countries (see Table 9-1).

In the words of the Ontario Federation of Labour: "Women get pregnant, men do not. If women are to have equal rights in the workforce, they must not be penalized because they are the ones in our society who bear children."[7]

A momentum had been established by unions struggling for paid maternity leave. The postal workers succeeded in their well-publicized strike in 1981, followed by the Canadian Union of Public Professional

TABLE 9-1
Maternity Leave in Europe

Country	Length of Paid Maternity Leave	Maternity Benefits
Sweden	9 months. Leave after birth may be taken by either parent	90% of wages of parent taking leave. Paid by employer
Czechoslovakia	26 weeks	99% of wages
Denmark	14 weeks	90% of salary or wages
France	16 weeks (26 weeks for third child)	90% of salary or wages
West Germany	14 weeks	100% of salary or wages
East Germany	26 weeks	100% of salary or wages
Hungary	20 weeks	Full pay if employed 270 days prior to confinement
Italy	20 weeks	80% of salary or wages
Netherlands	12 weeks	100% of earnings
Poland	16 weeks for 1st child 18 weeks for 2nd child 26 weeks in case of multiple birth[1]	100% of earnings
USSR	16 weeks	100% of earnings. No minimum length of service requirements

[1] Has been improved recently, no details presently available.

Source: Ontario Federation of Labour.

and Technical Employees and clerical workers of the Public Service Alliance of Canada. The federal government replied by instituting its wage and compensation controls, so subsequent groups have been forced to pay for maternity leave by accepting a wage increase under 6 per cent: home economists (5.6 per cent) and historical researchers (5.9 per cent). (There are variations in the costs for different proportions of women in the groups, and different time periods covered.)

Day Care

The position of the minister of finance is that the federal government does not wish to contribute to an increase in the labour participation rate of women by providing funding for day care.[8] However, we reject the implicit suggestion that entering the paid labour force is a privilege to which women do not have a right. Further, single, widowed and divorced women make up 40 per cent of the female labour force; many of these women are single parents and require day care for their children. Despite the continuing increase in the labour force participation of women, space in public day-care centres has decreased by 40 per cent since 1978 due to government cutbacks, and many women are forced to work part time because of the absence of affordable child care.

Equal Pay for Work of Equal Value

The pattern of ghettoization of women workers and the continuing wage gap of about 40 per cent between men and women indicate clearly the need for equal-pay-for-work-of-equal-value legislation in Canada. Canada has ratified an International Labour Organization (ILO) convention on the subject requiring that:

> Each member shall, by means appropriate to the methods in operation for determining rates of remuneration, promote and, insofar as is consistent with such methods, ensure the application to all workers of the principle of equal remuneration for men and women workers for work of equal value.[9]

The federal government implemented the principle in section 11 of the Canadian Human Rights Act, but despite consultation and agreement of the provinces at the time of ratification of the ILO convention, only Quebec has instituted equal value legislation.[10]

Unlike the equal-pay-for-equal-*work* formulation, the equal *value* concept allows comparison between work done by women and men whose jobs are equal in value, though not necessarily "substantially similar," using as factors of comparison the composite of skill, effort, responsibility, and working conditions within an establishment. Thus, it is an essential tool in ending the systemic discrimination associated with low-wage female ghettos by allowing comparison of the "women's" work with work of males in other jobs.

Section 11 of the Canadian Human Rights Act was implemented in March 1978, and a recent study of cases under it indicates that the procedures usually involve long delays and that the federal government as employer has resisted the struggle of women in various classifications to use the complaint procedure. Until very recently, the Canadian Human Rights Commission employed only one equal pay officer for the entire country so that:

> In general, one can conclude that enforcement of individual complaints is more difficult than enforcement of group complaints, and that the majority of successful complaints have been filed or supported by unions. In the federal jurisdiction, enforcement has been delayed

because of shortage of Commission staff. Some complaints filed in 1979 are only now in the initial stages of investigation.[11]

The review of the cases also demonstrates the importance of collective bargaining as a strategy for obtaining equal pay.

The federal government attempted to eliminate the equal value concept in its wage restraint bill of which the first form, tabled in the House of Commons by Donald Johnston, was to limit wage increases "notwithstanding any other Act of Parliament."[12] Lobbying by NAC resulted in an amendment, permitting complaints under all sections of the Canadian Human Rights Act, including section 11, to continue. Recent amendments to the regulations under section 11 have further undermined its effectiveness.[13]

The governmental obstructions to the attainment of equal pay for work of equal value, combined with employer resistance, is unconscionable and contrary to its international legal responsibilities. The government of Canada should in fact be leading an economy-wide enforcement of equal value, but the federal government has instead attempted to limit even the effects of the current legislation, considered by women to be only a necessary first step. This contributes to a continued subsidization of the economy by millions of low-paid women workers.

Lack of Effective Affirmative Action Programs

While women's groups have long emphasized the need for mandatory affirmative action programs to attack ghettoization, no legislation exists requiring such programs in Canada. Only permissive legislation, as in various human rights statutes and the Constitution, has been passed.

With its 85,000 female employees, the federal government is the largest employer of women in Canada, and its record in this area is instructive. Affirmative action "pilot projects" were conducted in three departments, Treasury Board, Employment and Immigration Canada, and Secretary of State, from 1980 to 1983. Julie White has analyzed the results:

Since 1972 there has been a small increase of women in the executive category (from 0.3 to 4 per cent) and in the technical category (from 8 to 12 per cent). However, the proportions of women in the scientific and professional category and the operational category have actually declined slightly (from 24 to 22 per cent and from 13 to 12 per cent, respectively). Major changes have taken place in only two categories. In the administrative and foreign service there has been a marked improvement in the proportion of women, from 14 to 30 per cent of the work force. The administrative support category also shows a significant change, but in the direction of higher concentration. In 1972, 68 per cent of administrative support workers were women, but the 1981 figure is 82 per cent. Thus, only in the administrative and foreign service category has significant improvement occurred. Women remain highly ghettoized within the federal public service.

Not only are women employed largely in certain limited categories, they are also found at the lower levels of the groups within those categories. Within the administrative and foreign service category, for example, the largest group is Program Administration (PM), employing over 25,000 workers. While 30 per cent of all PM workers are women, they comprise 42 per cent of the workers at level 1, 23 per cent of those at level 3, and at level 7 only 7 per cent of the workers are women. Within the administrative support category, the clerical and regulatory (CR) workers form the largest group, employing almost 39,000 women — 46 per cent of all women working in the federal public service. The following table [Table 9-2] shows that not only are women concentrated within the CR group, but also they work at the lowest levels within that group.[14]

The restriction of women to few types of employment and to the lowest levels within jobs significantly limits their opportunities to achieve equality of opportunity for advancement in the work force.

NAC advocates affirmative action programs which would focus on training and assistance to women at all levels of job categories to move into higher-paid positions and more-varied occupations.

TABLE 9-2
The Distribution of Women in the Clerical and Regulatory Group, 1981

Level	No. Men	No. Women	Percentage of Women	Pay Rates ($)
CR1	50	111	69	10.282-11,745
CR2	1,719	7,319	81	12,175-13,212
CR3	2,817	13,274	83	14,527-15,875
CR4	4,047	13,613	77	16,126-17,633
CR5	1,863	4,044	69	18,303-20,017
CR6	308	307	50	19,707-21,566
CR7	13	8	38	23,055-25,239
Total	10,817	38,676	78	

Note: Even in this group, where women outnumber men four to one in the lower levels, women are still drastically underrepresented at the higher, supervisory levels.

Source: Public Service Commission, unpublished data, 1981.

In 1983 the federal government announced a public service-wide affirmative action program. Does it have more potential than the previous pilot projects? We note that the plan is by guidelines only, not mandatory legislation, and has no structure in place to assure participation by women and their union representatives. The stated goal is to increase the number of women in management positions,[15] which is far from a real affirmative action plan which would have as its aim to improve the position of women at all levels by assisting them to move into higher and more-varied positions. Given that only about 10 per cent of positions are managerial, this will not assist the vast majority of women. The time periods proposed for the program (to December 1984 for departments to develop plans, and no evaluation before 1987-88) together with the lack of a mandatory legislative base give no reason to believe this program will be of any greater assistance to women than was its predecessor. Equally disheartening is the dissemination of the view that "affirmative action now exists in the public service," which, together with the five-year period before review, will doubtless silence further discussion of the problem before 1986.

Affirmative action is premised on the need to move positively to compensate for the systemic discrimination in the workplace that leaves women at the lowest rungs of very few types of employment. We remain convinced that a mandatory, legislated base is essential, in both public and private sectors, for any appreciable reversal of the systemic discrimination.

Contracting Out and Part-Time Work

The increase in numbers of women working part time has been documented elsewhere, as has the disadvantaged position of many of them.[16] In the federal government the position of contract worker has been described:

> The use of contract workers is expanding, a trend that causes concern because of the lack of protection for these workers. As they are not public servants, they have no security, no right to appeal on termination of their work, no seniority for recall and no access to training programs, and they are not eligible to apply for job openings restricted to internal candidates. Those on individual contracts make their own private arrangements for salary level, but are normally excluded from all benefits. Workers such as cleaners and office staff have their pay and conditions established by the private agencies that formally employ them. Since these workers are employed by agencies outside the government, they cannot be unionized by the public service unions and are not protected under the collective agreements covering other federal workers.[17]

The nation-wide increase in the contracting out of many public services ("privatization"), from office work to hospital cleaning, represents a continuing erosion of rights and pay for the women workers affected. NAC notes that despite the establishment of a federal commission of inquiry into part-time work, the federal government has not indicated any intention to extend recommended protections to part-time and contract workers. Such neglect contributes to the continuing impoverishment of these women.

Technological Change

The NAC submission to the Labour Canada Task Force on Micro-Electronics and Employment and our comments on the task force report contain our views on the profound effects on women of the technological revolution now occurring. We have continually underlined that policy initiatives are needed for the federal government to assure that the positive potential of the technological revolution is shared by the working people of Canada and that women, whose sectors of employment face a serious erosion of jobs, receive that retraining and social support services necessary for adaptation to the emerging world.

Instead, the government has not moved to provide mechanisms for worker decision making in technological change, and has not responded to the continuing anxieties of women regarding the health effects of work with video display terminals (VDTs). The Canadian Centre for Occupational Health and Safety reports new concerns regarding pulse-modulated, very low frequency electromagnetic fields, produced by VDTs,[18] but the federal government continues to ignore the undeniable clusters of miscarriages and birth defects among women VDT operators, as well as the impact on women workers of unemployment due to technological change, which we discuss further below.

Unemployment and Job Creation

With unemployment levels at 11 to 12 per cent of the work force, and no appreciable decline predicted for the foreseeable future, unemployment and job creation dominate the minds of all who are concerned with employment rights of workers.

NAC was involved in extensive consultations with the minister responsible for the status of women, the Hon. Judy Erola, on the New Employment Expansion and Development Program (NEEDs) in which we indicated our concern that the projects suggested in the program were not in the sectors where women work, and appeared to be directed disproportionately to reduce male unemployment.[19] The program continued to operate with this orientation, and at a recent meeting with the Hon. John Roberts, NAC was told that no program initiatives to reduce unemployment of women are planned.

The current Canada Works program precludes projects which replace volunteer work or duplicate existing services; these restrictions will prevent women from developing services on a voluntary basis, as has been done in the past, and then using these ideas to develop paid work. Further, in its orientation to development of projects by the private sector in areas of public works and capital expenditure, the program does not orient funds to the sectors where women work, and therefore deprives women of an equitable portion of the funds available.

The federal government response, as expressed in the 1982 budget and *The Rocky Road to 1990: A Staff Paper on Economic Development Priorities*,[20] is to reply to the profound problems of structural unemployment by reliance on "the importance of the overall business environment" as the strategy to increase employment. However, emerging employment trends in Canada and the United States indicate that the private sector's use of technological change and accompanying structural changes in the economy will not produce employment or involve an equitable distribution of the benefits of technological change.[21] Reliance on the private sector in these circumstances is therefore as wrong-headed as were the recession-inducing policies aimed at reducing inflation by the incalculable human and economic cost of high unemployment.

Full employment, especially for women, can only be achieved through the development of public sector employment. It is no accident that amongst the industrialized nations of the West, Sweden has the lowest unemployment rate, 4 per cent. Public sector spending in Sweden constitutes 70 per cent of the GNP, while public sector spending in Canada constitutes 45 per cent of the GNP.[22] Meanwhile, our unemployment rate hovers around 12 per cent.

We must emphasize that the participation rate of Swedish women is one of the highest in the world at 70 per cent, while ours is lower at approximately 53 per cent....[23]

Conclusion

Government policy in Canada has acted to limit the capacity of unions to act as income distributors; it has attempted to limit the remedial effects of human rights legislation; it has failed to expand employment opportunities for women; and it has denied the valid social and economic purposes served by the public sector.

The American example of an increasingly class-ridden society and the B.C. experience of a conflict-ridden one both loom on our immediate horizon as dislocation from massive unemployment and impoverishment of working people continues.

The scale of the injustice is enormous.

We urge you to resist calls for "the small business" approach to management of a national economy; to explore protection for women and other affected workers in the face of structural change; to make job creation the priority in economic development, including in the public sector; and to expand the bases for democratic participation in decision making on government economic policy.

10   Northern Neglect

MAKIVIK CORPORATION

Like all Native peoples, the Inuit are striving for more public and political recognition of their precarious position within Canadian society. There are approximately 5,800 Inuit in northern Quebec. This territory, a part of the Inuit homeland in which they are the predominant population, is about one-third the size of Quebec.

The Makivik Corporation is an Inuit organization created under Quebec law and represents the Inuit of northern Quebec on economic, social and other issues related to the James Bay and Northern Quebec Agreement. The agreement was signed in 1975 and is the only comprehensive land claims settlement presently existing in Canada. The corporation is also involved in various economic ventures, including a regional airline and construction company, within the northern territory. It participates in the ongoing constitutional process concerning aboriginal peoples, both at the national level and within Quebec.

The Makivik brief, entitled "The Future of Inuit in Canada's Economic Union: Northern Partnership or Neglect," describes in some detail the problems and challenges faced by Inuit, concentrating to a large degree on northern Quebec. It describes the fundamental goals and aspirations of a distinct people within Canada.

The alarming gaps that continue to widen between Inuit and non-Native Canadians in regard to economic and social development, the ineffectiveness of government programs and policies to alleviate such problems to date and the need for a new national perspective are all reasons why the Inuit seek a fresh approach that would contribute to growth rather than perpetuate dependency. The following excerpt is from the first portion of the ninety-three-page brief.

During the past few years, Inuit in northern Quebec and other parts of Canada have established economic and social development as a priority. However, whether through misguided government policies or outright neglect, we find ourselves, as a people, stripped of our economic rights and without adequate opportunities to significantly promote our self-reliance. As northern peoples, we will never accept a system which exploits the natural resources within our vast region at the expense of our rights and our own development — and which precludes our full participation. Government policies and practices are sorely in need of change. If the North is to contribute to strengthening Canada's economic union, a new consciousness must evolve which includes Inuit as full and active partners....

In order to understand the dynamics which have led to our present position within this country, it is important to examine briefly our recent history.

In 1975 the James Bay and Northern Quebec Agreement was entered into by Inuit of northern Quebec with the federal and Quebec governments.[1] Under the agreement, it was intended that our aboriginal rights in and to land[2] in Quebec were to be exchanged for other more clearly defined rights and benefits. Despite the signing of the agreement, many of the fundamental problems we experienced in our past history still remain.

From 1867 to the present time, governments in Canada have failed to confirm unequivocally the rights and status of northern Quebec Inuit. This continued state of uncertainty has had a destabilizing effect on our societies and has permitted the ongoing erosion of our rights and interests by both federal and provincial governments. Political and economic colonial policies have worked to deny us access to adequate resources. It has left us lacking in essential services and economic opportunities. It has offered us little or no cultural protection. We are today faced with unprecedented social problems, while our cultures and values are being eroded at an alarming rate.

This situation is unacceptable. The economic, social and political disadvantages we suffer are not mere coincidence. They are, at least in part, the consequences of perpetuating the uncertainty of our constitutional and other rights and status, while permitting their further erosion by the daily actions of governments.

If there are any lessons to be learned from our history, it is that we must fully determine our constitutional and other rights and status, as Inuit, and obtain further constitutional protections in order to enjoy positive growth and deter the constant pressures of assimilation. In so doing, it must be recognized that it is often necessary to provide different rights for different peoples or cultures. Otherwise, the rights of the majority would always prevail over those of the minority. In other words, equality of treatment for Inuit and other aboriginal peoples may often mean the right to be treated differently[3] from non-Native Canadians.

A further lesson relates to the constitutional arrangements which took place early in Canada's history.

When the British North America Act was drafted and adopted in 1867 as an integral part of Canada's Constitution, it was provided in section 91(24) that "Indians, and Lands reserved for the Indians" are exclusive federal legislative jurisdiction. This unique constitutional provision also signifies that the federal government has a political[4] if not legal obligation of the highest order and is often referred to as the "federal trust responsibility."[5]

Despite Canada's trust responsibility in regard to Inuit, our people were not made aware when Canada transferred jurisdiction over part of our homeland to Quebec by virtue of the Quebec Boundaries Extension Acts of 1912.[6] Nor were the repercussions of such transfer on our rights and our future adequately considered. The effects of this unilateral transfer were felt by us years later when we negotiated our land claims in northern Quebec. Although our aboriginal rights in and to the territory pre-existed the 1912 acquisition by Quebec by a few thousand years, Quebec insisted during negotiations of our land claims that it would only recognize ownership of Inuit lands in limited areas and where the subsurface contained no known mineral potential.[7]

Recently, a more enlightened attitude has been shown by federal and provincial governments in Canada in regard to constitutional issues. In matters affecting aboriginal peoples, governments appear committed to a constitutional process which includes the full and ongoing participation of aboriginal peoples. However, based on their historical experience, it is the position of most aboriginal peoples in Canada that the consent of each of them (Inuit, Indians and Métis) must be obtained for any constitutional amendments which directly affect them....

Constitutional Process

Constitutions are political as well as legal documents. They serve as fundamental expressions of values and cultures, of rights and freedoms and of human hopes and experiences. A constitution sets guidelines for the actions of both governments and citizens. In the Canadian context, it must reflect the principles of mutual respect and amity between existing communities of peoples, whether they be Inuit or Indian, French or English.

In this context, the recognition and affirmation of aboriginal and treaty rights in section 35 of the Constitution Act, 1982, and the creation of a separate part for the elaboration of the rights of aboriginal peoples, could provide the cornerstone for the eventual development of an aboriginal charter of rights under Canada's Constitution.[8]

Although a further elaboration of aboriginal rights did not materialize at the last First Ministers Conference, it did result in the signing of the 1983 Constitutional Accord on Aboriginal Rights. Consequently, there will be opportunities at First Ministers Conferences over the next years to further provide for our constitutional rights. In any event, other mechanisms are necessary to complement the constitutional process. Existing policies will have to change and new laws enacted, when necessary, if our present and future constitutional rights are to be fully implemented and respected on a consistent basis.

Another important avenue for change is the federal process for the settlement of comprehensive land claims established in 1973. While there may be many favourable aspects relating to land claims negotiations, the settlement of aboriginal claims is still predicated on the extinguishment and surrender of aboriginal rights. From a Native perspective, the government requirement for extinguishment or surrender is fundamentally inconsistent in spirit with the recognition and affirmation of aboriginal rights in Canada's Constitution.[9] Further, northern Quebec Inuit should not have been required to negotiate aboriginal land rights in order to obtain essential services and basic structures for their communities and region. Generally, such services and structures are readily provided by government to other Canadians.

A further limitation in the claims settlement process exists in regard to government programs. While it is possible to refocus normal government resources to enhance the efficiency of existing programs, it is not intended that new indeterminate programs geared solely to Natives be provided by the federal government in settlements.[10] Therefore, the comprehensive land claims process alone is not designed to meet all the socioeconomic and other needs of aboriginal peoples.

Government Departmental Process

Although a few exceptions exist, federal and provincial government departments generally do not provide policies or programs which adequately respond to the needs of Native Peoples. In many instances, the philosophies or attitudes of civil servants are less than helpful in dealing with our various issues.

As Inuit from northern Quebec, we encounter too often a prevailing attitude among federal civil servants that federal departments are no longer responsible for Inuit issues due to the signing of the James Bay and Northern Quebec Agreement.[11] Despite the continuing constitutional responsibility for Inuit and the specific terms of the agreement,[12] we do not have access to federal programs in an equivalent fashion to Indians.

The ineptness or unwillingness of government bureaucracies to adapt to the changes brought about by our land claims settlement has been recently commented upon by the federal government. In its February 1982 report entitled "James Bay and Northern Quebec Agreement Implementation Review," the Department of Indian Affairs and Northern Development (DIAND) concludes as follows:

Lack of proper mechanisms, structures and attitudes regarding implementation has been a major impediment to the smooth and efficient implementation of the Agreement. The establishment of more effective systems for implementation can do a great deal to prevent the buildup of the type of conflict and tensions which, in recent years, have consumed time and resources that could be used more productively in achieving the aims and objectives of the Agreement. No mechanisms, however, will make the Agreement work well unless all parties contribute their best efforts.[13]

Similar contradictions and inconsistencies are evident within Quebec government departments. On July 6, 1982, capital budgets for northern Quebec were frozen and programs suspended as a result of a Treasury Board decision.[14] No consultation took place with us prior to such decision.

The Treasury Board made no reference in its decision to Quebec's financial obligations under the James Bay and Northern Quebec Agreement. In addition, there is little evidence from Quebec that the government is willing to amend, when necessary, the agreement. While there is token acknowledgment of the "dynamic" nature of our land claims settlement, the government is generally reluctant to amend the agreement, either to reflect changing circumstances and conditions or to provide for the recognition of other Inuit rights not fully dealt with in the agreement.[15] Conversely, when changes are made to Quebec legislation related to the agreement, prior consent is not sought from Makivik as required by our land claims settlement.[16] Usually, Quebec's rationale is that such legislative amendments have not had the effect of amending the agreement.

Need for Global Review

As can be seen from the above, existing processes for change, while often useful, do not necessarily ensure that government policies, programs and laws will consistently respond to the interests of Inuit and other aboriginal peoples. The many interfaces between our economic and social issues and government decision making still require further evaluation. Federal and provincial policies affecting Inuit must still be formulated in collaboration with us. In many instances, the policies should flow from our own institutions of self-government and then be reflected in the policies of federal and provincial governments.

In addition, it is important to determine how national policies could be implemented uniformly in the provinces through joint cooperation or otherwise....

Inuit Aspirations and Goals

It is our position that national goals and policies must not only accommodate, but also foster the growth of Inuit goals and aspirations. In order to realize Canada's potential and to secure sustained economic and social progress, it is important to achieve greater understanding of our objectives and aims, our rights and our interests.

We elaborate on the nature of Inuit aspirations and goals under three main subheadings, namely, economic and social rights, cultural rights and political rights. However, the rights and principles enunciated under one classification may often include aspects of another.

Economic and Social Rights

- *Right to an adequate land base and to its management and use.* Land rights are an integral part of our aboriginal and treaty rights and, as such, are unique to aboriginal peoples. Land is the very essence of the Inuit way of life and Inuit identity. Protection of the land and control of its use are in fact protections of Inuit culture and Inuit economies. Consequently, our collective[17] and individual land rights must be so recognized as to be clearly enforceable against other users.
- *Right to harvest wildlife on a priority basis, subject to principles of conservation, and the right to fully participate in wildlife management.* Inuit harvesting of wildlife in the circumpolar region constitutes both an aboriginal right and a cultural right. As such, it is a fundamental human right worthy of protection on the regional, national and international levels. Denial of Inuit priority use of wildlife in the circumpolar region for subsistence is the equivalent to a denial of our human rights. Since our food base is viewed as our long-term security, our rights to wildlife must extend to the land and to habitat protection. Inuit must participate in wildlife management to define the relationship between subsistence, commercial and nonconsumptive[18] utilization of resources and habitats. In this regard, we must develop planning guidelines in order to satisfy the short- and long-term needs of our culture and economies.
- *Right to an economic base to promote our own self-sufficiency.* Governments have artificially severed our rights of access to economic resources which are intimately tied to our ability to exercise our other economic, social, cultural and political rights. Adequate recognition must be obtained for our right to participate fully in economic development within our region, as well as rights relating to renewable and nonrenewable resources, including subsurface rights.
- *Right to develop a balanced and diversified northern economy which accommodates and promotes both wage and subsistence economies.* The continued viability of our subsistence economy should be further developed, and we must ensure its stability and growth in the long term. At the same time, we should promote industrial employment in our wage economy, giving careful consideration to any potential adverse effects on our subsistence economy, environment and culture.

- *Right to adequate services in Inuit communities.* We must work towards eliminating regional disparities due to the short- and long-term economic, social and cultural implications of such disparities.

Cultural Rights

- *Right to ensure our survival as a distinct people.* A multitude of elements are required to ensure Inuit cultural survival. Ongoing use and development of Inuktitut as a working language in our region is crucial. We must also have culturally appropriate education services of high quality. In addition, further constitutional recognition and protection of Inuit rights and interests in our region, including the offshore, are needed to ensure our survival as a people. We must also have the economic resources to sustain the ongoing development of all aspects of Inuit culture.
- *Right to use and enjoy cultural property relating to Inuit culture and ancestry.* Artifacts and other evidence associated with Inuit use and occupancy of lands and resources represent a cultural, historical and ethnographic heritage of Inuit society. We have a special relationship with such evidence which requires further expression in terms of rights and responsibilities. The Inuit archaeological record is of spiritual, cultural, religious and educational importance to us. For educational and cultural purposes, a greater proportion of Inuit cultural property must find a permanent home within our northern region.[19]
- *Right to determine our own membership and right to our own culture, language and traditions.* Artificial distinctions as to who are aboriginal peoples have been created from time to time by governments. These distinctions have had adverse effects on aboriginal cultures. Only Inuit should determine who are members of their people. In addition, the Constitution must recognize more fully our right to our customs and traditions and the use and development of our language and history. The preparation of an Inuit history from an Inuit perspective would contribute significantly to our cultural development.[20]

Political Rights

- *Right to self-determination within the Canadian federation.*[21] Inuit must have greater control over matters affecting us in our region. Self-determination goes much beyond entitlement to culture, language, traditional customs and the development of identity. Self-determination implies constitutionally protected powers over ourselves, our lands and resources. Mutually satisfactory modes of expressing the internationally accepted principle of self-determination[22] can be determined through further discussions with government.

- *Right to self-government.* This right embodies to some degree the principle of self-determination and is a fundamental right of aboriginal peoples which should be recognized in the Constitution. The right to self-government should include the right to fully participate in the management of our region, including its land and marine environment and biological resources, in recognition of Inuit continuing use and Inuit dependence, in whole or in part, for survival upon the resources in our region.
- *Right to our own institutions.* Institutions of self-government must be appropriate to our way of life and to our rights, interests and values. Our institutions must have access to adequate economic resources in order to be able to fully exercise the powers vested in them.

The above represent many of our goals and aspirations as a distinct people. In order to determine what may be preventing or retarding their realization, we must look at the problems and challenges facing us. This is the subject of the next section.

Existing Patterns of Northern Neglect

If there is one word to depict the overall conditions in northern Quebec, it would be "neglect."[23] The reasons for such neglect are varied.

In some cases, inadequate budget allocations for northern Quebec may be due to a lack of political clout to prevent such treatment in times when governments are cutting their budgets. In other cases, federal-provincial disputes may retard or prevent cost-sharing initiatives from being implemented. On other occasions, concrete steps are actually taken but are later found to be ineffective or inappropriate, since the local population was not adequately consulted. Finally, some northern problems may simply be ignored.

In its February 1982 report entitled "James Bay and Northern Quebec Agreement Implementation Review," the federal government describes the existing conditions in Inuit communities in northern Quebec: "Many communities experience overcrowded housing, inadequate water and sanitation services, little fire protection, poor roads and little municipal infrastructure. Education facilities are often poor...."

It is worth noting that facilities and services available in Inuit communities in the Northwest Territories are clearly superior to those in similar communities in northern Quebec. This is at least partly due to the jurisdictional disputes between Canada and Quebec which took place in the 1960s and early 1970s.[24] As a result, essential services, such as airstrips, housing, schools and municipal services, were not maintained and experienced serious decline....

On May 6, 1983, the prime minister of Canada tabled Bill C-152,[25] which provides for more comprehensive principles in dealing with regional disparities and disadvantaged regions. However, this bill would set up a framework which requires federal-provincial agreements[26] in order for disadvantaged regions to benefit. Therefore, the regional entities of aboriginal peoples are not ensured of any direct involvement in the negotiation of such agreements. Based on our experience in northern Quebec, it is likely that Inuit would continue to be deprived of the benefits of such programs, since they are dependent on federal-Quebec agreement.

A further problem is that many federal programs generally end up being applied to status Indians and not northern Quebec Inuit, contrary to the federal constitutional responsibility for Inuit and the specific provisions of our agreement.[27] A notable exception is the recent creation of the five-year $345-million Native Economic Development Fund which applies to Inuit, Indians and Métis. However, it is still premature to determine to what extent Inuit will actually receive concrete benefits from this fund.

Makivik cannot accept the excessive unemployment which is rampant in our communities as a result of overt government neglect. Although governments may be well intentioned in their efforts to alleviate the situation, Inuit cannot afford to continue with piecemeal, disjointed and sometimes wholly inappropriate economic programs. The ongoing lack of economic activity and the presence of high unemployment are major contributors to our social problems such as alcohol, drug abuse and youth-related crime in Inuit communities. Moreover, by not providing for adequate economic and social programs, the federal and Quebec governments are inadvertently fostering Inuit dependence on welfare and unemployment. By not making a major investment in our economic future through adequate programs and funding, governments are enjoying little financial saving, since additional costs are therefore incurred under welfare, unemployment and rehabilitative social programs....

Canada's Constitution commits both Parliament and the provincial legislatures, together with the government of Canada and the provincial governments, to "furthering economic development to reduce disparity in opportunities."[28] Moreover, the Constitution provides specific provisions to enable affirmative action programs and policies to be implemented by governments so as to ensure equality of opportunity for aboriginal peoples as well as other Canadians.[29] While such fundamental principles have been included in the "spirit of the Constitution," as well as the letter, economic opportunities have not been created, nor have regional disparities been reduced, in northern Quebec.

Challenges for Economic Policy

11

The Need for an Industrial Strategy

QUEBEC TEACHERS FEDERATION

The Quebec Teachers Federation, known in French as the CEQ (Centrale de l'enseignement du Québec) has some 86,200 members, grouped in 150 affiliated units. It is recognized as being one of the principal forces for progressive change in Quebec. Its seventy-four-page brief to the Macdonald Commission emphasizes the importance of economic, social, political and fundamental human rights in any consideration of Canada's economic future. It calls for a full-employment policy and in the following excerpt shows how foreign control of the Canadian economy has contributed to our pitiful record on employment creation. The excerpt goes on to argue the case for an industrial strategy for Canada.

There is still more foreign capital invested in Canada than in any other country in the world.[1] In 1977 direct foreign investment in Canada amounted to some $47 billion. Nonresidents controlled 55 per cent of the capital in the manufacturing industries, 68 per cent of the capital in the oil and gas industries and 55 per cent of the capital in the mining industry.[2]

In 1979 there were 1,709 Canadian-controlled and 1,255 foreign-controlled companies with assets exceeding $10 million. Among the hundred largest companies, the foreign sector accounted for 47.5 per cent of sales, 29.5 per cent of share-holdings, 37 per cent of assets, 41 per cent of profits and 57 per cent of taxable income.[3]

Since the Second World War, these massive amounts of foreign capital, mainly American, have had a predominantly negative effect on the Canadian economy, subordinating it to the U.S. economy. Foreign capital has turned Canada into not only an exporter of raw materials (and therefore jobs), but also an exporter of capital in the form of interest and dividend payments to foreign investors. The commission of inquiry into the Canadian automotive industry headed by Simon Reisman, former deputy minister of finance, reported in 1979 that in thirteen years, from 1965 to 1977, American multinationals invested only $54 million in the Canadian automotive industry. However, the same multinational firms brought home $1.1 billion in profits. These figures do not take into account approximately $1 billion left behind to strengthen their hold over the industry. Where does the $1.1 billion go? Who decides?

The Canadian economy is in fact structurally linked and tied to the American economy. In Canada's balance of payments, any surplus recorded in traded goods is more than offset by the services deficit, which consists mainly of interest, dividend and royalty payments. Net interest, dividend and other payments leaving the country during the last three years alone (1980-82) totalled $36.9 billion.[4] The resulting overall deficit in the current balance must be compensated for by a huge inflow of capital to even out the balance of payments. This means keeping interest rates higher than in the U.S., which ensures that American policies are copied almost automatically in Canada. We have recently seen the disastrous results.

In the current crisis and recession, while the multinationals' profits are falling, funds transferred to head offices are increasing and creating economic problems for Canada as the host country.

Recently, the multinational Iron Ore Company closed its Schefferville mine, leaving 285 miners jobless after transferring $225 million in profits to American shareholders. Not only are interest and dividend outlaws on the increase, but the trend in the foreign capital account is towards disinvestment. Until a few years ago, direct foreign investment had always flowed into Canada, but now this has been reversed. From 1981 to the second quarter of 1983, direct withdrawal of foreign capital reached $6.4 billion,[5] which is equal to the total accumulated inflow between 1970 and 1980. This does not mean that foreign investment in Canada has stopped. It continues to increase, but it is generated through profits made in Canada.

Foreign control must be reduced if we are to consolidate our industrial structure and develop our own technology, gain economic control and become masters of our own collective life. Contrary to the direction of present government policies, more power should be given to the Foreign Investment Review Agency (FIRA) and national economic power should be developed by building up the economic role of the state.

The Debate

The debates which have taken place over the last decade on the development of an industrial strategy may be schematically reconstructed from various studies and policies. It is also possible to follow the progress of the debate.

- *In the late 1960s and early 1970s*, many analyses emphasized the extent of foreign control and the threat that it represents for the

Canadian economy. The studies and reports by Kari Levitt, Mel Watkins and Herb Gray come to mind. Also at the time, the Senate committee chaired by Maurice Lamontagne recommended a major reform of science policy.

- *The early 1970s* were marked by the elaboration of various policy papers and statements including: studies done by the Department of Industry, Trade and Commerce towards an industrial strategy; the arguments of the Science Council of Canada against foreign control and for "scientific sovereignty"; the 1972 policy statement by the minister of external affairs dealing with the "third option"; and the attitude adopted by the Economic Council of Canada in favour of trade liberalization.

- *Between 1975 and 1977* there was an effort made by the "DM 10" (deputy ministers) group to prepare the economy for the period following wage and price controls.

- *From 1977 to 1978* we saw labour-management committees in twenty-three industrial sectors; the creation of the Ministry of State for Economic and Regional Development (MSERD), in the guise of its predecessor, the Board for Economic Development; and Senator Bud Olson's eight-point agenda recommending a shift from subsidization of consumption to aid in generating capital.

- *During the 1979-81 period* economic strategies centred around two poles: the manufacturing industry and the use of natural resources. Several initiatives may be stressed: the fairly nationalistic position articulated by Herb Gray, as minister of industry in 1980, emphasizing production in the manufacturing sector; the "Medium Term Track Document" released in 1981 by MSERD proposing a strategy focused on resources on the basis that conditions of trade should improve; the National Energy Program (NEP); and the Blair-Carr Task Force on Megaprojects (1981).[6]

This all led to the statement entitled *Economic Development for Canada in the 1980's*, which accompanied Finance Minister MacEachen's November 1981 budget. Those who recommended resource development won out in the debate against the advocates of a strategy focused on manufacturing and state intervention. The economic development statement also maintained that the Canadianization aspect of the NEP was not appropriate for other sectors. Assurances were also offered that FIRA would not be given more power.

In the end then, despite all the twists and turns taken along the way, a strategy of promoting natural resource exports and reducing government intervention and limiting Canadianization emerged as dominant in the debate. However, in the very moment of victory, the fluctuation of oil prices, the collapse of energy megaprojects, the damage caused by high interest rates and the worsening of the recession reopened the whole question of economic policy.

Economic Policy, 1981-83

In an orientation paper from the Ministry of State for Economic and Regional Development entitled *The Rocky Road to 1990*, the federal government outlined the following prospects for the next decade. From 1981 to 1991, about one-quarter of the jobs in the traditional manufacturing sector will be eliminated, perhaps along with a quarter of the jobs in the financial sector. A total of one to two million jobs will be lost. At the same time, two million new people can be expected to enter the work force. The federal government nonetheless identifies three main areas of growth: resource-related industries (which are not known as job intensive); technological goods and services; and personal services (such as video products, health care and fast foods).

As a result, the employment situation is bound to deteriorate amid major structural disruptions. Far from suggesting means of countering this trend, however, the federal government paper advocated support for the emerging changes, considering any attempt to resist the current course of events to be futile.

The policy recommended is mainly aimed at helping people relocate in the urban centres that are expected to grow: the cities of southern Ontario and British Columbia, the four major cities in the Prairies, Halifax, St. John's and perhaps, although there is some doubt, Montreal and Quebec. The government also maintains that it should not try to force the hand of new "footloose" industries. If a company wants to set up business in Toronto, for example, it would be preferable to lend support to the company than to attempt to force it to locate in the province of Quebec, for fear that in the end it will locate in Boston. The orientations in this paper are thus a cause of great concern. They lead to a heightening of social and regional disparities and inequalities.

Today [late 1983 — Ed.], the federal government seems more confused than ever. It is resigned to allowing powerful international forces to shape the Canadian economy of tomorrow. The April 1983 budget did give slightly more encouragement to technological development; the volatility of raw material markets was finally appreciated. However, the government still adheres to a policy of international specialization in resources, as shown by the major infrastructure undertakings in the West to transport primary products to markets in the Pacific Rim countries. The Cold Lake Oil Sands Project was even revived on a modest scale.

There is also a resigned acceptance of a closer integration of the Canadian economy with the American one, as if this amounted to a question of economic rationalization between partners of equal strength.

In this connection, the minister of state for international trade, Gerald Regan, announced on September 1, 1983, that Ottawa had abandoned the "third option." This concept, put forward in 1972, was aimed at reducing Canada's dependence on the United States by increasing trade with the European Economic Community (EEC) and Asia. Even though common sense — backed by numerous studies — dictates that commercial interests lie in rapid growth markets, the federal government prefers to opt for the easier route, leaving uncontrolled the economic forces which are pushing Canada toward a satellite economy.

To concentrate commercial policy on the American market still more heavily, Ottawa also raised the prospect of sectoral free trade agreements in textiles and clothing as well as public transit. In the textiles sector, 120,000 Quebec jobs depend on tariffs and quotas, an obvious source of concern to us. The federal government spokesman added that these agreements foreshadowed others, notably in the alloy steel and petrochemical sectors. The laissez-faire doctrine, so dear to the Economic Council and Senator van Roggen, thus seems to be finding favour again with Ottawa politicians in this present utterly chaotic economic situation. We believe that the disruption this policy would cause in industry, not to mention the political repercussions, would compromise any possibility of bringing the economy back to a level of full employment.

Policies that give priority to adapting rapidly to the world market allow for the acceleration of technological change regardless of social consequences, and promote narrow industrial specialization with no concern for the effects on sectoral interdependencies. These policies increase regional specialization, even if it heightens disparities, and open the border to foreign capital investment and products without regard for the resulting dislocation and loss of jobs.

The precepts of the monetarist and neo-liberal cliques, as implemented by Thatcher, Reagan and, caught in the tide, a number of other industrialized countries, have only contributed to worsening human misery, without offering any prospects for improvement. The unlimited confidence in the virtues of the market that constitutes the theoretical base of these schools and the accompanying strategy of abandoning social policy jeopardize everything workers have struggled so hard to gain.

Elements of an Industrial Strategy

The development of social and democratic rights must be based on economic development that puts the interests of the majority first. This requires the implementation of an industrial strategy devised in a democratic fashion. Such a project should, in our opinion, proceed from the following considerations:

- A recognition of the need for an industrial strategy closely tied to job development, with the objective of strengthening the industrial framework so as to recapture the domestic market and increase the share of our industrial products on international markets.

- In consequence, both free trade and excessive protectionism must be rejected. Also to be rejected is North American integration, which would result in further American domination of Canada and lead to even greater neglect of the rest of the world.
- Indigenous technological development should be seen primarily as an alternative to a strategy oriented towards market access that would entail relinquishing entire sectors of the economy to foreign control.[7] The need to reduce foreign control over our economy must be acknowledged.
- The need for a financial strategy aimed at channelling savings into "domestic" economic development must be recognized. Such a strategy entails controls over the employment and use of profits and savings, since market incentive measures have proved ineffective.
- Recognizing the need for an international policy which serves the interests of the common people everywhere: international relations based on cooperation and mutual benefit; support for progressive governments; boycott of regimes that encourage the exploitation of workers.
- Considering the power of the interest groups that wield capital in our society, we would like to reassert our position that the government should be a driving force in establishing and implementing economic development strategies. This consideration goes hand in hand with the demand for a democratic transformation of government in order to ensure genuine participation of the people in the choices our society makes. The need for more democratic decision making also exists at the level of businesses. To start this process, the labour movement (and union rights) must be promoted.

Without going into great detail, we would like to give some of the underlying reasons for our position.

In a developed economy, the manufacturing industry plays a key role, even if it absorbs only one-third of the labour force (23 per cent in Quebec in 1980). The manufacturing industry stimulates the entire economy through numerous spillover effects on productivity and production, in both the primary industries (upstream) and the service industries (downstream). This was pointed out in the early Sixties by the economist Kaldor.[8]

When world demand stagnates, as it is doing right now, the competition faced by an open economy causes the domestic industrial fabric to unravel. Success on the world market helps the most efficient producers to penetrate the domestic market; this, however, disrupts the cohesiveness of the domestic production system. It has been pointed out that import penetration is heavy in certain key sectors of the manufacturing industry. What would happen if all protectionist measures were suddenly abolished?[9] Policies must therefore be devised to slow down deindustrialization and stop the process of penetration of the domestic market leading to loss of competitiveness and reduction of employment.

This requires a policy specifically geared toward developing industrial productive capacity. We nevertheless consider that seeking to adapt quickly to the world market by specializing in a few fields of expertise is not an acceptable medium-term solution for Canada, given the shortcomings of the manufacturing sector and the strong hold of foreign capital. Is increased international specialization a logical policy? Would it prevent U.S. subsidiaries from returning home to reap the benefits of economies of scale resulting from the concentration of production? Would there be anything to prevent Canadian capital from being redeployed to the U.S. market? From 1978 until 1983, direct Canadian investment abroad has totalled $16.3 billion.[10] The gaping holes in the economic structure of Canada would likely open further rather than close, thus weakening the dynamics of the manufacturing industry even further, under such a policy. Finally, in a match where one contestant outweighs the other by ten to one, the outcome in North America is easy to predict unless a handicap is introduced. This is not to deny that Canada can compete effectively in certain areas of the international market, but the interests of the Canadian economy and of the workers who are dependent on it are not the same as those of international capital, including so-called Canadian capital.

One of the major weaknesses of the Canadian economic structure is the capital equipment sector, which shows an enormous deficit. In order to consolidate the domestic market, a production strategy aimed at rebuilding the equipment industry should therefore constitute one of the major points of a strategy for industrial development objectives.[11] Such an approach would obviate the difficult problem of low productivity levels resulting from protectionism. In this area it is not necessary to start from scratch, since annual exports of equipment total approximately $8 billion.

To complement these developments, the telecommunications industry, where a good start has already been made, should be strengthened. Major investments should also be made in the pharmaceutical industry, in biotechnology and, generally speaking, in all health-related sectors; this is an area where, according to Stuart Smith, chairman of the Science Council of Canada, "we are not even in the running."

A dynamic renewal of industry cannot, in our opinion, be left primarily to the initiative of private enterprise. The success of such a strategy depends, on the contrary, on an extension and deepening of government intervention in order to solve the problem of developing the key sectors we have identified. For this reason we would like again to emphasize the important role to be played by the government in the implementation of an industrial strategy.

Deregulation, tax reductions on savings and profits, and decreasing government involvement in education, health and social services do not result in fair distribution of material and human resources. Rather, further reliance on the "free" market encourages those who wield financial power in Canada to move into those markets where they will be able to increase the scale of their operations, in other words into the U.S. The Bank of Montreal has, for example, recently obtained control of Harris Bankcorp of Chicago, so it can finance medium-sized projects in the U.S. This brings the Bank of Montreal's U.S. assets to $14.7 billion, or one-fifth of the bank's total assets, after completion of the merger.[12] When a major Canadian financial institution sets such an example, will not others be inclined to follow it?

In summary, to put the economy back on the road to full employment, the government must act more forcefully when it sees the need to pursue a strategy of compensating for the gaps and deficiencies in the industrial structure. Basically, economic policy must aim at regaining the domestic market and reworking the industrial fabric rather than seeking the illusory market "fit," whether this be a sectoral or regional specialization.

Therefore, in order to recapture the domestic market, control technical development and solve employment problems, ways of making capital flow into the most important sectors must be found. It is the responsibility of society as a whole to meet this challenge. We believe that in a more democratic state, initiatives taken by the people can help solve the problems facing us.

12 | The Pitfalls of Free Trade

CANADIAN INSTITUTE
FOR ECONOMIC POLICY

*The pitfalls of so-called free trade were analyzed by the Canadian
Institute for Economic Policy (CIEP) in its presentation to the
Macdonald Commission that is reprinted here. Its main submission to the commission, a comprehensive assessment of Canada's
economic problems, was released as a CIEP study under the title*
Rebuilding from Within *(Toronto: James Lorimer and Company,
1984).*

*The institute was created by some of the same individuals who
were active in the Committee for an Independent Canada. As a
think tank operating from 1979 to 1984, the CIEP published thirty-
one policy studies. Its brief to the Macdonald Commission was
written by Abraham Rotstein, a University of Toronto economist
and vice-chairman of the institute. It reflects the contribution of
other CIEP board members, most notably Walter Gordon, a cham-
pion of Canadian sovereignty and former Liberal cabinet minister, who was the institute's founder and chairman. The institute's
message is clear: industrial policy must be given first priority,
and trade policy made to accommodate, rather than direct, industrial policy.*

Renewed calls for "free trade" with the United States have become
widespread recently. This is a romantic and illusory notion. At a time
when double-digit unemployment is being projected for the Canadian
economy into the early 1990s, free trade with the United States stands
the risk of creating an economic quagmire in the Canadian manufacturing sector. The effects on manufacturing employment could be
devastating.

Canada has already made extensive commitments towards freer trade
in the last Tokyo Round of GATT (General Agreement on Tariffs and
Trade) negotiations. These tariff reductions will be fully realized by
1987. Further moves in this direction at the present time are fuelled
by economic illusions of the United States as the land of "greener
pastures," and gloss over the difficult problems of our branch-plant
economy. Calls for freer trade divert attention as well from the main

economic challenge: an industrial policy to deal with our high unemployment.

A brief review of our postwar economic strategy is followed by an examination of the concrete difficulties that militate against both "free trade" and the government's recent proposal of "sectoral free trade."

During the postwar period, mainstream economic thinking in Canada produced a surprisingly coherent outlook for the future. The three pillars of this outlook consisted of an orderly movement towards world trade liberalization, a neutral or modest role for government in the economy and "Quiet Diplomacy" in our relations with the United States.

These three pillars were internally consistent. When liberalized trade is made the primary policy thrust, industrial policy necessarily takes on an auxiliary or dependent role. The relative importance of various industries is established by the external verdicts and price signals that flow from our trade opportunities. Industrial policy, in that case, is merely designed to accommodate these trade opportunities and lacks an independent thrust of its own. "Quiet Diplomacy," in turn, is designed to smooth the way for "frictionless" transborder flows of goods, capital and even cultural phenomena, from television to magazines.

While such a general outlook necessarily suffers from the internal contradictions and exceptions of the Canadian experience, it has nevertheless had a powerful influence on the broad direction in which policy unfolded in the postwar period.

Our main theme is that all three policies have now run their course and have been overtaken by major changes in the global economy, in the domestic economy and in Canadian-American relations. A new economic outlook is required that departs sharply from the received wisdom.

The most serious symptom of our economic malaise is the double-digit unemployment now being projected to the end of this decade and into the early 1990s. This problem should receive the highest priority. Industrial policy should now become the main focus of our attention and trade policy subordinated to its objectives — a diametrical shift from our traditional stance. "Public Diplomacy" has now begun to replace "Quiet Diplomacy" in our relations with the United States. Its tactical success over the short term should now be followed by a longer-term strategy to support our industrial and commercial policy objectives.

A rather vocal sentiment is now emerging advocating closer integration with the United States, a return in effect to the vision of the status quo ante. In it we hear the rhetoric and sentiments of the traditional postwar perspective, a hope for the future that is essentially a more fulfilled version of the past.

The reader will hardly fail to recognize the reasoning:

- Canada was and remains a major trading nation and must follow the global path of gradual trade liberalization and learn to compete abroad.

- Domestic industrial policy must fall in line with emerging trends in our trade and comparative advantage. Diverting or distorting such "market forces" is bound to be costly and self-defeating. We must abide by the price signals of these market forces and adjust our labour rates, capital flows, management techniques and productivity accordingly. We must "make it in the big leagues," where the rules of the game are "clear" and "obvious."
- In a troubled world economy that may be headed for blocs of regional integration, an accommodation with the Americans that is trouble-free stands the best chance of realizing substantial gains for the Canadian economy. The large U.S. market would provide a competitive stimulus for the rationalization of Canadian industry and the benefits of economies of scale.
- The phasing in of further tariff reductions can be arranged over a longer period to ease the transition for both firms and employees. Generous assistance will be provided.

This vision, in our view, runs counter to many formidable obstacles that are being ignored or dismissed. It is animated by a "vie en rose" phenomenon, an attempt to escape from Canada's very serious domestic economic problems as well as to gloss over certain basic difficulties in the American economy itself. These new realities bear some closer scrutiny.

First are the existing Canadian commitments from the Tokyo Round. By 1987 the Canadian tariff on durable industrial products will have been reduced by some 40 per cent. This will bring the weighted average rate of tariff protection from 15 per cent in 1979 to 9 to 10 per cent by 1987.[1] How much further can this process of tariff reduction be extended before "diminishing returns" set in? In contrast to the pure theory of free trade, what are the obstacles and institutional realities we are likely to confront?

A glance, for example, at our preponderant export items, namely, passenger automobiles and chassis, motor vehicle parts, and trucks and related items, reveals that they are covered by the Auto Pact and generally move in an intracorporate framework, that is, at "transfer prices" rather than at "market prices" that result from the more conventional trade between partners dealing at arm's length. Indeed, it is not generally appreciated that more than half of Canadian exports to the United States, that is, about 56 per cent, take place between firms of which one partner has ownership of at least 5 per cent of the equity of the other.[2] The constraints on price formation are a clear departure from the classical notion of market forces and throw the entire basis of free trade into question.

The implications should be apparent. The full economic benefits from a genuine free trade program flow from the "ripple effects," so to speak, of flexible adjustments to market prices. The reverberation of these market prices from our export activities set in motion, at least in theory, a series of internal adjustments in the rest of the economy which ultimately realize the maximum benefits of these "gains from trade."

This process runs on an entirely different track when the economic adjustments in question are not at the behest of conventional market forces but under the aegis of intracorporate transfers. There is no clear indication in such a case where the bulk of the "gains from trade" will accrue, that is, whether to Canada or to the United States. If an increased volume of trade between the two countries is to run mainly in the parent-subsidiary channels, the outcome may be subject to the caprice of accounting and administrative decisions or to various political and protectionist pressures on the American economy.

It will be recalled that 48 per cent of Canadian manufacturing is foreign controlled, some 80 per cent of that sector being U.S. controlled. Many of these firms have been established in Canada to "leap over" the tariff wall and so to obtain access to the Canadian market. They have little interest in exporting abroad and would certainly find it peculiar to compete with their parent company in the U.S. market even if nominally allowed to do so. A recent statement by Austin Delaney, president of Bell and Howell (Canada), a manufacturer of photographic equipment, is typical of the position of many similar subsidiaries:

> Firstly, you have to understand our mandate here in Canada. Bell and Howell has been established here since 1954 with the prime objective of selling its products to the Canadian market and without intentions to export to other markets, as our parent company has other arrangements for export throughout Europe and the rest of the world.[3]

Aggregate data on this tendency to restrict exports are difficult to obtain, and experience of course varies among many firms. Yet the logic of the situation is clear for those firms expressly established to circumvent the tariff barriers in order to serve the Canadian market. It is, in our view, Alice-in-Wonderland economics to expect branch plants in Canada to compete with their parent companies on their home ground in the United States. Indeed, the reverse phenomenon is more likely: free trade will encourage the dismantling of Canadian branch plants and the Canadian market will be served either from the United States or from relocated offshore production in Southeast Asia.

The issue of the tariff, however, is itself of diminishing importance as the issue of nontariff barriers comes to the fore. A developed network of legal barriers, ostensibly for contingencies such as dumping, is now in place in the U.S. But as the recent Canadian government report notes: "The risks of our trading partners' systems of contingency import protection being misused for protectionist purposes are real."[4] (A fuller account of this legal network and "Buy-America" provisions is presented in Fred Lazar's study *The New Protectionism*).[5]

Americans have already had recourse to these nontariff barriers in order to restrict the imports of specialty steels, cement, defence equipment, and Canadian shipping services. Efforts to restrict lumber imports and trucking were very close to realization. Other legislation is pending. In the past year [1983], some sixty-three bills before Congress contained "reciprocity" clauses that could, if passed, restrict Canadian exports to the U.S. in many ways. Few of these bills will actually become law; yet they are indicative of a powerful protectionist mood in the American Congress.

Such political forces may wax and wane, depending on the economic climate. Yet they point up the continuing vulnerability of Canadian trade to these forces, particularly since 66 per cent of all Canadian exports are to the United States.

The more significant point, however, is whether it is realistic to expect that free trade agreements can be negotiated that are insulated from these pressures and the related network of nontariff barriers. Can American officials negotiate away their nontariff barriers, even if they are willing to do so, in the same way that they could negotiate tariff cuts? This is a moot point, and it is at least conceivable that American government officials may not be able to make good on such "free trade" agreements when a militant and protectionist Congress under heavy pressure from domestic unemployment holds sway.

The case against a bilateral free trade agreement with the United States thus rests on a recognition of novel institutional changes, changes which have called into question the benefits that are, on the basis of international trade theory, presumed to await us. An international economy replete with intracorporate activity, transfer prices, nontariff barriers, weak economies and high unemployment, and that is falling back on protectionist or defensive strategies, is a different world from that visualized by the nineteenth-century theorists of free trade. Free trade proposals thus rest on very shaky grounds.

Other substantive difficulties are summed up in the recent Canadian government document *A Review of Canadian Trade Policy for the 1980's* as follows:

- Canadian manufacturing industries enjoy few comparative advantages vis-à-vis the United States. Consequently, the removal of tariffs would simply lead to the replacement over time of Canadian manufacturing production by American. Canadian labour (and other factors) released from manufacturing would be drawn into the resources and services sectors, would seek to emigrate or, most probably, would swell the ranks of the unemployed.
- Heavy U.S. ownership in Canadian industry would, through the operation of "board room prejudices," tend to result in Canadian

production being relocated in the United States, even in those instances where Canadian production costs were lower.

- The exchange rate cannot be counted on as regulator of relative competitiveness and location advantages between Canada and the United States in the manufacturing sector. There are simply too many influences on the exchange rate.

- The structure of the Canadian economy following free trade would be less beneficial in terms of the future development of Canada. A strengthening of the resource sector at the expense of manufacturing might yield higher income but would nullify efforts to foster the indigenous technology and research and development (R&D) capability necessary for Canada's long-term success as an industrial society.[6]

After reviewing the arguments on both sides of this issue, the authors of the Canadian government report propose a compromise solution known as "sectoral tree trade." It involves a sector-by-sector negotiation of such possible items as urban mass transit equipment, textiles and petrochemicals. Not free trade but "the gradual movement by successive Canadian governments towards freer trade."[7] Shades of Mackenzie King!

There can be no objection in principle, of course, to simply opening up sectors of the American market where Canadians have or may acquire a comparative advantage. But what will be the quid pro quo? Would the Americans ask in return, say, for genuine free trade in automobiles, that is, the cancellation of the production guarantees of the Auto Pact and with it the erosion of our automobile industry? Are there likely to be any political concessions to the Americans as, so to speak, an "earnest of good faith"? This might become the occasion for the Americans to put their two "bêtes noires" on the negotiating table — the Foreign Investment Review Agency (FIRA) and/or the National Energy Program (NEP).[8]

How far are Canadians prepared to go to secure either "free trade" or "sectoral free trade"? The government's paper *Canadian Trade Policy for the 1980's* tilts in favour of a fine balancing act among all the recognized difficulties. But it reserves judgment on the crucial issues discussed here:

The task of managing the relationship smoothly is, of course, made more complex as the more aggressive pursuit by the United States of its interests clashes with the interests of its trading partners. Canada, for its part, has been and will continue to be preoccupied with regional and industrial development and with questions of investment/ownership. The effect will be that ownership policies, subsidies, regional development programs, investment incentives, duty remissions, offsets, export financing, and other trade-related measures will be factors in Canada-U.S. trade relations, as will similar programs and policies in the U.S. More than ever, in an interdependent world, *Canadian policies will need to be framed against the background of the likely foreign, particularly U.S., reaction* [emphasis added].[9]

On this latter point, the government report is entirely silent and leaves this issue in limbo. The net effect, as this particular document illustrates, is to postpone basic decisions to some indefinite future date, while hoping to wrest some "balanced" compromise out of an ongoing difficult situation. It is another way to manoeuvre at the margin within the status quo while hoping with wide-eyed innocence for the best.

For reasons that are set out in our full brief,[10] we feel that a full-scale industrial policy is our first priority in a rapidly deteriorating economic situation. If that is the case, then trade policy should cease to be our primary preoccupation and should instead be subordinated to industrial policy.

Trade will, of course, continue to be of vital importance to the Canadian economy, but it is doubtful that we can aspire to more than the retention of our existing market share in the United States. That in itself will require close to heroic efforts by our representatives in Washington, a major effort in Public Diplomacy.

Should Canada embark on a full-scale industrial policy, more onerous challenges will arise. We will have to counter and to deflect the negative impact of an industrial policy in the United States and the numerous pretexts which will present themselves for invoking countervailing legislation against Canadian imports. But we will not be without some allies: on the other side of this question are the trading partners and consumer groups in the United States whose interests would run parallel to our own in preserving access to cheaper Canadian products.

The basic issue is clear-cut. Should we try to shore up the status quo, as the government proposes to do, by a series of patchwork adjustments such as sectoral free trade, while edging the Canadian and American economies into a closer pattern of integration? Or has the time come when the question of an industrial policy must be given first priority and trade policy made to accommodate rather than to direct our industrial policy?

13 | Jobs and the New Technology

ONTARIO PUBLIC SERVICE EMPLOYEES UNION

*The Ontario Public Service Employees Union (OPSEU) repre-
sents over 75,000 employees in the public sector throughout Ontario.
Its members are employed by hospitals, community colleges, children's aid societies, municipalities, and by the government of
Ontario itself in some twenty-odd ministries.*

*OPSEU holds to the conviction that workers in a democratic
society have the fundamental right to organize and bargain collectively. This right was not handed to working people on a silver
platter, by the mere passing of laws. It was won in long and bitter
struggles. It is correspondingly prized, and defended when under
attack. However, the right to organize and bargain collectively in
the public sector has lately been under attack. In its seventy-two-
page brief to the Macdonald Commission, the union presents some
of the human consequences of Ontario's cutbacks and restraint
programs and suggests that Canada is in danger of failing the
tests of a civilized society. The following excerpt deals with the
all-important question of high-tech in the workplace and its consequences for future employment prospects for Canadians. The
introduction of new technology may well be the most important
issue facing the Canadian trade union movement.*

A new technological revolution is under way. Although its lynchpin is
the microchip, it includes robotics, fibre optics, laser technology, satel-
lites and so on. The new technological revolution will have widespread
economic and social consequences. But its pre-eminent impact will be
on work — on jobs and job content.

The new technological revolution has given rise to, among other
things, two groups of forecasters: the optimists and the pessimists.
The optimists admit that labour-saving technology is nothing new and
that it normally results in some job displacement. But in the long run,
they claim, many more new jobs have always been created than old
jobs lost. The pessimists disagree. They say the microchip revolution
will be deeply disruptive.

Except perhaps for the first Industrial Revolution, what has been common to earlier technological breakthroughs is their application to the demand side of the economy even more than to the supply side. Along with new methods of production and increased demand for capital goods came increased markets for new goods which consumers found useful and/or desirable. Increased output accordingly matched increased productivity.

By contrast, the microchip revolution is for the most part oriented to the supply side of the economy. Certainly, there will be household and consumer applications, such as computer games. But its applications to new methods of production, distribution, transportation and communication are its outstanding aspect.

In *The Collapse of Work*, Clive Jenkins and Berry Sherman have written:

> Most technological changes have been applied directly to the goods or services, and have directly stimulated the availability and production of new ones. This has enabled economies to expand and provide employment at one and the same time. However, we are not standing on the threshold of a new breakthrough which, at present, acts primarily on the process side alone.

Jenkins and Sherman further noted that:

> Unemployment, which has been synonymous with slumps and low investment, will, for the next few decades, be equally the product of high investment and booms. This quantum leap in technology will accelerate the structural changes in the pattern of employment which have been steadily advancing over the past decade and will exert an immensely destructive impact on both existing jobs and the future supply of work.

The characteristics of the microchip revolution which make it the most significant revolution of the twentieth century, and perhaps even more important than the first Industrial Revolution, are:

- it both extends and displaces a wide range of intellectual, intuitive and manual skills;
- it is all pervasive;
- it is still advancing rapidly;
- it is very cheap and getting cheaper;
- it will become abundantly available from international sources;
- it can both centralize and decentralize work processes at the same time; and
- it can vastly increase productivity.

The microchip revolution will affect jobs in three ways. It will create some jobs; it will destroy many jobs; and it will change almost all jobs. We share the view of those experts who say that more jobs will be lost than will be gained. Some believe that the job losses will fall mainly on the service industries and on women; others that the job losses have already fallen on the goods-producing industries and on men. Both may be right. Unemployment is thus the main threat. And this poses for Canada a cruel dilemma: jobs will disappear if we do not embrace the new technology because markets would be lost; Canada would not remain competitive, either at home or abroad. But jobs will also be lost if we do embrace the new technology. In other words, we may drown if we do swim with the tide; we will certainly drown if we don't.

In 1981, 9.9 million Canadians were employed for wages and salaries, 3.1 million in goods-producing industries, and 6.8 million in services. Of the former, 77 per cent were men; and of the latter, 49 per cent were women. It is generally acknowledged that women doing office work, including the office and clerical employees of the Ontario government who are members of our union, will be among those whom the microchip revolution will affect adversely. Some idea of the numbers at risk may be gained from the following:

- In the twenty years from 1961 to 1981, Canada's labour force increased by 5,358,000. Of this number, 3,450,000 were women. Women now make up 41 per cent of Canada's labour force, and they have accounted for 57 per cent of the increase since 1961. Women work mainly in service industries — trade, finance, community, business and personal services, and government — and in a much narrower range of low-paid, low-status occupations than men. The microchip revolution will increase this concentration.

- In the twenty years from 1961 to 1981, the number of service workers in Canada, including government workers, increased by 3,911,000. Of this number, 2,430,000 were women. Four out of five of the women who have entered the labour force since 1961 have been service workers. If service employment were to shrink back to its relative size of twenty years ago, 2,500,000 Canadians would be out of work — 970,000 men and 1,530,000 women. This would include 275,000 government employees, of whom as many as 35,000 would be employees of the Ontario government. Meanwhile, the number of production workers in relation to whom these figures are calculated will also shrink.

- In the twenty years from 1961 to 1981, the number of office and clerical workers in Canada increased by 1,227,000. Of this number, 1,110,000 were women. Not all office and clerical workers are employed in service industries, but the majority of them are. This includes in particular the many hundreds of thousands employed by the federal, provincial and municipal governments across the country. One out of four of the women who have entered the labour force since 1961 have been office and clerical workers. If office and clerical employment were to shrink back to its relative size of twenty years ago, 560,000 Canadians would be out of work — 55,000 men and 505,000 women. This would include 160,000 office and clerical workers employed by government, of whom as many as 15,000 would be employees of the Ontario government.

Consequences for Remaining Jobs

Besides increased productivity and the spectre of unemployment, the microchip revolution will have other consequences for employees. In changing the content of many jobs, it will change the required skills and qualifications. The brain work of the few who plan the installation of the new computer systems and who write the programs to make them work will become more demanding, and perhaps more interesting. The work of those who use the systems will become more routine, repetitive and dull. For example, the decisions and judgments which typists now make — and typing can be pretty dull at the best of times — will in future be made by word processors. The typists will simply type, press the right button, and the machine will do the rest. "Deskilling" of jobs, from which lower classifications and lower pay would follow, is a widely foreseen consequence.

Secondly, the microchip revolution will raise new problems of workers' health and job stress. Everyone knows of the health hazards of video display terminals (VDTs). Stress, fatigue, headache, impairment of eyesight, and the danger to pregnant women are well known and are being increasingly documented. We are not reassured by inadequate research, half-truths and soothing syrup. The trade union movement learned long ago that dealing with problems such as these, and ensuring that the safety and health of workers are effectively protected, cannot be left to those who stand to gain from the dangers to which others, but not they, are exposed. Current experience confirms this lesson.

Thirdly, the microchip revolution will give management new means of detailed, minute-by-minute, ever stricter and more inquisitorial supervision of employees. Management will gain a command over the labour process more pervasive and oppressive than ever before. For example, control mechanisms will record the rate at which text is typed into word processors and the speed at which figures are entered into accounting machines. They will also record the number of mistakes and the time taken to make corrections. They will record the time spent by employees at their work stations, and how much time they spend on the phone, how much time talking to other employees, how often they sneeze or blow their nose, and just about every other conscious or unconscious human action throughout the working day. All this information will be transmitted to management for scrutiny and corrective or disciplinary action. Thus, if the microchip revolution will not eliminate completely the requirement for human labour, it will on the other hand give management the means of making sure that every minute of working time is accounted for and devoted to 100 per cent efficiency and concentration in the service of the employer. It will create a working atmosphere of tension, insecurity and speedup which will aggravate the problems of workers' health referred to above.

Fourthly, the microchip revolution will present management with new opportunities and temptations to split up staffs and contract work out to non-union firms. It may in fact bring about a radical change in the organization of work. Computer terminals for word processing and a wide range of other functions are now available for use at home. The result is that just as computers link the head office of multinational corporations with their subsidiaries in other countries, so home computers can link individuals working at home with their superiors elsewhere. By sitting down at their home computers, people will be able to "go to work" in the same way as they now go the movies by watching TV and attend concerts by playing records or listening to the radio. People working at home can be instructed via their terminals about the work to be done as easily as when they are "at work," and the home terminals can be equipped with the same means of detailed supervision as "at the office." An apparent advantage of this arrangement is the time it would save in travelling to and from work. But it would also give management a big advantage in arranging part-time work and, as noted, would as well be a powerful incentive to the contracting out of work to replace the hiring and classification of permanent staff. The effects on people's health and morale of working in isolation from each other could be serious — no research has been done on this aspect. And one need only ask the simple question — How do you call a union meeting of workers who never meet and have no opportunity of seeing or talking to each other? — to see the potential impact on unions. Individual and social life will certainly be impoverished to the extent that it is reduced to sitting in front of and "interfacing" through the medium of video display terminals connected by fibre optics that make it possible to keep people physically apart. There could be no better way for management to divide and conquer.

Therefore, fifthly, the microchip revolution will, unless countervailing action is taken, tend to weaken the unions and lessen the sense employees have of their union's role in the collective defence of their rights and interests. Mass unemployment diminishes labour's strength. Job insecurity, staff dispersal, contracting out, together with speedup and relentless supervision — all these inhibit union activity and the discussion of union affairs, prevent the day-to-day contacts and diminish the energy normally devoted to union business.

An entirely new set of labour relations is necessary if these adverse consequences are to be avoided. These new relations require first of all that the right of unions to bargain with respect to technological change be recognized and fully implemented in the public as well as in the private sector. The laws governing crown employees' collective bargaining, which now exclude technological change, must be amended accordingly. The law cannot stand still while technology races ahead.

But more than this is needed…. Employees must be involved in the planning of production processes and in everything affecting the content and rhythm of their jobs. They must know and agree to the speed at which they will be expected to work and the degree of supervision under which they will be placed. They must be completely and honestly informed as to the toll in physical and nervous strain which their jobs exact, and the effects this has on their health. In all these matters, the role of unions is vital and must not be gainsaid. But governments must also be involved, not as disinterested referees, but as active participants in researching, defining, improving and enforcing standards.

Appropriately, these expanded functions will require staffing. The new jobs will be welcome. Some service industries will remain labour intensive, and as employment in other industries shrinks, in these it can expand. As Jenkins and Sherman point out, "It is in the labour-intensive industries that jobs can be created, and, typically, these are in the public sector areas — health, education and social services."

The Consequences of Technological Change

The wages of labour are the encouragement of industry, which, like every other human quality, improves in proportion to the encouragement it receives. A plentiful subsistence increases the bodily strength of the labourer, and the comfortable hope of bettering his condition animates him to exert that strength to the utmost. Where wages are high, accordingly, we shall always find the workmen more active, diligent, and expeditious than where they are low….

Our merchants and master-manufacturers complain much of the bad effects of high wages in raising the price, and thereby lessening the sale of their goods both at home and abroad. They say nothing concerning the bad effects of high profits. They are silent with regard to the pernicious effects of their own gains. They complain only of those of other people.

— Adam Smith, *The Wealth of Nations*

The outstanding characteristic of the Canadian economy in the medium and long term is technological change. As noted, microchips and fibre optics are combining in unprecedented methods of production, distribution, transportation and communication; they are creating an extraordinary rise in productivity and promise (or threaten) to continue this rise at an accelerated rate.

Much has been written about the slowdown in productivity since the mid-1970s, a slowdown which has affected most industrial countries as well as Canada. The causes of this slowdown are imperfectly understood and remain to be clarified. But whatever the causes may be, or rather may have been, we believe the slowdown is essentially a thing of the past. The productive potential of microchips and fibre optics is irresistible and compelling. Applications of the new technology are rapidly spreading throughout the economy, and their effect must accordingly be regarded as the dominating concern of economic and social policies.

What does this extraordinary rise in productivity mean? What are its likely consequences? In our view, they are the following:

- A rapid expansion in the economy's *potential* output. But expanding productive capacity will run into constraints because, on the one hand, the supply of raw materials and energy is not inexhaustible and, on the other hand, markets for new goods and services are limited by our present social arrangements for the distribution of income. At the lower end of the income scale, which for the world economy as a whole means the vast majority of the population, people cannot afford to buy what they need. For Canada and other industrially developed countries, at the middle and upper reaches of the scale, there is a limit beyond which people cannot be persuaded, in spite of all advertising efforts, to buy things they do not need, do not really want, and would probably be just as well off without. There are only twenty-four hours to the day, and few of us can or wish to spend all of them consuming and being entertained.
- There will therefore be a growing gap between potential output, assuming reasonably full employment of the labour force and the utilization of productive capacity, and actual output. The production both of capital and consumer goods and services is governed by the prospects of profitable sales. But since production will require fewer workers and will thereby generate less income to those who normally spend rather than save, actual as well as prospective sales will fail to grow at the required rate.
- For Canada and other industrial countries, the widening gap between potential and actual output will hit especially hard owing to the increasing export of capital investment and production by multinational corporations to the so-called newly industrializing countries. The output from the industrial enclaves in these countries, equipped with the latest industrial technology and employing labour at a fraction of the cost of here at home, is obviously not meant for sale in the newly industrializing countries themselves. The process of

production creates no market in them; in fact, every effort is made to prevent the creation of a market by the ruthless exploitation of an overflowing labour market, by the denial of health and safety measures both on and off the job, by support of repressive governments for these purposes. It follows that while markets there are deliberately neglected, the export of capital and the reverse flow of cheaply produced imports increasingly undermine and limit markets here.

- All of this means that the distribution of income in each country taken separately as well as internationally is becoming more and more unequal — a small number of multinational corporations and wealthy individuals at the top, larger and larger numbers at the bottom, and a diminishing number in the middle. The majority under the broad centre of the distributional bell are being squeezed out of their traditional position. The economic and social consequences of this are grave. But the overriding result is that the gap between actual and potential output, and thereby between actual and what might even approach full employment, is widened even more.

- There will therefore be a massive displacement of workers, many of whom will never find another job. This means massive and perhaps permanent unemployment of people who are now working or have worked. There will also be a large reduction in the requirement for new workers, and consequently in new job opportunities. This means massive and much longer, if not permanent, unemployment among young people who have never worked and whose prospects of ever working will be worse than they already are.

- Within a drastically reduced employed labour force, there will be a growing need for highly trained professional and technical people, balanced by a growing proportion of unskilled workers doing routine work, planned and programmed for them by others. Every moment and every breath, almost every thought, will be recorded and analyzed by computers in order to ensure maximum output. This means the wholesale de-skilling of jobs. Workers will be divided into a top and bottom; owing to what has been called the "disappearing middle," fewer and fewer will be in between.

- Finally, it must be emphasized that the microchip revolution affects not only the production of goods, where more or less objective measures of productivity can be applied with reasonable confidence. It also affects the provision of services of all kinds, where measures of productivity are fraught with difficulties and loaded with uncertainty. This is above all true of the new means of recording, compiling, transmitting and "producing" information, and it applies no less to the public sector, in which our members and those of other important unions are employed, than it does to the private sector.

We have two comments to make in this regard. The first is that since employment and gross national product increasingly consist of services rather than goods, the overall measurement of productivity in the economy as a whole becomes more and more liable to error, that is, to a systematic downward bias. It is for this reason that we are sceptical of recent figures indicating Canada's allegedly poor productivity performance. Here is a field where better questions might usefully be asked and better answers given than hitherto.

Our second comment is that, whatever the truth about productivity may be, there is no question as to the effect of the microchip revolution on jobs in the public sector across Canada and on our members in particular. Jobs in the public sector have been eliminated or de-skilled as they have been in the private sector, and thousands of workers have likewise been laid off or downgraded. These developments are combined with cutbacks in government services, with the result that job security for public sector employees is a thing of the past.

In short, far from being immune to and protected by some beneficent dispensation from the consequences of the microchip revolution which we have outlined, public sector employees in general and members of our union in particular are caught up in their throes along with the population whom it is our function and wish to serve.

Conclusion

There is a complacent view, which we have briefly referred to earlier and which historical experience is said to support, that as productivity improves, output will rise by roughly the amount needed to avoid the loss of jobs. We reject this view as unrealistic and in conflict with current facts. Although this view may have been true in periods of rapid growth, Canada and the world economy have for ten years been in a period of slow growth, marked by deep recession and feeble recovery. The complacent view may apply to the lucky few for whom the new technology provides good jobs, requiring unusual ability and thorough training. But it is a false hope for the many for whom no openings are available or whose abilities will be wasted in such de-skilled jobs as they may find — jobs which pay less, which are often non-union and where seniority and grievance protection against arbitrary layoffs are absent. This complacent view may be relevant for some favoured countries which can send their "guest workers" and "wetbacks" back home when they become redundant, but it is obviously not relevant for the countries to which these workers return, nor for Canada.

And the complacent view ignores the fact that never before have hundreds of thousands of workers been permanently *eliminated* from production. In basic industry, work itself is disappearing. By contrast, in some service industries, where the new technology can do many things which human beings could never do, or can do them at a speed which human beings can never equal, there has so far been an intangible but unmistakable increase in output. An overall reduction in the number of employees in the service sector has thereby so far been avoided. Thus, in communication, finance and branches of the public service, the elimination of workers may be delayed for a time. But after growth has ceased, reduction in the number of employees will soon follow. Cutbacks may not yet be widespread, but they will sooner or later, and probably sooner than later, become the general rule.

14 The Perpetuation of Regional Disparities

CONFEDERATION OF NATIONAL TRADE UNIONS

Known in Quebec as the CSN (Confédération des syndicats nationaux), this independent trade union central represents 210,084 members through its 1,624 union affiliates. Founded in 1921, it was at one time headed by Jean Marchand, later a Liberal cabinet minister under both Pearson and Trudeau. In recent years the CSN has been in the forefront of political struggle in modern Quebec. Its stands on social and economic issues and its strong commitment to workers' rights have led it to join with other trade union centrals in Quebec, most notably the Quebec Teachers Federation (CEQ) and the Quebec Federation of Labour (FTQ), in a common front to oppose restrictive government policies.

The CSN appeared before the Macdonald Commission on four occasions, in Quebec, Chicoutimi, Saint George de Beauce and Montreal. This excerpt is from the brief presented in Montreal. The presentation included a strong defence of labour rights, not reprinted here.

In our opinion, a careful analysis of Canada's economic problems must go beyond the specific conditions and policies which led to the 1981-83 recession. The first point to note is that although during the postwar years Canada experienced a relatively sustained rate of growth which compared favourably to the average for the industrialized countries, our unemployment rate performance was not as good. In 1960-81, it was the same as Italy's and was exceeded by only two of the twenty-four member countries of the Organization for Economic Cooperation and Development (OECD) — Ireland and Turkey. Canada's higher average unemployment is better understood when the great differences in the regional employment rates within the country are considered. During the period 1970-82, unemployment was, on the average, 45 per cent higher in Quebec than in Ontario and 63 per cent higher in the Atlantic provinces. So, although Canada could pride itself on having kept unemployment at a level which compared favourably with other industrialized countries in regions such as Ontario and the Prairies, the same could not be said of Quebec and the Atlantic provinces. Under both good and bad economic conditions, these regions have experienced unemployment rates among the highest in the industrialized world.

A History of Underdevelopment

The existence and persistence of such regional disparities are not, in our opinion, fortuitous. They are ingrained in the history of Canada, a country whose economy has been built on mining, forestry and farming, with the industrial manufacturing infrastructure (especially heavy and high-technology industry) concentrated in southern Ontario. Indeed, almost all manufacturing industry is located in Ontario, with the exception of a few industries which are concentrated in Quebec, such as the textile industry (requiring abundant cheap labour) and the shipbuilding industry (for geographic reasons). Even these industries have suffered a significant decline recently in Quebec, while gaining strength in other provinces.

Geographical factors have no doubt favoured southern Ontario as the industrial centre of Canada, in particular its proximity to the industrial heartland of the United States. But numerous interventions by the federal government have also encouraged the concentration of industrial activity in Ontario. By means of huge federal subsidies, all Canadian taxpayers financed railways to the Pacific which made possible the establishment of the iron and steel industries in Ontario. Only 12 per cent of Canada's track is located in Quebec, which has 26 per cent of the population. At the Canadian taxpayers' expense once again, the construction of the St. Lawrence Seaway in the 1950s saw Montreal lose its status of transshipper for all eastern Canada and caused its port activities to fall dramatically as ports further inland gained ground.

Also during the 1950s, the government devised the "Borden line," ordering that only Canadian oil could be used west of the Ottawa Valley. This prompted the development of petrochemical complexes in Sarnia and other Ontario cities. Montreal, which had until then been the petrochemical capital of Canada, saw its growth in this area halted abruptly by the federal decision. Ultimately, this has led to the closing down of 40 per cent of Quebec's oil-refining capacity in the early 1980s, jeopardizing Quebec's petrochemical factories, which are located primarily in the eastern metropolitan area and the St. Maurice Valley.

In the early 1960s, while the Canadian government was negotiating the Auto Pact with the United States, which involved some restructuring of the industry, the government had an excellent opportunity to force the automotive industry to decentralize. But instead, it was allowed to remain concentrated in southern Ontario, with only one factory in Quebec. Even in a sector as essential as housing, federal aid to Ontario has been double the aid to Quebec. At present, only 16 per cent of Canada's low-rental housing is in Quebec, despite long waiting lists for these units.

Federal crown corporations follow the same trends we have just outlined. The Canada Development Corporation was established in 1971 by the Canadian government in order to ensure a Canadian presence in certain dynamic industries in the private sector of the economy. It is evident that this corporation is similar to its partners in the private sector in practically excluding Quebec from its investment portfolio; only a tiny portion of its assets are located in Quebec (primarily in the pharmaceutical product and office automation sectors). Most of the corporation's investments are concentrated in Ontario and western Canada (if not in foreign countries) in the mining, oil and gas, and petrochemical sectors. Head office personnel are divided between Toronto and Vancouver. A similar pattern is followed by Petro-Canada, a crown corporation which made itself known in Quebec mainly by purchasing two oil refineries and the affiliated service station chains and then proceeding immediately to close one of the two refineries (the BP plant). The corporation is now in the process of cutting off supplies to several stations of the former BP chain.

Failure of Development Policies

Some viewed the establishment of the Department of Regional Economic Expansion in 1969 as proof that the federal government had established a means to decentralize the manufacturing sector in favour of disadvantaged regions. Several reasons can account for the failure of this program, which did not significantly reduce regional disparities. How many times has the federal government, by a simple order-in-council, intervened to grant a huge subsidy to a company to set up in Ontario, offsetting the hundreds of subsidies granted to small Quebec companies? Several years ago, the Pépin-Robarts federal task force tried to sort out the "numbers war" over Quebec's economic accounts which was waged before the referendum. It concluded: "Statistical evidence from recently developed provincial accounts fail to establish that Quebec has been a major net recipient of federal funds."[1] It is not surprising, in view of this rather dismal record, that the politicians who urged Quebecers to vote "No" during the 1980 referendum debate preferred to speak of the future rather than the past in promising, for example, an oil price which would remain lower than the American price, the Carmont heavy oil-processing project worth a billion dollars, and concentration of the results of the F-18 (fighter plane) project in Quebec. All these promises were quickly forgotten once the referendum was over, needless to say. It is therefore not surprising that many Quebecers remain sceptical about the economic benefits of Canadian federalism. For our part, we believe that the social and political instabilities which, in the past, have resulted from the economic disparities which persist in Canada will remain until the economic injustices are set right....

The decrease in world oil prices and in energy consumption over the past two years has destroyed the promising outlook presented in *Canada's Economic Development in the 1980's*, published by the government in November 1981. Since then, the only economic policy offered by the government has been "6 and 5," which means limiting the salary increases of Canadian working men and women even though salary increases in Canada during the past ten years have ranked among the lowest in the industrialized countries. In short, this policy, by restricting the purchasing power of Canadian workers, only contributes to slowing down the recovery and to increasing income disparities in Canada.

By searching for ways to link Canada's economic development to the traditional exploitation of resources and a few fashionable high-technology sectors, the leading federal government planners seem to have completely excluded any possibility for economic growth designed to better meet people's basic needs for improved clothing, housing, food and transportation. Yet many of the goods meeting these needs constitute growth sectors in which imports play a large part; Canadian products could attempt to replace these imports. In this connection, there have been many successes: by diversifying production and stepping up processing, Quebec has become more self-sufficient in food production; in public transport vehicle production, thousands of jobs have been created in Quebec in recent years to meet the new demand; and new types of housing have been developed which use energy and urban land more efficiently.

We would also like to discuss development prospects that exist in sectors which were simply left to deteriorate without the type of government assistance and protection which exists in other countries: sectors such as shipbuilding, textiles/clothing/shoes and fishing. In our opinion, the government would be making a mistake by cutting back these industries even further because few other employment possibilities exist in regions where these industries are located. In other sectors such as furniture and automotive parts, where at present Canada shows a very poor balance of trade, we also see development opportunities because of our access to raw materials and the size of the Canadian market.

Decentralized Development

The CSN believes that the mainstay of a development policy aimed at full employment for Canada must be support for the manufacturing industries that create the most employment. The energy/resources sector has, up to now, benefitted from far more tax breaks and financial support than the manufacturing sector. This is hard to justify, since manufacturing generates far more jobs. As for the types of personal services (such as entertainment, videos and fast foods) which the government considers as growth sectors, we believe that their development will take place without special government aid. However, the CSN supports maintaining the universality of public health and education services. It seems to us that the trend toward privatization in some provinces only reduces access to such services and contributes to the erosion of the principle of equal treatment for all.

A policy supporting the manufacturing sector should be accompanied by a policy aiming at the constant growth of overall demand. A policy of relatively stable interest rates obviously goes with a full-employment program, and we can only hope that the government will permanently renounce the disastrous monetary policies it followed from 1980 to 1983. Steady growth in overall demand also means allowing Canadians' income to increase regularly — that is, to increase security benefits, pension incomes, etc., on a regular basis and also to abandon unwarranted programs such as 6 and 5, while consumption is decreasing.

If Canada's economic union still means anything, the manufacturing sector has to grow in a more decentralized manner than hitherto — more decentralized than was suggested by the federal government economic development document mentioned above.

We have shown how the federal government's interventions are largely responsible for the concentration of the manufacturing industry in southern Ontario. It would seem to us that the government would even be justified in taking major compensatory action in order, for example, to restore Quebec's shipbuilding industry to the same position it once held in Canada, ensure the establishment of new automobile factories in Quebec and see to it that Quebec's petrochemical industry benefits from subsidized prices for raw materials which must be imported from Ontario. As well, in order to favour decentralized development, we suggest that the federal government cease to oppose the self-sufficiency efforts embarked upon by the Quebec government in the food and agriculture sector. Instead, the government should support such efforts as well as others of the same sort undertaken in sectors where economies of scale are not a major consideration.

15 Can Capital and Labour Cooperate?

UNITED AUTO WORKERS

In this second excerpt from the UAW brief (see also chapter 2), the issue of relations between employers and employees — capital and labour — is addressed from the perspective of individual workers. It is pointed out that all too often the goal of management is to get workers to cooperate on management's terms. Little consideration is given to society's objective of improved production, let alone workers rights. The UAW make the point that workers are not investors and argue that consultation is often seen by management as a substitute for improving working conditions. To some readers this defence of trade unionism may seem limited, but it reflects a reality of trade union existence. In good times few employers worry about consulting labour. In bad times management wants concessions and the benefits of cooperation.

The emphasis on becoming cost-competitive includes more than just costs. Increasingly, labour relations "experts" have emphasized the poor quality of labour-management relations in this country and the need for substantial reform in attitudes, if not in legislation. To reinforce their arguments, international models are repeatedly used.

We do not oppose examining what is happening elsewhere to find relevant examples for Canada. We do oppose selective and superficial comparisons that are taken out of context. And we're very sceptical of commentators who identify a particular model but, as the situation develops, silently discard it and find another. In the early Fifties, Sweden was the model; in the Sixties, problems arose in Sweden, and then West Germany became the new model; by the Seventies, West German workers were being asked — in words very familiar to us — why they couldn't be more like the Japanese workers.

The most frustrating thing about the discussion of "labour-management relations" is the way the issue is defined. Given the framework of international competition, and the inherent biases of most experts, "improving labour-management relations" is taken to mean how to decrease worker resistance and how to strengthen corporate performance.

In other words, the problem is posed as a competitive problem — improving efficiency and cost — rather than as a problem of *balancing* legitimate worker concerns with society's objective of improved production.

Interest in workers is, therefore, secondary. Labour's concerns must be addressed only because otherwise workers have the potential to frustrate corporate priorities: by our wage demands, by our resistance to sacrificing plant and office rights in the name of increasing management "flexibility," by our political demands for more equality, security and restrictions of corporate power.

It is in this context that our attitudes and responses to management "innovations" such as participation on boards of directors, quality-of-work-life (QWL) experiments, profit-sharing schemes and employee buyouts should be understood.

No one has convinced us that participation on corporate boards, as a token representative of workers, will do anything for working people. It may provide some information, but collective bargaining and ongoing union-company contact already exist as vehicles through which we can request information. A corporation that has made up its mind to keep information secret will also keep it from us if it allows us a seat on the board; a corporation that has agreed to share information needs no new mechanism for doing so.

We do not oppose QWL experiments. Contrary to popular conceptions, unions don't spend most of their daily lives dealing with monetary problems; dealing with the "quality of work life" of our members is already a dominant union concern.

When management raises this issue and introduces new programs to deal with it (Quality Circles, Employee Involvement, Worker Participation, etc.), no one should be surprised at our scepticism. After all, while talking QWL, management is often resisting our concrete demands to improve the quality of work life: demands related to health and safety, noise, cafeteria facilities, arbitrary discipline, speed of production, etc.

In other cases, management wants a new relationship with the union, but sees no connection with the fact that it is fighting the union's attempt to organize its office workers. And it should be noted that an environment in which concessions are demanded is hardly an atmosphere conducive to new forms of cooperation and QWL.

We do have QWL experiments currently taking place. Our position is that we will endorse them if two conditions are met. First, that their main goal is, in fact, to do what they claim: improve the quality of work life of working people. If they also improve productivity, that's fine and good — but it must be seen as a positive side-effect and *not* as the prime goal. Second, the program should not be a sophisticated mechanism for eventually weakening the union, and thereby leaving workers very much more vulnerable in the future.

As with QWL issues, we're obviously interested in "profit sharing." But the vehicle we've chosen to achieve this is collective bargaining. We reject rigid formulas to determine our wages and therefore reject any scheme in which profit sharing is seen as a substitute for our collective-bargaining program. (We do not oppose corporations giving us a profit-related bonus over and above our basic demands, but corporations haven't responded to this with any enthusiasm.)

The basis for our rejection of a formula which leaves our wages dependent to any significant degree on profits, is both a matter of principle and of practical considerations.

Workers are not investors. Workers are not trying to make money but to satisfy needs. Unlike investors, workers cannot gamble on upturns and downturns; workers have daily needs to meet and therefore look for a stable income. Workers can't wait for a potential investment return; they must be paid directly for their labour.

Futhermore, linking wages to the profits of the company means that workers with similar skills doing similar work would get very different rates of pay. A major UAW policy over the years has been "pattern bargaining." This means that workers at the four auto majors get essentially the same wages and benefits even though corporate circumstances differ. And it means that we attempt to apply this pattern to smaller companies, thereby achieving an important union objective — the reduction of inequalities which the market would otherwise impose within the work force.

At the practical level, there are all kinds of questions to be asked about linking wages to profits when we don't control the factors which determine and define profits (for example, how much is reinvested and where, how much goes to stockholders). These kinds of problems are accentuated when, as in Canada, we are very often dealing with subsidiaries of larger global entities, and so the data on local profits can easily be manipulated.

The issue of employee buyouts (workers buying facilities about to close) has received a great deal of publicity. Again, we are less than enthusiastic. In exceptional circumstances, workers with no other choices may decide to risk this direction, but these remain exceptions. They are certainly not a panacea in any broader way. It simply does not make sense for workers with limited savings to risk an investment in operations which business finds too risky and which the market has already rejected.

"Strike Happy" Unions

No matter how legitimate our demands are, it is the *unions* who have to initiate strike action. This reinforces the public bias of blaming workers for management-labour conflicts. And, sharing the basic assumptions of many labour-relations experts, unions are attacked as being too powerful.

It is rather incredible to see people arguing that unions are too powerful; the reality is that, whatever our potential, we remain relatively weak. In spite of our policies and demonstrations, our priorities remain unresponded to, while government budgets continue to cater to the corporations. We do not control investment or modernization; we cannot gain job security or adequate protection when bankruptcies occur; we have the most limited kind of control over technology and management rights; and, looking at a simple indicator, our real wages are actually *lower* today than they were in 1976.

Our union has had its share of strikes and a few comments on these strikes should provide some insight into the factors underlying worker militancy and the notion of being "strike happy."

- Some of our most bitter strikes, the ones that had a lot of media attention and therefore influenced public perceptions of union militancy, were strikes over the most basic of union issues: the recognition of the union as the elected representative of workers. Two such strikes were the eighteen-month strike at United Aircraft (now Pratt and Whitney) and the five-month strike at Fleck Manufacturing.
- Other high-profile strikes involved the issue of concessions, in which workers were not trying to make any breakthroughs but basically trying to hang on to what they had, or regain what they had recently lost (Chrysler is the most well-known example).
- A third example of industrial action by workers involved sit-ins as a response to plant closures and very inadequate pension and severance protection. One worker involved at Houdaille summarized the frustrations and the positions workers were forced into by asking, "Why do we have to do something illegal to get some justice?"

Workers *do* understand economic reality. They understand the threatening reality of economic competition and the consequent limits on the demands they can make of their employers. But they also understand that, whatever they have in common with their employer, there is also a conflict over priorities. And so tensions between management and labour will, under our economic system, inevitably remain.

Management is fond of telling us there's no free lunch. If management wants to reduce the tensions with labour, it must recall this "no free lunch" principle. There is no point in inventing new schemes, or new names for old schemes, if they are just gimmicks to increase productivity or lower costs. Creating a more satisfied worker requires management expanding how it traditionally views "investment": management must be prepared to invest in its workers by devoting resources to decent pay, better working conditions and greater work rights.

It is also essential to note that any attempt to sincerely improve labour-management relations requires going *beyond* what happens directly between the two parties; the external environment is critical. Our earlier discussion ["Can Canada Compete?" — Ed.] on international competition leads to the conclusion that an emphasis on the priority of an export-orientation strategy — and therefore on a policy that aims to further strengthen the corporations at the expense of workers — will intensify labour-management tensions.

This point should also be made at a more general level. Governments, in the name of a "more favourable investment climate" and "becoming internationally competitive," may try to get labour's cooperation in programs of restraint. But an immediate dilemma emerges.

If workers are being asked to make personal sacrifices, we will obviously ask what guarantees there are that we will eventually benefit. Furthermore, since collective bargaining is the primary function of unions, limits on collective bargaining affect our *organizational* strength. Unions which surrender their main function will wither into "... nothing more than one institution among many in the service of capitalism: a convenient organization for disciplining the workers, occupying their leisure time, and ensuring their profitability for business."[1]

Because of this permanent risk to the workers' primary institution for self-defence, their unions, labour will obviously demand very stringent changes in the economy to guarantee workers' well-being before we would seriously consider any cooperation in these government programs.

When these guarantees are spelled out in more detail, it becomes clear that "free enterprise," by definition, cannot make such guarantees. As the president of the Canadian Chamber of Commerce, Sam Hughes, stated: "It is almost impossible for a corporation to pursue the private enterprise objective of profit and, at the same time, to observe the government's social objectives."[2] And, as we've argued, within the anarchy of international competition and free trade, even well-meaning governments face severe restrictions on what they can, in fact, guarantee.

In short, as we spell out our needs, and the restrictions on corporations and the market necessary to provide guarantees to workers, the corporations will quickly identify such a program as "damaging the investment climate." Under our economic system, and particularly in these economic times, the government cannot simultaneously improve the investment climate by attacking the living standards of working people *and* guarantee working people that they will eventually come out ahead.

And so, as in British Columbia, business leaders continue to support restraint: "Bennett has said front and center he is going ahead with restraint and that is what *industry* needs."[3] And, as in British Columbia, labour has no choice but to lead the resistance to this rolling back of the clock.

Those who believe that the recession frightened workers into accepting a new, ongoing and more cooperative position vis-à-vis management are misreading history. Fear and force are not solid nor permanent foundations on which to build cooperative relationships.

16 Going Broke on the Farm

NATIONAL FARMERS UNION

The National Farmers Union (NFU) was founded in July 1969. It brought together into a common organization the membership of four autonomous provincial farm unions and opened the door for direct membership involvement of farmers across Canada in the formulation of farm policy.

Though major contributors to the economic well-being of Canada through the production of food, farmers' concerns are poorly understood. As the major farm policy issues can only be resolved at the national level of government, it follows that farmers need comprehensive policy approaches that eliminate conflicts among producers and then seek implementation of these policies at the various levels of government. The following excerpt from the NFU thirty-page brief outlines the dismal outlook for Canada's farm population and warns against a future where Canada is more and more dependent on foreign food supplies. While Canadian farmers have been regarded by governments as expendable, the resources the farmer produces are not.

No political party can today claim to have an agricultural policy that is either comprehensive or committed to any more than the further economic exploitation of food production and farm people. The greater potential of farm people for the advancement of farm policy issues clearly is through organization. While farmers in Canada do not lack organizations, as the NFU says, "They definitely lack organization...."

In Canada, governments in general do not welcome the concept of a powerful farm lobby group. Rather than negotiating on farm policy in a comprehensive way, governments prefer to deal with policy in an ad hoc and fragmented manner through the encouragement of several separate self-interest commodity groups....

The total of capital invested in farming in Canada was, according to the 1981 Census of Agriculture, $130.3 billion. That represented an average investment per each of the 318,361 census farm operators in Canada of over $400,000. In 1981 that amount of farm capital investment returned $18.5 billion in cash receipts but only $4.2 billion in realized net income. This was an average per operator return of $58,110 in cash receipts and $13,192 in realized net income — a return of less than 3.3 per cent on capital. Canada Savings Bonds offered over 19 per cent. In 1982 average cash receipts per operator rose to $59,176 and realized net income declined to $11,032, an apparent return of 2.7 per cent on capital.

The index of farm production increased by 3.3 per cent from 128.9 in 1981 to 133.2 in 1982 (1971 = 100). Higher productivity was rewarded by lower net income. It is this chronic low return on investment in food production that will continue to force farmers out of agriculture in future years.

We realize these figures are useful as rough indicators only. The 1981 Census of Agriculture defines a "farmer" as anyone who had sales of agricultural products exceeding $250. That, of course, is ridiculous. A commercial farm is defined as one having sales of $5,000 or more, which includes 243,876 producers. Average capital investment of this group is $490,413.

However, even if the total realized net income of $3.5 billion recorded in 1982 were divided among commercial farmers only, the average net income would increase to $14,351 per operator and return on invested capital would rise to 2.9 per cent. In 1971 the total outstanding farm credit of farmers in Canada from all sources was $4,616.7 million. By 1980 this had increased to $16,583.3 million or by 359.2 per cent.[1]

The ratio of farm debt to realized net income in 1971 was 3.7:1 ($3.70 of debt for every $1 of realized net income). In 1980 this ratio stood at 4.9:1. The risk in earning a livelihood from farming has increased as margins of return narrow. An increasing amount of the value of farm productivity is spent on the costs of inputs and debt servicing. In 1982 total farm operating and depreciation charges reached nearly $15.6 billion or 82.6 per cent of cash receipts.

As margins of return narrow, it often means that cultural practices on farm lands become less than ideal. Agricultural land is a vital natural resource of this nation, but its purpose is increasingly being distorted and exploited at times for nonproductive or speculative purposes, much as are other commodities. Conventional wisdom has always dealt with the problem of low farm income within the context of there being too many farmers to share available income. In 1982 it would have required only about 100,000 farmers, less than one-third the present number, if each were to attain a realized net income of $35,000.

The dilemma of low farm income is reflected in the increasing dependence of farmers upon earnings from off-farm work. The Census of Agriculture statistics of 1981 report that 123,136 or 39 per cent of all farms reported off-farm work averaging 171 days per farm in 1980. This was higher than the number reported by the 1976 interim census at which time 114,625 farms representing 34 per cent of the total number of census farms reported off-farm work averaging 172 days in 1975. Of the off-farm work reported in the 1981 census, 87.2 per cent was non-agricultural. In a period of relatively high unemployment, the competition for work from farmers who experience insufficient on-farm income has at least some measurable impact on the general rate of unemployment.

Not only is the production of food in Canada generously subsidized through earned income from off-farm employment but from the active contribution through unpaid family labour. A research study on the *Employment Practices of Farm Women* undertaken by the NFU in 1982 indicated that among farm women surveyed who did not work off-farm, the hours of work in physical labour averaged 40 hours per week in the fall, 30 hours weekly in summer, 35 hours in spring and 15 hours during the winter. Of farm women engaged in off-farm work, 55 per cent indicated that earnings were used for family living, household expenses or for farm operations.

National Agri-Food Strategy and Objectives

According to Hedley and Anderson:[2]

> Canada has two particular interests in global agricultural development. *One stems strictly from self-interest.* The Canadian government is committed to agricultural development as a predominant feature of Canada's *economic development strategy*. The other is Canada's acceptance of a share of responsibility for world agri-food development, that is, general international trade liberalization, and the transfer to developing nations of technology, suitable forms of capital and essential food aid.

The "economic development strategy" referred to above is linked to the government's trade balance concerns. The export of agricultural products has nearly doubled over the past five years, increasing from $4,800 million in 1978 to $9,306 million in 1982. Our food imports have in the same period increased only from $4,016 million in 1978 to $5,058 million in 1982, resulting in a healthy agricultural trade balance in 1982 of $4,248 million.

Continue the authors:

> With respect to the domestic development of agriculture, the fortunes of the Canadian agri-food sector are inextricably tied to macro-economic international variables over which Canada can exercise only a minor influence. The Canadian agri-food sector is exceedingly vulnerable to policy decisions taken abroad, relative currency values, interest rates, and the effects of the physical environment on world

crops and yields. But Canadian policy decisions and production variabilities are barely discernible influences in the context of the global food economy.

The main thrusts of agri-food policy are market development, resource productivity, international development cooperation, and limited price intervention. The purpose of domestic policies and programs is to enable private operators under competent management to earn normal profits and rates of return to resources, and thereby ensure an adequate supply of good quality food for Canadian consumers and for export.

In the matter of Canadian agri-food price policy there are three overriding considerations. First, prices of grains and oilseeds are major determinants of food prices in Canada. Second, such large amounts of those commodities are exported that external prices largely determine domestic prices. In fact, agricultural export sales are equivalent to one-half the value of farm cash receipts and three-fifths of agricultural export revenue from sales of grains and oilseeds. It follows that export prices of grains and oilseeds determine not only the prices of cereal products in Canada but strongly influence those of animal products, since grains and oilseeds are significant inputs for animal production. And the third consideration is that price and output variability are both high and the two seldom offset each other. The resulting high level of income instability makes stabilization a major policy consideration.[3]

In summary, federal policy toward agriculture is clearly committed to a strategy whereby:

- Farmers in the sale of their products must be competitive with every other producer in the world as well as the treasuries of numerous foreign countries.
- It is assumed that farmers who qualify as "competent managers," or by inference who are able to survive, will provide the needed production for domestic and export markets.
- Cheap grains and oilseeds are seen as essential in a cheap food policy, since they are linked to livestock production. Hence, if farm gate prices for grain and oilseeds are lowered through the imposition of high freight rates, for example, a major gain in policy objective will be assumed to have been attained.
- When the "competent managers" can't any longer make it, stabilization will be used as an instrument of income transfer, and as the authors explain: "The purpose of stabilization is to protect producers against those price variations which play havoc with the cash flow of farm business and thereby threaten the viability of efficient enterprises. However, stabilization measures have been designed so that

they are oriented to market prices and neutral with respect to resource allocation."

Stabilization and Orderly Marketing

As we have witnessed in numerous instances, the concept of federal stabilization programs has not been acceptable to provincial governments who top-load[4] federal programs in order to maintain production within their provinces. While this may result in distorting the balance of production based on "natural advantage," it does slow down the rate of farm decline.

We submit that contrary to its pronouncements of commitment to preserving the family farm structure in food production, the federal government has no policies or intent to live up to such a commitment and that it basically supports the increasing industrialization of the industry. We believe the government is committed to the ideal that "bigger is better" in food production.

As an organization, we do not in principle support the concept of provincial top-loading of stabilization programs. We support the concept of sound national initiatives in production marketing and pricing. However, provincial governments sometimes feel forced into structuring stabilization programs to preserve their economic self-interests as they perceive them to be. Balkanization of the country results.

Grain

The Western Grain Stabilization Program is another kind of stabilization that is unrelated to production costs. Its macro-approach to maintaining a level of income over the entire grain-growing region that does not fall below the previous five-year average, is intended more to maintain cash flow within the region than it is to support the income needs of individual farmers.

In a payout year those participating producers who have been in the position of making maximum contributions to the plan in previous years will receive the largest payouts, even though their income in the payout year has not declined. Those producers who through misfortune have not done well in the previous five years will receive proportionately less. The fund now boasts a credit of over $800 million, and although many producers have experienced tight economic times, no payments have been made since 1978.

Dairy and Poultry

Interestingly enough, Hedley and Anderson refer to the administered supply management programs that apply to dairy and poultry products as follows:

Supply management, on the other hand, with import protection for dairy and poultry products, enables the formation of administered domestic prices insulated from direct price forces in foreign markets. Thus supply management of dairy and poultry products is the feature of Canadian price and marketing policy that clearly expresses Canada's determination not to allow her economy to be dominated by prices. However, the strong influence of external grain prices extends even to the administered prices of commodities under supply management. Although protected by import quotas from direct international competition, these commodities are priced by cost-of-production formulas in which feedgrain and oilseed prices are major components.

There is little doubt that the potential for expansion of production of both dairy and poultry products is great except for the low world prices for these products, as dairy producers in particular are aware. The National Farmers Union supports the concept of administered price programs such as those for dairy and poultry products; however, we do not support the concept of placing a price on production quotas, as is too frequently the case for these products.

Canadian Wheat Board

We also strongly support the orderly marketing principles of the Canadian Wheat Board (CWB), which is an example of an effective export marketing structure operating at producer expense and pooling returns of wheat, oats and barley sold into export for payment to producers. In spite of its marketing success, the board is under constant pressure from self-interested groups within the industry who seek less regulation than is necessary to maintain an orderly system.

The federal government, in our view, has given only lukewarm support to the marketing concepts of the CWB. Jurisdiction over the marketing of domestic feed grains was removed from the board in the 1971-72 crop year and released to the private grain trade. The board was doing too good a job in maximizing returns on feed grains for grain producers. This apparently was inconsistent with federal policy objectives. Since domestic feed grain requirements get first priority from supplies, the board is releasing supplies at domestic prices that at times are below export prices. The federal government in 1982 reimbursed losses of up to $8 million against the difference between the board's domestic and export sales prices, thereby allowing the private grain trade and speculators "to have their cake and eat it too."

The passage of Bill C-155[5] by the House of Commons, obstensibly to improve the grain transport system, brings with it extremely negative implications for grain producers and for national unity. The existence of the Crow rate on export grain has indisputably assisted grain producers to remain competitive in world grain markets. Difficulty in maintaining this competitive edge will be increasingly experienced as rates projected to rise by 100 per cent by 1985-86 and 500 per cent by 1990-91 fall into place. Farmers have been made scapegoats under this legislation, which essentially will allow the financing of the railway companies' megaproject of upgrading a transportation system that will primarily be utilized for the movement of commodities other than grain.

If the government had a genuine concept of "economic union," it would regard transportation as an essential service needed for regional development rather than as entrepreneurial profit organizations seeking a 20 per cent return on capital. The railway companies should be integrated and operated as a public utility.

The marketing of rye, flaxseed and rapeseed continues to remain under the open marketing system in spite of repeated requests of many producers and producer organizations to have these grains placed under CWB jurisdiction. The "spot" price and "street" price spreads of these crops, particularly rapeseed, have at times been scandalous. If the government was genuinely interested in improving the economic interests of producers, these crops would be included under CWB jurisdiction. The NFU has gone further and recommended the establishment of a Canadian Grains Board that would take responsibility for the orderly marketing of all major grains produced in Canada, including corn.

Livestock

It should not be necessary to relate to this commission the instability of prices and markets experienced by livestock producers. This has in turn created wide periodic swings in production patterns as well. The current free market system of selling livestock is a major cause of instability in our livestock sector. Farmers are cast in the role of "price takers" as they compete for markets controlled by relatively few buyers. The inevitable effect is that "competition destroys profits." As a consequence, when producers are unable to recover costs, there is no incentive or reason to produce.

Our voluntary meat import law is basically ineffective in protecting farm prices for livestock. The importation of live slaughter cattle is exempted. Under the General Agreement on Tariffs and Trade (GATT) we are committed in the importation of dressed beef to a minimum 139.1 million pounds, based on 1980 population. As population increases, the quota increases proportionately.

From time to time attempts have been made through organized effort to "change the system." The organization of cooperatives and some marketing boards serve as examples. But in every case they continue to rely on an imperfect market system for setting prices. Some provincial pork marketing agencies have sought and attained export market contracts and at times have acquired them through underbidding other provincial marketing agencies.

The NFU has for some time recommended the organization of a National Meat Authority for Canada with a view toward:

- attaining full self-sufficiency of the regulated products;
- developing sufficient export markets to achieve, as a minimum goal, balanced trade in volume for each commodity;
- encouraging the production of the regulated products on as broad a basis as possible, consistent for the retention of family farms as the basic production unit;
- providing for consumers adequate and high-quality supplies of the regulated products at stable prices; and
- returning to producers prices for their products which will reflect their costs of production and a reasonable return on investment, management and labour.

It is of more than passing interest that a red-meats marketing study (by E.H. Anderson, chairman, and Henry Vandermuellen) commissioned some two years ago by the federal minister of agriculture, on the basis of press reports, apparently came to conclusions similar in a number of respects to those of our own. The report only recently found the light of day as a result of its release to a news reporter under freedom of information legislation.

Potatoes

Of all commodities produced and marketed in Canada, none perhaps have been more unstable or erratic in price return than potatoes. Our organization has for a number of years promoted the concept of an Eastern Canada Potato Marketing Commission designed on the principle of the Canadian Wheat Board.

Conclusion

The major obstacles in the way of bringing income stability and equality of marketing and pricing opportunities to producers have been the private trade, narrowly based provincial marketing organizations and provincial governments that would be required to transfer marketing authority to a central selling agency.

Efforts of the federal government over the past four years to bring about an agency of only limited purpose have failed. Lack of agreement to transfer powers sometimes runs parallel to self-interested considerations based on market shares or the desire to encourage greater self-sufficiency and economic spin-off in processing and employment.

In the meanwhile, producers continue to go broke.

Take potatoes as an example: the only way a meaningful market structure with control over supply may emerge is through the development of a federal price guarantee to producers, the payment of which is conditional upon participation in and transfer of powers by provinces to an interprovincial marketing structure.

In summary, we regard the organization of effective marketing structures as a top priority in creating a meaningful concept of "economic union" for farm products. Without the presence of income stability, our family farm structure in Canada will continue to shrink drastically, as will the economic viability of rural communities supported by food production.

PART IV

An Alternative Vision of Canada

17

Economic Development and Social Justice

THE UNITED CHURCH OF CANADA

The eighteen-member Working Unit on Social Issues and Justice took responsibility for the United Church's submission to the Macdonald Commission. Great care was taken to draw attention to policies related to the economy that have concerned the United Church for some time and to show how these concerns are widely shared among a number of Canadian churches, and indeed depend on ecumenical thinking. The United Church focuses on the values and goals of economic development, believing, as it does, that if this activity is to have any meaning, it must be related to human fulfilment in justice and peace. The United Church is Canada's largest Protestant denomination and has a strong traditional concern for social justice. In the excerpt that follows, the order in which the topics are introduced has been changed from the original brief.

A relatively few large corporations have come to dominate the global economic scene. It is increasingly clear that these giants are no longer accountable to not only the public or unions, but to governments as well. The transnational corporations, in particular, have shown the capacity to form monopolies and oligopolies, to disrupt national economies, to export jobs, to interfere with social progress, and evade taxation.[1] The growth of both electronic communications and transnational banking has removed monetary control from nations, and beyond the international agreement established at Bretton Woods in 1944, into the relative anarchy of an uncontrolled and largely unregulated international market. Canada is one among many nations today that will never be able, in any near-adequate way, to organize its resources in the fight against unemployment and marginalization under current circumstances of monetary disorder. A new international monetary agreement, which would re-establish fair practices for weaker nations, is much needed.

Through the National Energy Program (NEP) and the Foreign Investment Review Agency (FIRA), Canada intervened in the "right" of foreign capital, concentrated primarily in the hands of transnationals, to pre-empt Canadian control. In the years ahead we need to continue such policies of a moderate nationalist bent, at least in key sectors which are related not simply to short-term financial considerations, but to long-term social implications. Since the economy, in the end, is simply a means to provide a living for ordinary people, the question must constantly be raised in all economic ventures as to the effect on the quality of life, on land use, on pricing, on environment, on foreign policy, etc. Ownership and control that can take a cavalier posture to social implications must be held accountable to the public, and kept within reach of that accountability at all times.

As we foresee an economy that conforms to the pattern of the just, participatory and sustainable,[2] it would be one that encourages accountability at a number of levels, that allows for increasing worker participation in planning and control, and that is targeted on basic necessities ahead of frills. There is room for more community and municipal control and management in some industries and for a much wider cooperative style.

The technological revolution is bound to create economic imbalances for years to come that can be both liberating and threatening. The kind of employment that used to be called "toil" will all but disappear except where human labour costs make it "economic" to use hands rather than machines, for example, in the Third World. Whole industries will be retooled, or rendered obsolete by developments, thousands of breadwinners will be displaced with the dim prospect of varying lengths of unemployment. To assume that market forces and the private sector can be relied on to sort this out for the best long-term human good is to be fanciful beyond measure and to base hope where there is no historic precedent.

The role of the government, therefore, as arbiter of the common good is not going to fade with the years. Rather the challenge becomes ever more acute to develop in government the capacity to constantly respond to new developments in employment patterns, and to do this in a manner that is discrete, nonpartisan, flexible and accountable.

From the vantage point of 1983 it would appear that a variety of work opportunities must be opened outside the traditional channels of public service or private industry. Local initiatives and community programs — not unlike those mounted in the early Seventies — should be re-examined with a view to extending their potential to provide goods and services. The local initiative can also be a source for new developments in education and the arts.

In the remainder of this decade it would seem that there is little hope of providing the traditional kinds of jobs for all who want employment. And yet there are countless useful activities to be performed: forests to be replanted, housing to be restored, new transport schemes to be developed, environmental cleanups to be done, etc., etc.

During the Local Initiatives Program of the early Seventies thousands of junk yards were tidied up, parks created, cemeteries restored, etc., and Canada became a more attractive place from coast to coast. Local initiative programs should become a permanent part of our future, with safeguards against political patronage. These initiatives should allow for a much wider range of activities than they did in the Seventies, including the start-up, under guidelines, of small competitive businesses.

Canada should in both the near term and long term avoid pinning its economic destiny on any one or more "great white hopes" — whether these be of a resource megaproject nature or in the race for high-tech supremacy. Rather, we think the capacity to produce food, provide adequate affordable housing, improve transportation, and develop soft-path energy options should become the base of the economic future.

It must be explicitly understood that a sustainable future should be based on a conserver mentality rather than a growth mentality. Canada is part of a planet that is a closed system, and the implications of this awareness are absolutely critical in our stewardship of limited natural resources. Much, if not most, economic activity in the industrial and postindustrial age has been at cross-purposes with good stewardship. This is now evident almost everywhere, and is the result of economic activity premised on pushing "The Limits to Growth" to the extreme.

What this implies for the later Eighties is a reaffirmation of social planning and environmental protection as invariable concomitants of economic planning and activity. Productivity is the activity that creates wealth; but some forms of productivity must be eliminated, other forms must be limited, and many forms must be regulated.

The Sin of High Interest

The Church has had a long struggle with usury. In Psalm 15 we find that those who have the right to enter Yaweh's tent are those "who do not ask interest on loans."

We understand the necessity of interest in an economy more dynamic than that of the ancient world. But usury (excessive interest) is still a sin. During the past two years our country's policy of high interest rates has crippled most sectors of the economy, with massive layoffs, record bankruptcies and great human hardship. A policy which has as its premise the need for thousands to be unemployed is unjust. Interest rates in Canada must be kept down and held much closer to the inflation rate. This may be the biggest single factor for economic recovery in the immediate future.

The Rights of Labour

Human labour has always been the indispensable factor in economic development. Historically, labour has often been exploited and regarded as expendable. Unions, collective bargaining and labour legislation have changed that in good measure, but not altogether. There are those in Canada today who would be glad to turn back the clock. And for transnational companies there are a score of cheap-labour countries to turn to who actively suppress labour's rights to organize and take collective economic action.

If economic development derives its raison d'être as a way to social development, then the future of our economic relations will pay attention to not only the bread and butter needs of workers, and their right to bargain collectively, but also their capacity for creativity in the workplace and their potential to contribute to world peace.

In the future there will be little tolerance in democracies for the disregard of labour's rights either at home or abroad. The loss of jobs in Canada premised on cheap labour overseas will not be tolerated. Instead, measures will be taken to encourage transnational communication between workers, particularly within the work force of the same parent company. The example of Ford workers from the United Kingdom, Europe, Japan and the U.S. who are already reaching out to one another on mutual concerns should be followed with deep interest by those who want economic development that is just, creative and harmonious.[3] Another example for the future is that of the workers at Lucas Aerospace Burnley in the U.K. who have taken the initiative on socially useful production as an alternative to "defence" production.

Native Culture and Identity

For some years the United Church, along with other churches, has attempted to stand in solidarity with Native Peoples as they seek justice, a way to participate and a sustainable future. The chief means to this solidarity has been through our involvement in Project North.

Since the Berger Commission, Canadians have become aware, as never before, of the heritage of Native Peoples and their claim on us to keep that heritage intact.

For the Native Peoples, aboriginal rights do not mean exclusive jurisdiction over parcels of real estate, but rather equity which flows from aboriginal title. They expect, then, royalties from renewable and nonrenewable resources; acknowledgment of past revenues and payment of past claims; and a continuing share of resource development revenues. Aboriginal rights apply to Métis and nonstatus Indians as well as those holding treaties. We support the desire of Native People to share in decisions on:

- environmental protection, and development planning;
- economic programs which emphasize collective and cooperative organizational styles; and,
- measures that promote local self-government related to both communities and interests within a region.

We stress again, as we have in other submissions to the federal government, that aboriginal rights be guaranteed within the Constitution of Canada, and that the implementation of the guarantee in particular instances be conducted in a process which is deemed fair.

Development in the North should break with scenarios for the lifting and export of nonrenewable resources, and where such initiatives are pursued, there must be guarantees of protection for tundra, forestry, wild life and water. This, of course, is also predicated on a determination to create in Canada a conservation and soft-path energy future.

In the event that large resource projects are continued through the North there must be:

- resources for communities to help cope with the socioeconomic impact; and
- Native participation in decision making, monitoring and profits.

Future development in the North will be situated in a context where local pride and personal dignity are the result of self-government in such matters as health and social services, administration of criminal justice and education. Social development programs should encourage local economic initiatives and gradually replace the need for current social assistance programs.

Francophone and Other Identities

The economic climate that evolves to the year 2000 must take account of the special nature of both francophone and anglophone groups in Canada. During the past thirty years these communities have displayed a growing sense of identity. The most notable manifestation of this has been within Quebec, although variations have been seen in other provinces.

It should first be noted that this growing sense of identity resembles the maturing process experienced by peoples in various parts of the world. As such, it is part of a process that is universal in nature.

Secondly, we recognize and believe that governments must affirm that such movements can be liberating and ultimately ensure a sounder social and economic climate. In actualizing their identity (primarily through language and culture), individuals are enabled to explore their creativity through education and other means and are, as a result, better able to assume a place in the work world. In short, identity is ultimately linked to work and serves to liberate the individual to a creative expression through work.

Identity is also related to a liberation of society. The affirmation of identity, as experienced in Canada, has challenged individuals to become involved in society, to become committed and to care about the social good. As such, society is seen again as an extension of self, a relationship that is destroyed by mass society and mass economy. In our view, mass societies and mass economies create alienation that translates into economic inertia and indifference. Creative potentials are frustrated when subjected to narrow, traditional political views and when economic sanctions are employed as a form of punishment.

Further, we believe that all peoples in Canada have much to learn about liberation from these movements to strengthen identity. Real involvement in the problems and solutions to economic and social questions cannot come from those alienated from society. Only by experiencing and perceiving economic and social life as an extension of self can Canadians begin to bring about creative and committed economic and social change.

As a result, we believe that governments must affirm the liberating nature of community-identity movements in Canada and encourage others to learn from them in order to produce a better society and a more fully functioning economy. To do this, Canadians must come to recognize that identity movements have matured by virtue of their openness to ideas and models from elsewhere. These movements can no longer be interpreted as based solely or primarily on traditional forms of nationalism. This implies a need for openness in the rest of Canada in order that other Canadians learn from the exciting experiments nearby and thus become better equipped to create new social and economic futures. Without such openness, we cannot learn and we are condemned to repeating the economic past over and over again.

Finally, we believe we are called upon to actualize a form of democracy which relies upon the building of consensus among all members of society. Building a constitution or an economic future without the full participation of both official language groups is totally unacceptable. What is necessary is a climate in which consensus can take place and whereby it can become a major operating principle in our social, economic and political life. Majority rule has traditionally implied that there is always one winner. We respectfully suggest that social, economic and political democracy based on the principle of consensus implies that there will be many winners, and a society in which the well-being of the whole community is paramount.

Into the Mainstream of Canadian Life

In our paper on income security of 1982, we quoted approvingly these principles enunciated by David Hollenbach:

- the needs of the poor must take priority over the wants of the rich;
- the freedom of the dominated must take priority over the liberty of the powerful; and
- the participation of marginalized groups must take priority over the preservation of an order that excludes them.[4]

One way of looking at the "economy" is to consider it as the domain and prerogative of a select few. The term itself is abstract and impersonal, and even where it touches down, the human level appears to be an art or science where financiers, managers, union leaders, academics and politicians are the soothsayers of its wisdom. In fact, all of these roles are indispensable, but happily this commission wants to hear from those who do not have general access to economic planning, as well as those who do.

We refer to that large part of the Canadian population who participate only marginally, if at all, in the production of goods or the provision of services. A short list of such people will include the elderly, those who survive on social assistance, the handicapped, Native People and those who cannot find work. As has been repeated through innumerable reports on unemployment, the list must include a growing number of young people.

Joining those who live lives marginal to the mainstream of the economy and its benefits are the working poor and that group of people who have come to be described as the "near poor."

The present system has been created and modified in a disjointed and unplanned manner mainly because there are two and sometimes three levels of government delivering services. Some programs operate at cross-purposes to others. Some overlap. And several operate with conflicting objectives. Some supplements, credits or allowances had their origin in political motivation. The system is so fragmented that some clients receive benefits from as many as six or seven different sources. As one government adds a benefit, another government subtracts a like amount. There is little hope of this changing until provincial and federal governments can agree on a new program to be designed, delivered and cost-shared.

There should be a long-range goal to create a new comprehensive and integrated system which would replace much of the present maze of programs and would deliver adequate income support with a minimum of intervention into the personal lives of the clients.

In the planning for Canada's economic development, we are concerned that due recognition in policymaking be given to closing the income and wealth gap in Canada between those who presently profit in the system and those who don't. In order to do this, we believe that at minimum the following measures will have to be taken:

- An overhaul of the tax system in line with the recommendation of the Royal Commission on Taxation of the Sixties (the Carter Commission). In 1979 the federal government lost $13.8 billion in foregone revenue on personal income tax, and $30 billion if corporate write-offs are included.[5]
- An untangling and clarification of federal and provincial responsibilities in areas of social responsibility. At present there is too much

slack in the lines of accountability respecting social housing. Whose responsibility is it anyway? The same can be said with respect to industrial incentives and job creation, job retraining, income support, social services, and many other social and economic areas of overlap.

- Protection for equalization grants to provinces related to both economic and social programs.
- Innovations in employment patterns such as work sharing, shorter work weeks, codetermination in plant management, local initiatives, income supplements through expanding tax credits or negative income tax mechanisms for working people.
- Pensions and income support pegged generously to average income levels so as to guarantee every Canadian a life above the poverty line. Income support from the present social assistance category should be a right and delivered through the tax system in tax credits or as a negative income tax.
- The protection of a universal medical and health-care system that is fully accessible to everyone, comprehensive in the range of services provided, and portable.
- The United Church opposes government lotteries as regressive taxation. The lotteries distract from the need to set social priorities, legitimate gambling in general, and widen the gap between haves and have-nots. The Working Unit and many other parts of the United Church have respectfully called on church members to boycott lotteries, to refuse to accept lottery grants for church-related projects, and to call on governments to remove themselves from the sponsorship of lotteries.
- However, given that governments are becoming more competitive rather than less so with lottery promotion, and given that lotteries, which recycle hundreds of millions of dollars annually, are regressive both at the sales end and at the benefits end (the poor pay disproportionately more and receive in grant benefits disproportionately less), we believe that the ends of social equity would be better served if lottery revenues were placed in general revenue for use to improve welfare measures rather than to be used for cultural and athletic facilities, etc.

The Third World

In recent years the churches, through the Taskforce on Churches and Corporate Responsibility, have made repeated interventions with corporations, banks, crown corporations and federal officials, concerning the impact of Canadian foreign investment, lending and trade on the most vulnerable people within the host countries. In general, we have accepted the argument that the presence of foreign capital will be a liberalizing influence that will ameliorate the situation for human rights and will allow the benefits of economic development to trickle down to the poorest within the society.

Our review of the data has led us to conclude that the thesis has not been proven true in the concrete cases we have examined over the past ten years. In fact, we find that we have benefitted as shareholders, and indirectly as consumers, from investment undertaken during a time of severe and growing repression in the Third World. We also find that we have had to pay a price as shareholders when conditions have worsened and the Canadian company has had to mothball the foreign operation.

Our experience indicates that it is not only bad for the disenfranchised of Third World countries to build our prosperity on the misery of the poorest; it is also bad for Canadian business.

This experience led us to make several suggestions to the Sub-Committee on Latin America and the Caribbean of the parliamentary Standing Committee on External Affairs and National Defence.[6] We believe they are relevant to the concerns of this commission.

In order to ensure that Canadian investment and lending is flowing to parts of the world that have potential for development into strong trading partners, we recommend that the Canadian government needs to gather the information required and conduct a regular review of human rights and Canadian foreign policy, including such matters as foreign investment, aid and trade.

Two types of information should be sought:

- information regarding the operations of publicly owned or supported national and international bodies, including the EDC (Export Development Corporation), CIDA (Canadian International Development Agency), Canadian crown corporations, and such international financial institutions as the World Bank, the Inter-American Development Bank and the IMF (International Monetary Fund), as well as in regard to publicly chartered and regulated corporations, particularly the private sector banks;
- up-to-date human rights assessments in countries of significant interest, in absolute terms or relative to their relationship with Canada.

Canada needs the same sort of concrete and accurate information as background to decisions regarding the activities of the World Bank and the International Monetary Fund, of which it is a funder and a voting member. The need is demonstrated in the recent debt crisis and the decision of donor countries to increase the reserves of the IMF to help debtor countries cover their loans to commercial lenders and international financial institutions. The decisions of private commercial banks to increase their loan exposure to foreign governments are usually an internal matter. However, in the current economic situation, governments of the North are being asked to share the burden of easing the problems created for debtor countries and for commercial banks by the lending practices of the 1970s. The Canadian taxpayer surely ought to expect that, in future, lending institutions will disclose their overseas lending on a country-by-country basis. If not, it is possible that another drain on the Canadian economy could be created by private banking, in concert with the international financial institutions, without our knowing about it. Responsibility demands accountability and disclosure.

We have further recommended that the Export Development Act be amended to ensure that decisions about the uses of its facilities for a particular country include a review of the country's human rights record. Further, the EDC should withhold financial support facilities for trade with countries that engage in a consistent pattern of gross violations of human rights until internationally recognized human rights organizations such as Amnesty International, the International Commission of Jurists and the United Nations Human Rights Commission have reported an undisputed cessation of gross and systematic violations of human rights.

We are not suggesting that Canada can cure the world of its human rights and underdevelopment ills. But the least we can do is ensure that public money and government services are not used to help private companies supply those who are carrying out human rights violations against their own citizens....

Peace

In 1983 the world spends upwards of one billion dollars a day in the manufacture of armaments. Not so long ago it was less than half this amount. Although Canada is not one of the major arms manufacturers, there are certain factors in our organization as a nation that make this sector rise and fall in proportion to the rise and fall of the global arms trade. Therefore, its impact on our economy rises and falls according to factors largely beyond our control. Since the Second World War, we have experienced cycles in demand for military goods — and, hence from one point of view, opportunities for job creation — that depend on the state of East-West relations, the programs of the major military alliances to retire old equipment and modernize their weapons systems, and the interest of smaller countries in purchasing military and military-related equipment. The revival of the Cold War and the rise of "national security" doctrines in many parts of the world have created a lucrative "market" for military goods and spare parts.[7]

We believe it would be both immoral for Canadians as a people and unhealthy for the Canadian economy as a whole, to seek to capture that market, either for nuclear weapons or for so-called conventional weapons. In fact, we believe it is in Canada's long-term interests to end the production of arms, except for the use of our own armed forces.

UN and other studies have demonstrated that the global arms trade is entrenching current global economic patterns in the North and providing an effective block to development in the South. What is new for us in the North is the extent to which the global arms trade is draining our own economies through its inefficient use of capital, human labour and resources.

In 1959 Canada and the United States entered into defence production sharing arrangements, known as DPSA. In those arrangements, we agreed to buy our major weapons systems from the United States. In 1963 the arrangements were amended to include a provision to ensure that Canada would buy from the U.S. as many military commodities as it sells to the United States. In a sense, the price of creating jobs in Canada in the military-parts industry was the purchase of weapons systems from the United States, with the familiar pressure on balance of payments and the need for more markets abroad.

The impact of DPSA is illustrated most recently. Between 1980 and 1981, military spending in the U.S. grew, producing a larger market, which could be tapped in the interest of Canadian sales and job creation. Table 17-1 shows the increase in sales during the preceding years.

The problem with arms manufacture as an immediate panacea for unemployment is that it requires large amounts of capital in return for very few jobs, which can evaporate for reasons beyond our control. American protectionism as a means of protecting jobs in the U.S. is creating resistance to imports, even from countries like Canada, which enjoys privileged status because of DPSA.

The boom in the American arms market could disappear for other reasons, including American balance-of-payments problems. When that occurs, as it inevitably will (given the experience of the Canadian arms industry during the pre- and post-Vietnam eras), Canada will have to find new markets to use its arms and space parts manufacturing capacity.

The easy market will be Third World countries, where social unrest, border disputes, military regimes, and national security doctrines create ready markets for military and military-related goods. Canada is certainly not the primary supplier of such goods to Third World coun-

TABLE 17-1

Increase in Canadian Military Sales Over Previous Years, 1978-82

(per cent)

1978 to 1979	35
1979 to 1980	35
1980 to 1981	75
1981 to 1982	40 (projected from first six months of 1982)

tries, but exports to the Third World, as a component of total sales, have been rising since the early 1960s level of approximately $25 million (Can.) per year to approximately $125 to $150 million a year in 1980. (See Tables 17-1 and 17-2. Since the figures are not disclosed precisely, they must be estimated by subtracting other amounts from total sales.)

Furthermore, in the 1970s Canada entered into a new phase in its weapons exports. Prior to that, our exports had primarily been in military transport aircraft, such as the Cariboo, Beaver, Buffalo, etc. However, in the 1970s we began to export electronic and aircraft components to Third World countries. While our customers were primarily Commonwealth countries in the 1960s, in the 1970s we broadened our customers to include those countries that were purchasing from the Americans.

At the beginning of the 1980s, this trend seems to be increasing. Indeed, some public figures have openly said that it *should*, as a means of revitalizing the economy and the industrial base of Canada. (In the 1980s, our exports now include not only transport aircraft and components, but also electronics, military rockets, some artillery, and light armoured vehicles. In other words, our export of munitions is creeping upward.)

We believe this is immoral and economically unhealthy. We are not saying that officials have deliberately taken a decision to do something immoral, but that these trends have developed as part of our effort to break out of the boom-bust cycle that plagues the Canadian military industry because our market is primarily outside the country, with the bulk of it in a single customer. To diminish the impact of decisions taken in the U.S., it would *appear* to some to be to our advantage to broaden the base of customers overseas. This is not the option to be embraced. Rather, we must get out of arms production, except, as noted, for use of the Canadian armed forces.

TABLE 17-2
Canadian Military Exports, 1978-82

(current millions of dollars)

	1978	1979	1980	1981	1982[1]
United States	267.0	367.7	481.7	826.6	724.2
Non-U.S.[2]	217.5	200.6	240.0	324.2	342.8
Total	484.5	568.3	721.7	1,150.8	1,067.0

[1] First nine months (Jan.-Sept.).
[2] About 50% NATO (non-U.S.) and 50% non-NATO.

Source: Department of Industry, Trade and Commerce, Canada.

FIGURE 17-1
Destination of Canadian Arms
Production, 1981

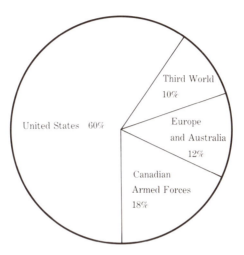

Source: Project Ploughshares.

The federal government should set a course to disengage from the global arms market. This would involve a phasing out of the Defence Industry Productivity Program (DIPP) grants, which took some $143 million of Canadian tax money in 1982. (See Tables 17-3 and 17-4. Through DIPP the government helps companies in the military industry to allow them to compete more effectively in the global arms market.) The DIPP grants could be much more wisely and productively spent on job creation in nonmilitary industries, where the investment would create a larger number of jobs for the money and contribute more effectively to the creation of a sustainable economic base.

Military spending comes down in the end to spending for waste in human, as well as in raw, resources. There are no industries under the sun less "economic" than those based on arms production. There are no industries whose existence is more blatantly set against good stewardship of the earth's finite resources and the good of humanity as a whole. It is crucial that the federal government take steps to pull Canada out of a trade that is rapidly impoverishing the entire world.

Development Prospects That Are Just, Participatory and Sustainable

Present and future directions will have the happiest outcome for Canadians, and others on this shared planet, when social justice, broad and

TABLE 17-3

Defence Industry Productivity Program (DIPP) — Federal Grants to Canadian Defence Industry, 1977-82

1977-78	$ 43,109,638
1978-79	52,200,000
1979-80	57,936,115
1980-81	94,931,422
1981-82	154,934,982

Source: Public Accounts of Canada.

TABLE 17-4

Top Twenty Defence Industry Grant Recipients — Dip Program 1980-81

1. Canadair Ltd., Montreal, P.Q.	$40,483,337
2. Pratt and Whitney Aircraft of Canada, Longueuil, P.Q.	37,198,885
3. Litton Systems (Canada) Ltd., Rexdale, Ont.	18,407,297
4. Canadian Marconi Company, Montreal, P.Q.	6,367,740
5. De Havilland Aircraft of Canada Ltd., Toronto, Ont.	6,232,296
6. McDonnell Douglas of Canada Ltd., Toronto, Ont.	4,340,877
7. Garret Manufacturing Ltd., Rexdale, Ont.	3,077,096
8. Dowty Equipment of Canada Ltd., Ajax, Ont.	2,107,705
9. CAE Electronics Ltd., Montreal, P.Q.	2,088,813
10. Magna International Inc., Kitchener, Ont.	2,009,799
11. Spar Technology Ltd., Ste. Anne, P.Q.	1,753,866
12. Ebco Industries Ltd., Richmond, Ont.	1,614,877
13. Linamar Machine Ltd., Arris, Ont.	1,492,745
14. Algoma Steel Corporation Ltd., Sault Ste. Marie, Ont.	1,301,124
15. Erie Technological Products Ltd., Trenton, Ont.	1,284,406
16. Canadian Aircraft Products Ltd., Montreal, P.Q.	1,171,556
17. Haley Industries Ltd., Haley, Ont.	1,165,971
18. Aviation Electric Ltd., Montreal, P.Q.	1,112,877
19. Computing Devices of Canada Ltd., Ottawa, Ont.	1,090,790
20. Walbar Machine Products of Canada Ltd., Mississauga, Ont.	914,507

Source: Public Accounts of Canada.

active public participation, and measures to protect indefinitely the resources of nature are kept together....

The concept of *social justice* is involved in the belief that fairness and equity should mark the sharing of wealth based on our common heritage. It creates in us a desire to close income gaps between Canadians; to honour the collective rights and traditions of our "first people" and of the French-speaking descendants of our first European settlers; to provide a safe home and healthy environment for dozens of ethnic and religious groupings that have come into Canadian life; and to conduct trade and commerce internally and externally in a way that will ensure the future for peace. Social justice requires protection of human rights as described in the UN Charter of Human Rights — rights which have been grossly violated by many countries in recent years.

The concept of *participation* arises out of increasing pluralism within and among nations. National and international economies, politics and technology have become increasingly complicated and complex. In these interrelated spheres is found the nexus of most contests for power, and the real or potential possibility of social injustice to either the living or to future generations.

In such a world, with so many things to be considered in order that fairness can be exercised, a deepening and extending of the democratic attitude and practice is imperative. Participation means sharing power. It means involvement in decision making and implementation by all affected groups. In more exact terms it requires an increasing role for hourly paid workers in all sectors; for recipients of social assistance and social services; for consumers; for farmers and fishermen; for small communities removed from centres of power; for city tenants; for women; for the Native Peoples; and for the French-speaking communities of Canada whether concentrated in Quebec or scattered throughout the country.

The concept of *sustainability* brings us to the consideration not only of the economy and its reward to this generation but of the economy as it will sustain generations yet unborn. The wealth we have and on which we have built our nation is a heritage. Social justice demands that a productive resource base and clean environment be passed on to those coming after us. The decisions made during this decade on land use, forestry, water resources, industrial waste, and energy development will mark the integrity of the stewardship we exercise toward our common heritage.

With the view that the economy is something we share in common; that it is the way we put together human and natural resources for the good of the common life; that it is a vast collective enterprise and the domain of no particular subgroup in society; ... this raises concluding questions:

- In the choices concerning our future, will ethics come before technology? Will persons come before things?
- Will our future be just, participatory and sustainable?
- Will the needs of the poor take priority over the wants of the rich?

18 The Informal Economy and the Will to Work

THE VANIER INSTITUTE OF THE FAMILY

The Vanier Institute of the Family is an independent research agency. Based in Ottawa, it is governed by a board of directors drawn from across Canada. It has become known for its innovative research into the relationship between the course of economic development and societal development more generally. Its particular interest has been patterns of family life and patterns of economic organization. The Vanier Institute is impressed with the way that community groups, such as New Dawn in Sydney and Sudbury 2001, are implementing new approaches to development.

This excerpt from their seventy-six-page brief focuses on the vital role of what the institute calls the informal economy, a social foundation necessary to any sustainable economy, though rarely recognized in conventional analysis. In essence the Vanier Institute has developed a new paradigm that permits a redefinition and rethinking of the most basic economic concept of all, work. The institute maintains that Canadians now see clearly the need to address "economic" issues from a more inclusive and comprehensive frame of reference.

How meaningful is the blind pursuit of increased GNP (gross national product)? Hugh Stretton, an Australian economist, points out the questionable nature of this measure of the quality of life in very simple terms. In so doing, he demonstrates clearly and with humour that an increase in GNP does not necessarily represent an actual increase in economic activity, productive work, productivity or well-being.

How easily we could turn the tables on the economists if we all decided that from tomorrow morning, the work of the domestic economy should be paid for. Instead of cooking dinner for her own lot, each housewife would feed her neighbours at regular restaurant rates; then they'd cook for her family and get their money back. We'd do each other's housework and gardening at award rates. Big money would change hands when we fixed each other's tap washers and electric plugs at the plumbers' and electricians' rates. Without a scrap of extra work the gross national product would go up by a third overnight. We would increase that to half if the children rented each other's backyards and paid each other as play supervisors, and we could double it if we all went to bed next door at regular massage parlour rates. Our economists would immediately be eager to find out what line of investment was showing such fabulous growth in capital/output ratio. They'd find that housing was bettered only by double beds and they'd recommend a massive switch of investment into both.[1]

Beyond these shortcomings, GNP also fails to differentiate between activity that originates from "goods" production and the production of "bads," such as cancer treatment, crime prevention and so on. Again, by focusing on current productive activity alone, GNP discriminates against durability and secondhand goods. A new car every year adds to the GNP; a used one does not.

The formal economy, which is monitored closely by reference to GNP and related indicators, is not the whole economy. It is not the whole context within which the problems of economic management need to be seen. It is only market, read "business," activity or public sector equivalents. What is being measured by those indicators is only goods and services produced for market exchange or in return for taxes, and the rate and efficiency at which land, labour and capital are employed to those ends.

What, then, is the whole economy and what, in particular, is the commission currently omitting from its consideration?

Figure 18-1 summarizes what the institute understands to be the whole economy. Although the figure shows eight discrete sectors of productivity, it is more accurate to think of the whole economy as a continuing spectrum of activities of many more forms than the eight sectors shown, with much overlapping, interpenetrations and shadings into one another....

The informal economy embraces a vast range of perfectly legal productive activity which is not intended for market exchange.[2] Nor is it normally measured by the conventional indicators. It includes much of the production of such essentials as food, clothing, shelter and heat for one's own use or for exchange within one's family or community. It incorporates those services such as child rearing, housework, home maintenance and renovations, provided these services are not hired out. A study done for Statistics Canada estimates that the household production sector would contribute another 40 to 50 per cent to the GNP if recorded.[3]

There is also a broad range of volunteer and community work which does not enter the market. There are also various forms of cooperative,

FIGURE 18-1
The Whole Economy

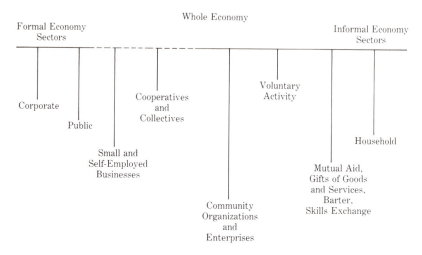

collective, community enterprise and unconventional small-business activity that fit uncomfortably within the traditional economic frameworks, analyses and measuring devices....

In describing the informal economy, it may also be helpful to make clear what we are *not* talking about. There has been some attention in recent years to the "black" or "underground" economy, which involves theft, black marketing or tax evasion. This economic activity has sometimes been labelled as part of the informal economy. We believe this to be misleading, but, more to the point, we do not intend to include this in our definition here.

Characteristics of the Informal Economy

There are two facets of the informal economy.

The first of these is *small-scale production*, much of it for domestic consumption within the household. Examples include small-scale agriculture and coastal fisheries, and Indian and Inuit hunting and fishing communities in the North. This type of informal activity accounts for a relatively small part of the output of the Canadian economy, although it is very significant in Third World economies.

The second involves both the production of goods and the provision of services in our homes and at the *community level*. These activities may be carried out in nonconventional or nonindustrial ways — nonprofit businesses, co-ops, collectives, community development corporations, voluntary organizations and mutual aid such as bartering or skills exchange, gifts of goods or services — or within a more conventional small-business framework. These activities are neither illegal nor remote, and occur daily to some degree in every household and every community.

There are some characteristics of production and exchange that become more visible as activity becomes more informal:

- an increasing number of transactions taking place without the involvement of money;
- production tends to become more decentralized and under local control;
- technology, though sometimes very sophisticated, is generally simpler;
- less recording of the activities involved;
- more emphasis on cooperation and mutual aid that people give to one another;
- a weaker direct link between work and income;
- a growing absence of contractual obligations;
- increased participation by women;
- more emphasis on the conditions of work and the importance of work activity itself;
- less stress on the profit motive and the objective of capital accumulation; and
- in general, a greater sensitivity and awareness of how the structuring of economic activity affects the well-being of people not only at work but in their overall lives, and in their relationships with others in their families and communities.

"Economic" versus "Social" Policy

Why do we seek to draw attention to the informal facets of the economy? In brief, we do so because there has been a grave neglect of the informal economy in economic thinking and texts which has resulted in shortsighted policies that have unintentionally proven disadvantageous to families and communities.

For example, conventional wisdom has it that production is performed solely by firms rather than households and community groups. The economic functions of householders, it is assumed, are limited to consuming the output of firms, giving birth to children, rearing and training them, and nurturing the adult worker. The success of the household as a social unit is now commonly judged by the quality of the labour (the "human" capital) that it provides to the larger institutions, and by the quantity of goods and services it can buy back.

But how are we to interpret the knowledge that households and the business community each purchase around $25 billion worth of capital goods or durables? If a household buys a refrigerator or a car, it is labelled capital "consumption"; yet if a firm buys these identical items the purchase is labelled "capital" investment. In both cases, however, the purchase is a means to produce further goods and services. Therefore, the only significant difference appears to be that the firm which sells its output is accorded a higher social value than the familial household and is thereby granted public financial advantages denied the latter. It is now time to question "sales" as the criterion by which to categorize parallel activities as being either productive or consumptive.

Households fulfill their responsibilities to provide adequate food, clothing and shelter for their members within social and economic circumstances prescribed by a variety of public policies. As noted, these policies often reflect the latent attitudes and values of an industrial way of life. Oriented toward the maximization of efficiency, these policies stimulate the process by which previously informal economic activities are transformed into formalized production methods and monetized exchanges carried out within the marketplace. For example, we see today a dramatic increase in the number of meals consumed away from home. These restaurant meals have added to the growth of the GNP when, in fact, no real additional meals have been prepared per capita. The GNP, as a concept, would now suggest that Canadians are eating double suppers. Because it is assumed that households are private units of consumption and that firms are public units of production, taxation policies as well as other policies designed to stimulate the economy often carry the unintended effect of undermining the social foundation of the informal economy. Consider, for example, that if McDonald's purchases a cooking range, it is, for purposes of taxation, treated as a capital investment, whereas if a household purchases the identical range, it is regarded as a consumer expenditure. But, in each case, the expenditure is made in order to facilitate economically productive activity. In strict economic terms (in contrast to accounting terms), McDonald's enjoys, by virtue of such public provisions, a competitive advantage over the household that chooses to cook its meals at home. The formal economy is stimulated, the GNP goes up, and increasingly we ask ourselves where our important times together, as members of families, have gone.

Like the familial household sector, the community service sector has also seen its productive activities go unrecognized. For example, how do we account for the (conservatively estimated) quarter of a million person-years of work donated freely to volunteer work in Canada if we do not recognize the productive importance of community service?

The conventional interpretation of the economy, which neglects the informal economy, is the product of the mass industrialization and monetization of our economy. As such, it has been underwritten by our value system. Our notions of work, income, success, progress, modernity and development are thoroughly rooted in the narrow and inverted perceptions of the industrial state. What is done on the job is production and work; what is done away from the job is consumption and leisure.

As soon as we regard such indices as GNP, rates of inflation, person-years of employment and what have you as the exclusive indices of economic performance, not to mention of social well-being, work is equated exclusively with those activities upon which a wage or salary is conferred. It follows that anything we do for which we do not receive payment — washing the dishes, caring for children, re-roofing the house, growing vegetables, cooking meals, changing a diaper — is, to the economist, leisure. And, as well, it follows that one's job has become the most important judgment of a person's social status regardless of the actual work he or she does or the contribution he or she makes to the economy and to the society.

In the formal economy, rationality and large-scale technology prevail. Until recently it has been seen as a place for men alone. The informal economy, and especially the household sector, is seen as the private and personal sphere, in which feelings dominate and, indeed, to which feelings should be restricted. It is also not seen as being productive because it has no measurable economic output. It is seen as the place for women, children and "the retired."

Unfortunately, this has affected public policy, in which there has arisen a false and injurious dichotomy. A fundamental division has been fostered between so-called economic and so-called social policy matters. Family allowances, child tax credits, and child-care subsidies, which are payments to families, are treated as matters of social welfare. Tax breaks, incentives and subsidies to industry and commerce, which comprise both direct and indirect payments to firms, are by contrast treated as matters of economic development and thereby accorded a higher social purpose and greater social value. In this view, economic and social matters are generally unrelated except insofar as greater productivity in "the economy" allows us to "pay" for social well-being. This is an example, of the first order, of inverted perception and value, to wit, that people depend on the economy whereas the reverse is true — the economy depends firstly on the imagination, initiative and energies of people, as the evolution of any economy clearly demonstrates.

In short, our society has developed two sets of language — the economic and the social — to describe what are in fact all part of the same reality, a continuum of a multitude of interrelationships between various units — persons, groups, organizations, unions, firms, corporations, public agencies and organs — that comprise the totality of our economic activity.

The value of the contributions of the so-called economic and social players can be better judged in light of this sounder understanding of the larger context. Beyond judging an economy or producing sector in such familiar terms as the volume of production (output), the amounts and combinations of labour, capital and resources required (inputs), the amount of employment, and the income, rents, revenues and profits generated (the returns to the various inputs), we need also to recognize that people enter into and interact within relationship patterns, for good or ill, when they engage in economic activity. They may be seen as relationships with institutions (banks, companies, etc.), but in the final analysis these relations are with other persons. Thus, it is telling that in our society we are surprised to encounter an empathetic bank manager, doctor, teacher, electrician or mechanic. As the Vanier Institute has stated previously, economic activity is

> ...*fundamentally a human activity*, not primarily an exchange of things and money. Very simply, what we regard as the economic system needs to be seen as a particular historically-limited human answer to the fundamental question about how human beings should relate together with regard to what is produced for survival and development. We need to learn that we cannot refer to the economic system as though it were somehow separate and apart from our own daily activities. Rather, it is an inseparable part of our whole life and we, in all our living, are parts of it. The economic system is, at root, a patterned set of human relationships.[4]

The Vanier Institute believes that people do not want to reduce and trivialize the meaning of their activities and relationships to that of commodities alone. They do not want human services to be provided as if they can be dispensed like soap powder, however well the quality control standards are established and monitored. And yet this is what has been happening for many decades....

Our present circumstances have been shaped by an historical trend toward increasing dependence on the formal monetized economy at the expense of the social foundation of the informal economy and the viability of informal community networks of support; as such, a simple withdrawal of programs and support is, at present, unrealistic. Thus, it is important to give more attention to the informal aspects of the economy and its relations with the formal economy because policies and programs need to be reoriented to support and enable the efforts of people to redevelop once more, over time, their capacities to help themselves and each other in more informal (more human, natural) ways.

Today, we have unemployment insurance systems that discourage and penalize people who perform nonindustrial work even though they cannot find jobs within the system. To receive an unemployment benefit means being at the twenty-four-hour beck and call of industry and government. It means not making any long-term commitments, not getting involved in other activities because there may be a job at a moment's notice. To do otherwise means losing the benefits.

When the number of "unemployed" in Canada runs at a million and a half, public policies that tie people to a fading industrial way of production are dysfunctional. Rather we can institute policies that encourage more people to create their own jobs in more informal ways, moving our industrialization pattern into another mode, that is, one which emphasizes small-scale enterprise and small working groups.

In light of the importance of the activities in the informal sector to the quality of life enjoyed by Canadians, we are also concerned at the extent to which the formal, industrialized production has crowded out the informal production methods. Pollution of the rivers and expropriation of the lands of thousands of Indians and Inuit bear testimony to this. More subtly, conventional mortgage systems and construction standards effectively prevent most people from building their own homes and gaining the satisfaction from so doing.

In short, many arrangements in the economy are undermining the social basis of the activities in the informal economy and thereby undermine the general economic and social health and capacity of Canadian society. Clearly, we need to focus on the different institutional forms of production — corporate, government, small business, community development corporations, co-op craft and skills exchange guilds, household — and assess the merits of the social patterns and behaviour associated with the different processes. Instead of choosing preferred economic structures simply on the basis of narrow financial and commercial criteria such as profitability, efficiency, export potential, we will choose also on the basis of the social behaviour and patterns they generate.

The Magnitude of the Informal Economy

In a study by David Ross and Peter Usher, entitled *The Whole Economy*, done for the Vanier Institute, the authors convey an impression of the relative sizes of the six sectors comprising the informal economy and give some indication of how much these various economic activities are omitted from conventional GNP accounting. (We have not dealt with the activities of the corporate and public sectors because they are well recorded.)...

In some instances, the federal government is now collecting some data on these sectors. It is safe to assume, for example, that most *small-business and self-employed activity* is recorded for inclusion in the GNP, although there are doubtless some exceptions, such as the unpaid labour input of spouses and other family members into family enterprises, such as farms. But it is only recently that data on the small-business sector (that is, those firms with sales of less than $2 million a year) has been collected systematically. This is surprising, given that these firms constitute 97 per cent of all firms. The data reveals that these firms account for some $25 billion, or 29 per cent, of the total contribution by all business to the GNP. In contrast, the very largest businesses (that is, those with sales of more than $20 million) account for 48 per cent of business GNP. We also know, even though there are on average only four employees in each small business, that these add up to some 2.7 million people, or 42 per cent of all business employment in Canada.

It is also of interest, but perhaps not surprising, to note that whereas 20 per cent of large firms are foreign controlled, less than 1 per cent of small firms are so controlled.

Unfortunately, although the activities of most self-employed are recorded for purposes of GNP, small-business statistics exclude other data on the self-employed. This gap is significant in that we do know that this group (excluding farmers) is growing at a rate of about 6 per cent a year — over twice the rate of paid employees. It may be useful to know more about the group.

Likewise, much *cooperative and collective activity* is included in the GNP. What is missing, though, is any allowance for the time contributions of members of smaller co-ops which result in the lower prices enjoyed by members. These lower prices would simply enter the GNP accounts as a lower volume of business, and no imputing wage adjustment is made to reflect the effort of the co-op members. Consequently, GNP is bound to understate the economic contribution of co-ops and collectives (especially the smaller ones). What is also of interest about this sector is the decline in the importance of manufacturing cooperatives and the rapid growth in the number of small retail and worker cooperatives.

With respect to *community enterprise activity*, we see that while estimates can be made for the GNP generated by paid employees in the charitable sector (excluding community hospitals and teaching institutions), the figure of $2.5 billion is very much a "guesstimate."

While some activity is recorded, there are numerous instances where nothing is recorded. For example, under the Local Initiatives Program (LIP), a federal direct job-creation program, no activity was recorded because payments were regarded as transfers like old age pensions, social assistance and unemployment insurance. Economic production was occurring but not being recorded.

A more serious omission is the exclusion of an implicit evaluation of the labour and goods provided by the *volunteer sector* to community enterprises and organizations. What can be estimated, however, is that some 2.7 million Canadians volunteer the equivalent of about 200,000 person-years of work each year. Ross and Usher suggest this might, on an admittedly artificial basis of conversion, be the equivalent of a $2.0-billion contribution to the GNP.

Mutual aid, barter and skills exchange are almost totally excluded from the GNP. However, the significance of these is considerable in Native communities and in remote rural areas such as parts of Newfoundland and Labrador. There are obvious policy implications stemming from the fact that Native communities can produce as much food as they do. This production ranges from about 240 pounds per head in the Mackenzie Valley and western Arctic to about 1,000 pounds in the Inuit-occupied areas of northern Quebec. This, naturally, reduces the need for wage employment because the imputed value of this production amounts to several thousands of dollars per household.[5] Similarly, through the process of mutual aid, about 80 per cent of the houses in rural Newfoundland are owner built; this has produced a far healthier situation in terms of mortgage-free housing as compared with, say, Ontario.

Again, the examination of the *household sector* reveals that although we are able to gain a good sense of its size in terms of the number of households, their occupants and their income, little or none of their activity is recorded in the GNP. And yet, from studies by Jonathan Gershuny in the U.K., we know that households are providing more and more of their own services. This has been helped by new technologies (such as washing machines) which have enabled substitution for services (such as laundry) formerly purchased in the formal sector. This shift has been considerable. Between 1954 and 1974, Gershuny estimates that as a percentage of all household expenditures on services, those expenditures on services purchased outside the home dropped from 56 per cent to 20 per cent whereas those expenditures on durables to produce services at home increased from 44 per cent to 80 per cent.[6]

This certainly underscores the argument for regarding the purchase of durables by households as capital investment in much the same way as we regard the purchase of equipment by firms as capital investment. The fact that the scale of these household purchases, at $26.4 billion in 1981, compares so closely with business investment of $28.7 billion in machinery and equipment in the same year, further underscores this point.

The analysis of the time budgets of members of households is also very revealing. The traditional dichotomy between paid work and leisure time used by mainstream economists does not hold up well. There is clearly a large block of time given over to informal work. What would be interesting to know more about is the rate at which this time block is expanding. We sense that this would give further insights into the distinction between formal productivity in the formal workplace and creative productivity in the informal work setting.

In conclusion, it would seem that Canada's GNP at market prices of about $350 billion in 1982 would be increased considerably if there were ways of calculating the value of economic activities in these sectors of the informal economy. An estimate by Statistics Canada suggests that the household sector alone might increase the GNP by about 40 per cent, and Ross and Usher estimate that the other sectors might add another 10 per cent. This would amount to another $175 billion added to the GNP. We point this out more to portray something of the magnitude of the activities in the informal economy than to suggest that we should make this adjustment simply to increase the GNP. That, in itself, would of course be no more than an act of self-delusion. What its inclusion would do, however, is lead economic policymakers to realize that the sound functioning and understanding of the informal economy in itself and in its relations with the formal economy have to be an integral part of the formulation of any set of public policy concerns...

Work and Social Benefits

Increased productivity, efficiency and control are essential goals of industrial production and technological innovation. Predictably, the closer we come to realizing these goals, there is a reduction in the number of persons involved in the process of industrial production. Over time, human labour has become less necessary in order to maintain and increase the aggregate national output of production. Recent technological advances in microelectronic technologies present to us the need for a quantum leap in the necessary adjustment processes as we face a further reduction in demand for human labour. The formal labour market has, to date, adjusted to this new reality by simply putting 10 per cent or more of the labour force on the dole.

The goals of mass industrial production processes have been to break down and rationalize as many tasks as possible into routine, constantly predictable acts. Our large, well-organized and closely administered labour forces in recent decades indicate the degree to which we have been successful in so shaping people toward these human labour and management practices. Increasingly, we have equally well prepared the ground, accordingly, for massive transfers of such acts to robotic devices and entities. This well-prepared ground is now beginning to experience that transfer, which is further advanced than most of us realize. It has not only imperceptibly touched us through our quartz watches and microwave ovens; but, our jobs — once a human preserve — are being sucked out from under our work forces at all levels by an unplanned yet radically effective tide of transfers. There are yet huge amounts of formal work and employment in Canada. However, more and more of it is going to robots rather than to people.

If we examine the issues of work and employment in the context of the whole economy, it quickly becomes evident that people want to work and, indeed, are working even though they may be unemployed. The notion of the "leisure society" is, frankly, a nonstarter. The prospect of such is, in reality, attractive to no one because our identities and the meanings of life are tied to what we can create through our skills, knowledge and perceptions. Although technologies have changed dramatically the ways in which production is accomplished, people have changed little, to the extent that their sense of self-worth, participation and people-contact, contribution and satisfaction is still mainly derived from work.

In this sense, the "work ethic" is still very much alive and well.

19 The Potential of Public Enterprise

CANADIAN UNION OF PUBLIC EMPLOYEES

In this second excerpt from the CUPE brief (see also chapter 4), an alternative economic strategy based on public enterprise is advanced. While neo-conservative critics have maligned the public sector, CUPE demonstrates the great potential of public enterprise.

We need a new strategy to address the real problems faced by ordinary Canadians.... This strategy must constitute a clear break with past and present economic policies. It must confront the serious structural economic problems we face in an honest and creative way. It must state what needs to be done, even if the remedies outlined are not popular at present. And it must challenge, directly, the prevailing argument propounded by business interests that the only way to resolve the crisis is to give private investors a completely free hand to restructure the economy according to their priorities.

The purpose of an alternate economic strategy must be to satisfy the basic social and economic needs of ordinary Canadians, rather than to maximize the profits of wealthy investors. It must create jobs, rather than use unemployment as a means of undermining the wages and job security of workers. It must promote socially useful investments, rather than speculation in finance, banking, real estate and foreign currency, no matter how profitable the latter activities are. It must focus on raising real wages and living standards, rather than sacrificing these to provide a more "favourable investment climate" for private capital.

And it must seek to improve the scope and quality of public services which are so essential to providing a decent standard of living for all Canadians, rather than to attempt to dismantle the social progress which working people have fought so hard to achieve over the past fifty years....

Fundamental to the implementation of an alternate economic strategy is the recognition that it is a mistake to give more say over economic decision making to private investors. What we need is to establish genuine public control over economic policy. This will entail new forms of involvement by — and accountability to — ordinary citizens....

The corporate sector has waged a remarkably successful campaign to discredit all forms of public ownership and control. This campaign has been immeasurably assisted by the actions of business-oriented governments, who have made no attempt to explore the very real possibilities which public ownership provides for democratic control by citizens.

Public enterprises have been modelled on the same hierarchical, authoritarian pattern as in the private sector, with the understandable result that the rights of workers, consumers, community residents and other groups of citizens have been largely ignored. All too often, failing industries and bankrupt corporations have been "nationalized" in a last-ditch effort to save them. This nationalization has usually been little more than bailing out private shareholders and transferring their debts to the public treasury.

When such enterprises fail to recover under public ownership, "government inefficiency and incompetence" are fingered as the culprits. At the same time, the former private investors who have too often been overcompensated for their property are free to place their capital into more promising areas of the economy.

Where public enterprises have been successful, they have frequently been sold to the private sector, or their profits have been channelled back to business via favourable pricing policies. With a few notable exceptions, governments in Canada have not wanted, nor attempted, to create model public enterprises. For such experiments, where successful, would pose a very real threat to their business supporters.

The reason government involvement in economic decision making is viewed with scepticism by many Canadians is precisely because, too frequently, it has *not* been carried out in the interests of citizens and taxpayers. Nor has it provided avenues for genuine democratic input. Government policies which reflect the priorities of business are unpopular, and quite rightly so.

Continued management of our economy according to the priorities of private investors, many of whom do not even reside in Canada, is inherently undemocratic. This dominance is also the reason why governments have followed economic policies which have sacrificed the interest of the majority of Canadians. But this does not mean that the public sector cannot be used to implement popular policies. Rather, it means that the subservience to private interest, which has characterized government economic policies until now, must be ended if we are going to use the public sector to rebuild our collapsing economy.

The choice we face is not between a continuation of prosperity resulting from the successful operation of private market forces on the one hand, and stagnation under greater public control on the other. It is between watching our living standards and job security erode as a result of policies designed to bolster profits at the expense of the majority of Canadians, and establishing new priorities which place the social and economic needs of working people first. More public ownership and effective, democratic public involvement in shaping economic policy is the only way the latter objective can be achieved.

Public Planning

When most Canadians hear the term "economic planning," they immediately envisage an impersonal, bureaucratic decision-making process by people who are removed from, and insensitive to, the problems and concerns of those affected by their decisions. Planning is viewed as too cumbersome, too top-heavy and too inefficient. Unfortunately, too much of the planning done by governments has conformed with this image.

What we need, instead, is a concept of planning which embodies widespread consultation throughout economic enterprises, including consultation with those who will actually do the work. We need a concept of planning which involves workers, local communities, popular organizations and all the various constituencies which will be affected. Instead of being secretive and modelled on the hierarchy of business organizations, it must be open and accessible to the public at all levels.

Moreover, economic plans must be widely discussed. There is little doubt that one of the principal reasons why public enterprises, crown corporations and government services are not popular is that they have prevented ordinary citizens (and employees) from participating in their decision-making process. Too often they have actively deterred popular involvement, viewing it as an obstacle to be overcome rather than as an integral part of the way they ought to be operating.

Economic planning at the national, regional, local and enterprise level must also take full account of the knowledge and skills of the people at each level. Planning is not a process where a handful of so-called experts determine the objectives and the means by which these objectives are to be implemented: it is a process which attempts to draw on the full resources of the people who will be involved. For example, workers at the level of the enterprise often know far more about certain aspects of the productive process than more senior staff who are remote from the job site. Competent planning will entail obtaining their views and incorporating these into the plans in a flexible and ongoing manner. It will also entail accepting their proposals for changes and modifications to the plans.

Similarly, local communities may be aware of problems or possibilities which would not be obvious to economists and planners who did not live in the area. (Too often local residents watch with amusement and disdain as inflexibly administered government projects come to grief because those in charge are unaware of local conditions.) Again, full and open discussions with people in these communities would ensure that appropriate additions or modifications were made in the plans....

The sense of alienation from government and government policy which most Canadians experience can only be overcome by ensuring that they have a real voice in economic decision making in the communities where they live and the enterprises where they work....

Investment Strategy

There is no shortage of investment funding in Canada. In recent years the ratio of savings to personal income has climbed dramatically. Economic insecurity has led many Canadians to limit their consumption so that they will have a nest egg if economic hardship comes. The following table shows the growth of the savings rate since 1974.

Despite the growth in savings, business investment declined in 1982 and is projected to decline further in 1983 and 1984. The problem, then, is not a shortage of capital, but an unwillingness of business to invest. In the face of such evidence, the need for government to take the lead in expanding investment is even more urgent.

Investment is the key to Canada's economic regeneration. But not any type of investment. The capital we invest should be targeted to the development of industries which will satisfy the social and economic needs of Canadians. This means that the criteria used to evaluate different investment opportunities must be broader than that of profitability. The impact on employment, the needs of local communities, the skill development of workers, the impact on our balance of payments and other considerations, especially of a social nature, must be also taken into account. Of course, such factors must be weighed carefully

TABLE 19-1
Growth of Savings, 1974-82

	Savings Rate (% Gross National Expenditure)
1974	9.9
1975	10.9
1976	10.0
1977	9.7
1978	11.1
1979	11.1
1980	11.2
1981	12.4
1982	13.7

Source: Marc Lalonde, *The Economic Outlook for Canada* (Ottawa, April 19, 1983), p. 21.

— no one wants to pour money into projects which are simply not viable.

But there are many projects which are rejected by the private sector on the grounds that they do not make quite as much profit as other, more speculative, ventures. There are investments — such as in the economic infrastructure — which contribute to improved efficiency throughout the economy. And there are other investments — energy conservation, for example — which make us less dependent on fluctuating world energy prices while contributing positively to our balance of payments. All these factors should be taken into account in determining an investment strategy.

There are many components of an alternate economic strategy which merit extensive consideration, including the questions of preventing a flight of capital, ensuring investment is channelled into the appropriate sectors of the economy, dealing with the balance of payments and developing a viable strategy for rebuilding our manufacturing industry.

At the same time, there are two questions of economic strategy where we feel we do have something constructive to put forward: public ownership could be used as a strategy for dealing with some of the key structural weaknesses of the economy; and basic public services could be expanded to satisfy the many unmet needs of Canadians and at the same time provide jobs for the growing number of unemployed.

The Need for More Public Ownership

There are many reasons why public ownership should be the central component of an alternate economic strategy. The first, and most important, is that it is necessary to break the stranglehold of the large multinational corporations over many areas of the economy. Public ownership provides the means to challenge the power of private corporations, limit their monopolistic practices and ensure that profits generated in our economy are used for further investment in socially desirable projects.

For example, the creation of downstream processing and manufacturing facilities to enable us to process our raw materials into manufactured goods will require substantial sums of investment capital which the corporations are unwilling to provide. Yet such investments are necessary if the objectives of new jobs and balanced economic development are to be achieved. Similarly, we need to give priority to investment in areas which will address major social needs, create jobs, reduce our dependence on foreign goods and services and improve our ability to control our pattern of economic development.

While an alternate economic strategy at this stage cannot provide a comprehensive blueprint on how public ownership can be used to get us out of our economic mess, there are a number of key economic sectors where it is possible to give a basic outline of what needs to be done. These are: resources, manufacturing, microtechnology and public housing.

One of the basic weaknesses of the Canadian economy is that far too much of our investment capital has been channelled into resource-extraction industries, such as the oil megaprojects. These projects are largely foreign owned. They provide few jobs. The profits are not widely shared among Canadians. They are highly capital intensive. They have resulted in an enormous expansion of our foreign debt. And, despite the huge subsidies and tax write-offs given to the resource companies, they have not been accompanied by the development of downstream processing facilities because the multinationals concerned are not interested in manufacturing in Canada.

Private control of our oil, mineral and forest industries has been accompanied by other major problems. These include pollution, regional dislocation, poor workplace health and safety, environmental abuses, and the exploitation of Native People. Public ownership would facilitate the adoption of policies designed to take account of the broader social and economic needs of Canadians, and especially those in communities directly affected by such investments.

Public ownership is also the only effective method to ensure that we benefit from the enormous profits being generated from our rich natural resources. The tax returns from this sector over the past decade are only a tiny fraction of what Canadians should be receiving. And they are diminishing as the companies become more and more adept at concealing their real rates of return.

Moreover, the past decade has seen a growing number of government assistance programs for these companies, resulting in even less of the tax revenues taken by federal and provincial treasuries being available to fund other programs.

Turning to mineral mining, the need to nationalize companies such as Inco has been recognized for many years. The disaster which has now befallen Sudbury as a result of Inco's failure to build downstream processing facilities or to reinvest its profits in the local community underlines why public control of our mineral resources is so vital.

The need for public ownership in forest products is also clear. While forestry, like mining, is now in a slump, this has been made far more severe because the forest companies have failed to develop a wood-processing industry.

It is incredible that we are importing furniture from Scandinavia, while exporting raw logs to the U.S., Japan and Europe. Much of the disruption facing towns affected by the present slump in export markets for lumber and pulp could be alleviated if large numbers of workers were employed in the manufacture of wood products for markets which do not fluctuate so wildly.

We desperately need a coherent manufacturing strategy designed to stop the collapse of our basic industries such as autos, farm machinery, electrical equipment, aviation components, transportation, metal fabrication, appliances and the like.

At present, we have nothing more than a series of ad hoc, unplanned interventions by governments to bail out, or subsidize, near-bankrupt firms. Not only are these policies not working: they do nothing to deal with the real structural causes of our manufacturing decline.

What is needed is the development of new crown corporations in key areas of manufacturing. A new crown corporation in auto parts, as recommended by the United Auto Workers (UAW), is long overdue. Indeed, there is a strong case for the development of a publicly owned auto industry producing a Canadian car.

In the transportation area, we need a massive expansion of our capacity to manufacture public transit equipment. Rising energy prices, environmental problems, safety considerations and the needs of urban residents all point to the urgent need for modernization of public transport across Canada. Rather than waiting for a crisis in urban transit, measures should be taken now to build a visible public transit industry which could supply our cities with Canadian-designed and Canadian-built equipment.

By providing municipalities with financial assistance, federal and provincial governments can guarantee a market for the output of new crown corporations in this sector.

The benefits of a new publicly owned, publicly controlled transit industry would be enormous. They include lower energy consumption, less reliance on imported oil, savings on the balance of payments, and employment growth in manufacturing, construction and the operation of the service itself. Such an industry would also facilitate reduction in pollution and other environmental hazards, open up the possibility of exporting Canadian technology, provide improved transport safety and lower health-care costs (as the use of accident-prone automobiles declines).

Public expansion in this area thus provides numerous positive advantages for the economy as a whole. It would not be a make-work project or a means of hiding the unemployment figures. Rather, it would constitute an important step towards creating a more rational and more economically viable transport system.

Public broadcasting also needs a major infusion of government resources if it is to do an effective job of satisfying the cultural, social and news requirements of Canadians. Private firms have already taken control of far too large a share of the television industry, to the detriment of Canadian content and the overall quality of service.

The decision by the CRTC (Canadian Radio-television and Telecommunications Commission) denying CBC the right to establish a second network, CBC-2, constituted a serious blow to the Canadian industry.

The private sector has demonstrated time and again that it is not interested in developing a major, independent Canadian television and film industry. It is therefore up to the public sector to step in and do the job.

Another area where public ownership and control is vital is microelectronics. Federal and provincial governments are currently providing generous subsidies for research and development in this area (especially in Ottawa's "Silicon Valley"). But they are allowing private companies to reap the entire benefit of this investment.

Increasingly, control over microelectronics means control over the future development of industry and commerce. The decisions now being made will have a profound effect on the lives of all Canadians. Yet the decisions of the corporations now guiding this development are not being taken with the needs of ordinary Canadians in mind. Rather, the private sector is guiding its development with the view to reducing employment, cutting labour costs, increasing worker productivity and tightening management control over the work process, regardless of the social impact and health consequences for workers.

As Canada's Telidon system confirms, we can develop, produce and sell new products in this sector of industry. However, if there is no systematic planning, and no attempt by governments to ensure that patent rights and production are maintained in Canada, our lead in some of these areas will quickly disappear and we will experience all the adverse consequences associated with foreign-controlled, branch-plant operations in other sectors of the economy.

Indeed, one of the key arguments supporting public ownership in microelectronics is that it will give us the opportunity to guide the development of our technology in a manner which will take into account the social and economic needs of Canadian workers. Instead of focusing on tightening work discipline and reducing employment, we can ensure that the microelectronics industry is used to expand services and provide workers with more control over their jobs.

The housing industry is another area where public expansion is vitally needed. At a time when the cost of housing is beyond the reach of young families; at a time when there is a critical shortage of new houses; and at a time when labour, technology and capital in the construction industry are lying idle, the need for public intervention is obvious. Yet the federal and provincial governments have been running down our public housing program.

In many western European countries, governments have entered the housing market in a major way, both as owners of public housing and as builders. As West Germany, Scandinavia and the Netherlands illustrate, public housing can be model housing if it is properly built and competently administered.

Aside from fulfilling an important social need, the construction of substantial numbers of public housing units would provide much needed jobs in the construction industry and in related building-supply industries. And, through the multiplier effect, it would also result in a major increase in spending and employment in other sectors of the economy. It would check profiteering by private landlords, while giving tenants an opportunity to rent decent accommodation at affordable prices.

Expansion in this sector would also have the beneficial effect of not being dependent upon significant amounts of foreign imports. Almost all the materials used are produced in Canada, while labour is also supplied domestically. Thus, it would have little adverse effect on our balance of payments. From the viewpoint of the economy as a whole, investment in domestically built public housing makes a good deal more sense than importing foreign-made consumer goods which exacerbate our balance of payments and produce no jobs in Canada.

Autos, public transport, communications, forest products and microelectronics illustrate the kind of public sector expansion required to deal with our economic problems. Conscious public planning, rather than acquiescence to the priorities dictated by multinational business, is vital to overcoming the economic crisis and the growing financial difficulties which the crisis is imposing on governments at federal, provincial and municipal levels....

Extend Public Services

Yet it is a mistake to assume that future growth in the above-mentioned sectors of the economy, even with significant public ownership, will generate the jobs Canadians so urgently require. If anything, the opposite is true. The number of people employed in industries such as manufacturing will fall because high-technology equipment is replacing workers at an accelerating pace.... An improved manufacturing base is a vital component of an alternate economic strategy. But it cannot, by itself, provide the key to full employment.

Service industries are not capital intensive. They are people intensive. The cost of creating jobs in the service sector is far less than in manufacturing, and only a tiny fraction of the cost in mining, forestry or oil extraction. Consequently, to expand employment, we must expand the service sector.

But it is not any type of service employment which ought to be expanded: public, rather than private, services should be the cornerstone of this expansion. There are persuasive reasons for this position. The social needs of Canadians are simply not being met at present....

Many of the services provided by the public sector are absolutely vital to a decent, civilized existence. They are of far more value in improving the lives of ordinary Canadians than alternate private sector spending.

For example, the provision of free, universal public education has been of incalculable benefit to millions of Canadians. True, it also provided the trained labour force that business required. But in the process it gave millions of Canadians opportunities they would otherwise not have had. Similarly, hospital insurance and medicare have also had an enormous — and positive — impact on the lives of most Canadians. Public hospital and medical coverage is cheaper, more comprehensive and of higher quality than that formerly provided by private enterprise. The problems we have with our health-care system stem not from the fact that it is publicly funded or that it is inherently inefficient but, rather, from the fact that it still has too many vestiges of the private sector encumbering its management and administration. For example, health insurance premiums constitute a source of unnecessary administrative costs. Funding through tax revenues, rather than insurance premiums, would sharply reduce administrative costs and still ensure that no Canadians fell through the safety net by missing payment of insurance premiums.

In a wide range of other areas of the economy, there can be little doubt that what is produced in the public sector is more socially valuable than that produced in the private sector. The problem is not that we have too much public spending, but rather that we do not have enough. Moreover, too much of the public spending we do have is of the wrong kind, that is, its purpose is purely to bolster business development.

Far from necessitating a reduction in the public sector, the present crisis underlines the need to begin a basic restructuring of economic priorities. If we cannot have more of everything, then we must at least ensure that what we do have is likely to satisfy our basic needs. At a time when the economic pie has stopped expanding, it is more — not less — important to see that our resources are allocated in the most socially desirable manner.

There is a pressing need for universal, high-quality day care. Only a tiny fraction of preschool children now have access to proper day-care centres. Surveys conducted by various provincial governments have repeatedly established that there is a large, unmet need for this service. Yet the development of day-care facilities has come to a virtual standstill as a result of restrictions on financing at federal and provincial levels.

We also need to restore funding to our educational system and provide new programs to satisfy the demand for adult education, special education for disadvantaged children, language education and similar concerns.

The state of our nursing homes across the country is abysmal. Virtually every week there is another horror story revealed about inadequate facilities or negligence on the part of nursing home operators. Old people are not being given decent care because we have failed to allocate sufficient resources to providing this service and because we have allowed unscrupulous private operators to profit from the needs of the elderly.

Our system of preventative medicine leaves much to be desired. Medicine has been viewed in terms of curing disease rather than promoting good health. Thus, we allow cigarette companies to claim tax deductions for advertising and promotion, while spending enormous sums on care for patients with lung cancer. The priorities are upside down.

We should also be expanding facilities for music, art, dance, the theatre and many other areas of popular culture. If our society can afford an Atari in every home and a video store on every street corner, it can also afford to provide funding for the facilities needed to encourage artistic creativity.

Municipal services in Canada are also in need of major improvements. It is true that Canadian municipalities have not witnessed the collapse in services which has occurred in many U.S. cities. But continued underfunding is a growing threat. It is very easy to ignore the importance of high-quality municipal services in making our communities pleasant, safe and interesting places to live. Parks and other recreational facilities play an important role in making cities liveable. Efficient garbage collection and street cleaning ensure high standards of sanitation. Community centres make an important contribution to local neighbourhoods. All these facilities which add to the quality of life are easily taken for granted.

Moreover, there are many other municipal services which remain inadequate. This is particularly true of social services. Care for the elderly, the disabled and others in need is not provided on a universal or consistent basis. In most cities, social and recreational facilities for the elderly, to give one example, are inadequate or nonexistent. Where they are provided, it is normally on the basis of demeaning means tests which attack the dignity of senior citizens and deter many others in need from applying. In these and many other areas, the need for greatly expanded municipal services is clear.

Urban public transit is another area where municipal services need major injections of funds. Compared with public transit in most western European cities, our facilities are rudimentary. Aside from the obvious benefits of reduced pollution, noise and congestion, public transit provides a vital service to those who do not have the option of owning cars. Moreover, increased use of public transit lowers consumption of gasoline (as car drivers leave their vehicles at home) and, in the process, reduces our dependency on imports of foreign oil, especially in eastern Canada.

The preceding list of new public services takes into account the one unused resource which we now have in great surplus — our two million unemployed. If we do not create public sector service jobs, those presently unemployed will have no jobs at all. There is no point in asking whether it would be better if they were to work in the private sector; the private sector has no jobs to offer them. Despite all the rhetoric about private sector expansion leading to job creation, the stark reality is that we have two choices: accept an unemployment level of over two million into the indefinite future *or* provide socially valuable public sector jobs. To us the choice seems perfectly clear.

The expansion of the public sector has other advantages. Insofar as it changes the pattern of consumption from private sector consumer goods, many of which are imported, to public sector services, it reduces imports and therefore assists the balance of payments. It also makes the economy less vulnerable to fluctuations in world markets.

The kind of public expansion outlined above does not involve make-work projects. It is not designed to conceal the number of unemployed. Rather, it fulfils pressing social needs — needs which our economy has failed to meet....

As Canadians we must begin to make a choice about the kind of society we want to live in and the way in which the resources generated within our economy are allocated. We must be prepared to assert that, in the future, social needs will take priority over the demands of business. We must be prepared to use public planning, public ownership and the expansion of the public sector as a means for resolving our present economic crisis.

20 | Moral Vision and Political Will

CANADIAN CONFERENCE
OF CATHOLIC BISHOPS

Canada's Catholic bishops electrified the country with their New Year's Day 1983 statement Ethical Reflections on the Economic Crisis. *No other source was as widely cited before the Macdonald Commission. In their presentation before the commission the bishops clarified their perspective on our socioeconomic order and identified Canada's major problems from the standpoint of social ethics. This excerpt includes the third part of their brief, together with a part of the introduction. In it the bishops, with their customary moral courage, set out the challenges facing Canadians.*

As was the case with Ethical Reflections, *the document for the Madonald Commission was prepared by the Social Affairs Commission of the Canadian Conference of Catholic Bishops (CCCB). This commission, composed of eight bishops from regions across Canada, has the major responsibility for elaborating the social teaching of Canada's Catholic bishops on matters of justice and peace. The document was approved in principle by the Executive Committee of the CCCB.*

In recent years, we have tried to stimulate some critical ethical reflections on Canada's economy through various social statements, working instruments and education projects.[1] Our experience to date, however, indicates that this is not always an easy endeavour. Ethics and economics have become separate disciplines in the historic evolution of liberal capitalism itself. The emphasis on economistic and mechanistic approaches has managed to drain the moral content out of economics as a discipline over the past century or more.[2] As a result, serious ethical discourse about the Canadian economy rarely occurs in our culture and society.

The Roman Catholic church, through almost a century of social teaching, has consistently maintained that there is an ethical order to be followed in the organization of an economy. This is evident, for example, in the writings of Pope John Paul II. In Catholic social teaching, the value and dignity of the human person lies at the centre of an economy based on justice. This means, in turn, that all persons in a given society should have the right of common access to, and use of, the goods produced by the economy.[3] In this context, peoples are meant to be the agents of their own history. Through their labour, workers are to be the subject not the object of production.[4] In turn, "capital" and "technology" are seen as the instruments of production. It follows, therefore, that people in general, and human labour in particular, take priority over both capital and technology in an economic order based on justice.

In general, this is the perspective from which we have attempted to stimulate some ethical reflections on the Canadian economy. This ethical perspective, in turn, is rooted in several major themes and principles developed in the scriptures and the social teachings of the church.... In addition, a particular pastoral methodology is generally used in the formulation of our ethical reflections.[5] This pastoral methodology involves a number of steps:

- being present with and listening to the experiences of the poor, the marginalized, the oppressed in our society (for example, the unemployed, the working poor, the welfare poor, exploited workers, Native Peoples, the elderly, the handicapped, small producers, racial and cultural minorities, etc.);
- developing a critical analysis of the economic, political and social structures that cause human suffering;
- making judgments in the light of Gospel principles and the social teachings of the church concerning social values and priorities;
- stimulating creative thought and action regarding alternative visions and models for social and economic development; and
- acting in solidarity with popular groups in their struggles to transform economic, political and social structures that cause social and economic injustices....

Given our perspective, we believe the fundamental challenge involves a combination of moral vision and political will. The primary task, in our view, is not simply a question of how governments can better manage the economy in the new high-tech industrial age. It is not a question of how to make people adjust, accommodate, adapt, retrain, relocate and lower their expectations. What we are facing are some basic structural problems in our economy that reveal a moral disorder in our society.

The challenge before us, therefore, is to search for alternative visions and models for the future development of our socioeconomic order in the new industrial age. As we emphasized above, the basic social contradiction of our times is the structural domination of capital and technology over people, over labour, over communities. What is required is a radical inversion of these structural relationships. In other words, ways must be found for people to exercise more effective control over both capital and technology so that they may become constructive instruments of creation by serving the basic needs of people and communities. This requires, in turn, that efforts be made to stimulate social imagination concerning alternative economic visions and models.

There are, of course, some built-in problems in our culture and society which limit our capacities for social imagination.[6] For example, the restricted ideological choice between two systems, either capitalism or communism, tends to stifle social imagination. At the same time, the dominant forces of transnational capital and technology largely dictate what is desirable and feasible, thereby limiting the capacities of nations and peoples to develop viable options. In addition, social imagination is further hampered by the kind of technological rationality that prevails in our culture today. This is the kind of reasoning that avoids fundamental questions by reducing everything to factual and quantifiable knowledge through a technical means-ends process. Finally, the continued problems of personal selfishness, possessive individualism, pursuit of narrow self-interest and collective greed prevent some people from developing a capacity for creative social imagination.

It is essential that people find ways of breaking out of these dominant modes of thought and develop new ways of thinking about social and economic alternatives.[7] We believe that the moral principles outlined above [not reprinted here] provide some guide posts for thinking about alternative visions and models. At this point, we do not intend to put forward detailed proposals or strategies. Our primary concern is to stimulate more creative thinking about social and economic alternatives. We do, however, have several questions, comments and suggestions regarding alternative directions.

Moral Purpose

First, what can be done to develop a clear statement of purpose regarding Canada's socioeconomic order that reflects basic moral principles? From our perspective, the primary purpose of our socioeconomic order should be to develop our resources to serve the basic needs of all people for a more fully human life in this country. This includes such basic life needs as adequate food, clothing, housing, education, employment, health care, and energy. It also means putting an emphasis on the integral development of peoples, the value and dignity of human work, the preferential option for the poor and the marginalized, and the priority of labour. What can be done to develop a process that leads towards a consensus on these and related principles as the foundation stone of our economy?

Social Goals

Second, what can be done to develop a new set of social goals that adequately reflect these basic purposes and principles? From our perspective, this involves a renewed national commitment to full employment, with an emphasis on permanent and meaningful jobs, and to new patterns of work, with adequate personal or family income. It also entails a fresh commitment to the development of more meaningful and effective forms of providing basic social services (for example, education, health care, social security benefits, etc.). These social objectives, in turn, require a commitment to finding new and more effective ways of redistributing wealth and power among both people and regions in this country. What can be done to develop a consensus around these and related social goals for the future development of this country?

Empower the Powerless

Third, what can be done to empower the poor and the marginalized to play a more meaningful and effective role in shaping the future development of our socioeconomic order? Across this country, there are working and nonworking people, men and women, in communities — small farmers, fisherpeople, factory workers, forestry workers, miners, Native People, office workers, people on welfare, public service workers, small-business people, and many others — who have a creative and dynamic contribution to make in shaping the social and economic future of this country. A clear social commitment is required to enable these people to truly become subjects of production and subjects of their own history. What steps can be taken to develop or redistribute resources and means for production in order to achieve this objective?

Economic Planning

Fourth, what can be done to develop more participatory and effective forms of economic planning for the future development of our society? From our perspective, a new approach to both centralized and decentralized planning may be required. The new economic forces of transnational capital/technology mean that nation-states must engage in centralized planning in order to ensure the realization of the common good and basic moral principles.[8] This may require the nationalization of key sectors of Canada's economy. Yet, experience has also shown that nationalization does not, in and of itself, guarantee popular participation in economic planning. Thus, decentralized forms of economic planning and decision making are required to ensure the participation of workers, the poor and the marginalized. What steps can be taken to develop this kind of approach to economic planning in this country?

Economic Strategies

Fifth, what can be done to develop new economic strategies based on integral, self-reliant models of development? As a country, we are blessed with an abundance of resources required to serve the basic needs of all our people for food, clothing, housing, employment, education, health care, energy and related needs. A new commitment, however, is needed to break the bonds of dependency and develop new economic strategies based on self-reliance. At one level, this means increasing the self-sufficiency of our industries to manufacture our natural resources as finished products for markets. At another level, it means increasing the capacities of local communities and regions to design models of economic development to serve the basic needs of their communities. What steps can be taken to make these kinds of self-reliant economic strategies a priority in this country?

Social Ownership

Sixth, what can be done to promote new forms of social ownership and control by communities and workers in our society? Indeed, the road to self-reliance itself requires new forms of ownership and control over the means of production. If communities are going to develop their resources to serve basic human and social needs, it is essential that they have effective control over the kinds of capital and technology required to achieve these objectives. If working people are going to exercise their right to become subjects of production, then new forms of worker-controlled industries need to be developed. Across the country, there are a few significant experiments in community- and worker-controlled enterprises that may offer some insights into the problems and possibilities to be faced. What steps can be taken to put a priority on stimulating new forms of social ownership and control by communities and workers?

Social Production

Seventh, what can be done to design more sustainable and socially useful forms of production and development? This means, for example, giving serious attention to developing forms of industrial production that make greater use of renewable energy sources (for example, electricity, sun, wind, methane, tidal power, etc.) rather than maintaining sole dependence on nonrenewable energy (for example, oil, gas, coal, etc.). It also means developing strategies to assist workers and industries involved in military production to redirect their energies into more socially useful forms of production. These social objectives, along with corresponding conversion strategies, need to be given serious attention in future economic planning. What steps can be taken now to design and implement more sustainable and socially useful forms of production for the future?

Global Solidarity

Eighth, what can be done to develop economic strategies in the context of global solidarity? Given the international realities of economic interdependence today, any significant changes in Canada's economic strategies are bound to have an effect on working people in other countries. This is especially critical for the poor countries of the Third World. It is important, therefore, to establish new forms of consultation, not only with the countries affected but especially with the workers in relevant industries. If, for example, specific strategies were proposed to strengthen the textile and clothing sectors of our economy, then direct consultations should take place with the workers in related Southeast Asian industries that would be affected by such changes. What steps therefore could be taken to ensure that this kind of global solidarity is actualized in the process of developing new economic strategies?

Taken together, these challenges involve basic value choices about what kind of nation and people we want to become. As a country, we have the resources, the capital, the technology and, above all else, the aspirations and skills of working men and women required to build an alternative economic future. Yet, the people of this country have seldom been challenged to envision and develop alternatives to the dominant economic model that governs our society. What is required, in the long run, is a dynamic public process designed to stimulate social imagination, develop alternative models and forge a new cultural vision in this country.

Notes

Introduction

[1] Hugh Thorburn, a well-known political scientist from Queen's University, was hired by the Macdonald Commission to analyze which interest groups made submissions to it. Among other things, he found that there were many new types of groups submitting briefs to this commission that had not done so to the previous royal commissions on the Canadian economy. Macdonald received 741 briefs in total compared with 297 to the Gordon Commission (1957) and 331 to the Rowell-Sirois (1937). Business associations and private companies made 250 submissions compared with 59 for labour. For the popular sector, the breakdown was as follows: Native Peoples' organizations, 27; women's groups, 34; religious organizations, 12; social service and health agencies, 37; and voluntary and special interest associations, 97. As a quantitative study, Thorburn's paper shows which groups participated, but it does not attempt any qualitative analysis of the briefs, and for this reason its perspective is limited. This study will eventually be published by the commission along with other papers and materials relevant to its work.

[2] For a mainstream view of what a royal commission is supposed to do, see Robert Fulford, *Saturday Night*, February 1985.

[3] In some instances, royal commissions are also a way to showcase the leadership potential of a "political heavyweight" who is being groomed for a new leadership position in a political party or in the state.

[4] Many of the commissioners and staff were openly critical of the value of the public hearings on the grounds that groups like trade unions or church groups were speaking on behalf of special interest organizations. By contrast, when business presented its briefs, the commission members believed that the private sector was speaking in the national interest.

[5] Recently, royal commissions are turning more and more to lawyers for advice. Lawyers have replaced political scientists and sociologists as government troubleshooters. It is significant that the executive director of the commission, Gerald Godsoe, is a corporate lawyer from Halifax and well connected with the business elite in Toronto. High-priced legal talent not only provides a certain kind of expertise but makes it appear as if justice has been done.

[6] See, for instance, Richard Simeon's fine study, *The History of Canadian Federalism*, which will be published by the Macdonald Commission.

[7] The Macdonald Commission bravely collected all the press reaction to it in two volumes. In a nutshell, what these volumes show is that the commission had been blown out of the water by its ineptitude.

[8] D.J Daley, "Canada's Comparative Advantage: Implications for Industrial Strategy," in *International Business: A Canadian Perspective* (Addison-Wesley, 1981), p. 701. Daley believes that workers get higher wages as a result of moving to the high-productivity sector. Strikingly absent from this discussion is any mention of workers losing their jobs through technological change.

[9] *The People's Report: A Social and Economic Alternative for B.C.* (Vancouver, 1985), p. 11.

[10] The data regarding savings from inventory control and better materials-handling techniques is from the *Globe and Mail*, "Firms urged to adopt flexible manufacturing," November 16, 1984. For a scathing account of North American management techniques, see Robert Reich, *The Next American Frontier* (New York: Times Books, 1983).

[11] Barbara J.C. Smith, "Adjusting to structural changes key to new growth," *Globe and Mail*, March 11, 1985, p. B-6.

[12] Donald Daley et al., "Corporate Profit Drop Is the Worst Since the 1930s," *Canadian Business Review*, Autumn 1982, p. 7.

[13] The figures come from the U.S. Bureau of Labor Statistics.

[14] Daley, "Canada's Comparative Advantage."

[15] Bruce Wilkinson calculates that free-traders estimate that income gains from broad free trade arrangements will be in the order of 7 to 8% maximum. Canada's productivity differential is of the order of 20 to 25%. This leaves a productivity gap of 15%!

[16] Barbara J.C. Smith, *Globe and Mail*, November 19, 1984, p. B-4. She adds that because Canadian utilization rates are significantly below American levels, this adversely affects business's decision to invest in plant and equipment.

[17] Daley, "Canada's Comparative Advantage," p. 698.

[18] The quote comes from Kristan Palda, a Queen's University economics professor, and is cited by the *Globe and Mail*'s business columnist, Ronald Anderson, in his daily column, February 7, 1985.

[19] *Globe and Mail*, April 23, 1983, p. B-11.

[20] *Globe and Mail*, March 13 and 15, 1985, Report on Business.

[21] This statement was originally made on November 19, 1984. Subsequently, Macdonald reiterated his stand in a number of public statements. See *Toronto Star*, February 24, 1984, and *Globe and Mail*, March 5, 1985.

[22] *The People's Report.*

[23] See Fred Lazar, "The Unresolved Debate: Free Trade/Industrial Policy," *The Atkinson Review of Canadian Studies* (Toronto: York University, April 1985).

[24] For a detailed critique of the literature and a summary of the arguments of Canadian economists, see Bruce Wilkinson, "Commercial Policy and Free Trade with the United States," in Brian Tomlin and Maureen Molot, eds., *Canada Among Nations 1984: A Time of Transition* (Toronto: James Lorimer, 1985).

[25] The list is cited in Fred Lazar, *The New Protectionism: Non-Tariff Barriers and Their Effects on Canada* (Toronto: James Lorimer, 1981), pp. 53-54.

[26] Ibid., p. 67.

[27] Alain Lipietz, *Le Monde Diplomatique*, le 8 juin 1983.

[28] *Globe and Mail*, February 13, 1985.

[29] Lazar, *New Protectionism*, p. 57.

[30] Ibid.

[31] In a recent background document on small business released by the minister of regional industrial expansion, 96% of all firms in Canada had sales of less than $2 million in 1980. Department of Regional Industrial Expansion, "Consultation Paper on Small Business" (Ottawa, 1985).

[32] For a detailed account of American legislation, consult Lazar, *New Protectionism*.

[33] Robert Lawrence, *Can America Compete?* (Washington D.C.: Brookings Institution, 1984), cited in *New York Review of Books*, September 27, 1984, p. 30.

[34] *Globe and Mail*, March 25, 1985.

[35] Wonnacott, *Canada/United States*, p. 16.

[36] Daley, "Canada's Comparative Advantage."

[37] Wonnacott, *Canada/United States*, p. 9.

[38] Marie-France Toinet, "Les risques de la seconde phase reaganienne," *Le Monde Diplomatique*, janvier 1985. I have drawn extensively on her excellent article for the information in this and succeeding paragraphs.

[39] "Do We Need an Industrial Policy," *Harper's*, February 1985.

[40] Ibid., p. 37.

[41] Ibid., p. 39.

[42] *Globe and Mail*, March 28, 1985.

[43] S.F. Kaliski, "Trends, Changes, and Imbalances: A Survey of the Canadian Labour Market," Study prepared for the Macdonald Commission, 1984. Women who are already trapped in low-paying job ghettos are going to be worse off, without any possibility of finding regular and decent employment each time they look for work.

[44] André Gorz, *Farewell to the Working Class: An Essay on Post-Industrial Socialism* (London: Pluto Press, 1980), p. 70.

[45] The government does not speak with one voice on this essential issue. It has released a spate of policy positions *grosso modo* on the need for an industrial strategy. These different position papers review the options as well as propose a new economic policy framework for the 1980s and 1990s. The most articulate and comprehensive statement by the former Liberal government is a position paper prepared by the Department of External Affairs, *Canadian Trade Policy for the 1980's* (Ottawa: Minister of Supply and Services Canada, 1983).

[46] Robert Boyer, "From Growth to Crisis: Changing Linkages between Industrial and Macro-economic Policy" (CNRS/CEPREMAP, Paris, France), paper presented to the Brookings Conference on Industrial Policy in France and Implications for the United States, September 22-28, 1984.

[47] Ibid.

[48] The Economic Council of Canada has published an endless number of studies devoted to this partisan position. See, for instance, Peyton Lyon, *Canada-United States Free Trade and Canadian Independence* (Ottawa, 1975). For one of the most highly ideological attacks on the concept of an industrial strategy, see the recent study commissioned by the Ontario Economic Council, William G. Watson, *A Primer on the Economics of Industrial Policy* (Toronto, 1983).

[49] For an excellent account of the importance of technology in Canadian discourse, see Arthur Kroker, *Technology and the Canadian Mind: Innis/McLuhan/Grant* (Montreal: New World Perspectives, 1984).

[50] Rudolph Bahro, *Socialism and Survival* (London: Heretic Books, 1982), p. 57.

1: Economic Decline in Canada

[1] Statistics Canada, *The Labour Force*, Cat. no. 71-001 (March 1983).

[2] Richard Deaton, "Unemployment: Canada's Malignant Social Pathology," *Perception*, Spring/Summer 1983, pp. 14-19.

[3] See Social Planning Council of Metropolitan Toronto, "Unemployment in Toronto, Hidden and Real," *Working Paper for Full Employment #1* (1980).

[4] Statistics Canada, *The Labour Force*, Cat. no. 71-001 (December 1982).

[5] Ibid., Table 41, p. 78.

[6] Social Planning Council of Metropolitan Toronto, *And the Poor Get Poorer* (1983).

[7] Ibid., p. 101.

8 We have commented on these arguments in our review of *The Task Force Report on the Labour Market* and *The Task Force Report on Unemployment Insurance* in Social Planning Council of Metropolitan Toronto, *A Job for Everyone: A Response to Unemployment Policies in Canada* (1982).

9 Employment and Immigration, *The Canadian Economy and Its Implications for Immigration* (June 1983). Reported in *Globe and Mail*, September 13, 1983, p. 8.

10 Statistics Canada, *The Labour Force*, Cat. no. 71-001 (August 1981, December 1982).

11 *Globe and Mail*, October 11, 1983, p. B3.

12 Department of Finance, *The Current Economic Situation and Prospects for the Economy in the Short and Medium Term* (November 1981).

13 John Britton and James Gilmour, *The Weakest Link* (Science Council of Canada, 1978).

14 Economic Council of Canada, *The Bottom Line* (Ottawa, 1983), p. 14.

15 Arthur Donner, "How Big Is the Public Sector?" *Toronto Star*, October 22, 1983.

16 Economic Council of Canada, *The Bottom Line*, p. 15.

17 Social Planning Council of Metropolitan Toronto, "Poverty and the Labour Market," *Working Paper for Full Employment #4* (1981).

18 James Bagnall, *Financial Post*, August 27, 1983.

19 *Financial Post*, August 27, 1983, p. 1.

20 H. Clare Pentland, "A Study of the Changing Social Economic and Political Background of the Canadian System of Industrial Relations" (Ottawa: Privy Council Office, 1968).

21 Economic Council of Canada, *The Bottom Line*, p. 12.

22 S. Bowles, D. Gordon and T. Weisskopf, *Beyond the Wasteland* (New York: Anchor Press/Doubleday, 1983), pp. 122-49.

23 Robert Reich, *The Next American Frontier* (New York: New York Times Books, 1983).

24 *Globe and Mail*, "Report on Business Report on Productivity," April 25, 1983, p. B11.

25 Capital stock refers to the machinery and equipment used to produce goods and services. The quality of capital stock depends on the level and type of investment by private industry. — Ed.

26 Economic Council of Canada, *The Bottom Line*, p. 115.

27 Interview with Barry Bluestone and Bennett Harrison, *Working Papers*, January/February 1983, pp. 43-44.

28 Office of Economic Policy Planning and Research of the State of California, "International Economic Performance and Comparative Tax Structure," Unpublished report, January 20, 1981. Cited in Bowles et al., *Beyond the Wasteland*, p. 421.

29 Kenneth N. Matziorinis, "The Effectiveness of Tax Incentives for Capital Investment," *Canadian Taxation*, Fall 1980, pp. 172-79.

30 Ibid., p. 179.

2: Can Canada Compete?

1 *Financial Post*, October 29, 1983.

2 Jack Wayman, "Electronics Industries Association, U.S.A.," *USA Today*, March 1, 1983.

3 *Business Week*, March 29, 1982.

4 Workers in these three industries comprise the UAW membership, although it is usually thought of as just auto workers. — Ed.

[5] Local-content requirements are sometimes a part of government policy for developing an industry. This is the case for the Mexican auto industry and Japanese aerospace production. — Ed.
[6] *Business Week*, March 28, 1983.
[7] *Wall Street Journal*, November 7, 1983.

4: Scapegoating the Public Sector

[1] Hugh Stretton, "Business and Government," *Australian Journal of Public Administration*, vol. 36, no. 1 (March 1977).

5: The Rise and Fall of the Welfare State

[1] Social Planning Council of Metropolitan Toronto, "The Erosion of Unemployment Insurance," *Social Infopac*, vol. 1, no. 5 (December 1982).
[2] Social Planning Council figures.
[3] Ibid.
[4] Gosta Esping-Anderson, "After the Welfare State," *Working Papers*, May/June, 1983, pp. 36-41.
[5] Ibid.
[6] Social Planning Council of Metropolitan Toronto, "With No Stigma Attached: Family Allowances and the Question of Universality," *Social Infopac*, vol. 2, no. 1 (February 1983).
[7] Michael Mendelson, *Universal or Selective* (Ontario Economic Council, 1981), p. 16.
[8] Canada, Department of Finance, *Analysis of Federal Tax Expenditures for Individuals* (Ottawa, November 1981), pp. 12, 13.
[9] Kenneth Matziorinis, "The Effectiveness of Tax Expenditures for Capital Investment," *Canadian Taxation*, Fall 1980, pp. 172-79; and Social Planning Council estimates.
[10] Bob Kuttner, "Growth with Equity," *Working Papers*, September/October 1981.

8: The Exclusion of Women from Economic Planning

[1] H.A. Innis, *The Fur Trade in Canada* (Toronto: University of Toronto Press, 1930).
[2] Lourdes Beneria, "Some Questions about the Origin of the Division of Labour by Sex in Rural Societies," in *Women in Rural Development: Critical Issues* (International Labour Organization, 1980), pp. 11-15.
[3] *Vancouver Province*, April 30, 1980.
[4] Thompson, Berwick and Pratt, *Social Plan, Tumbler Ridge, Northeast Sector, B.C.*, Submitted to B.C. Ministry of Municipal Affairs and Housing (Victoria, B.C.: Queen's Printer, March 23, 1978).
[5] See, for example: Alice H. Amsden, *The Economics of Women and Work* (Penguin, 1980); Scott Burns, *The Household Economy: Its Shape, Origins and Future* (Beacon Press, 1975); Helga E. Jacobson, "Women, Society and Change: Perspectives on the Division of Labour," in G.B. Hainsworth, *Southeast Asia: Women, Changing Social Structure and Cultural Continuity* (University of Ottawa Press, 1981), pp. 19-25; Dorothy E. Smith, "A Peculiar Eclipsing: Women's Exclusion from Men's Culture," *Women's Studies International Quarterly*, vol. 1 (1978), pp. 281-95; Kate M. Young, "A Methodological Approach to Analysing the Effects of Capitalist Agriculture on Women's Role and Their Position within the Community," in

Women in Rural Development: Critical Issues (International Labour Organization, 1980), pp. 4-10.

6 See: *Northern B.C. Women's Task Force Report on Single Industry Resource Communities* (Vancouver: Women's Research Centre, 1977); and *Beyond the Pipeline* (Vancouver: Women's Research Centre, 1979).

7 Public Commission on Social and Community Service Cutbacks, "Commission Interim Report" (Vancouver, B.C., July 1982), p. 8.

8 Women's Research Centre, "Energy Development and Social Institutions," Presentation to the Second International Forum on the Human Side of Energy, August 1981, p. 12.

9 National Council of Welfare, *Women and Poverty* (Ottawa: NCW, October 1979).

10 B.C. Federation of Labour, "Submission to the Federal Task Force on Micro-Electronics" (Vancouver: BCFL, July 23, 1982).

9: The Persistence of Inequality

1 Julie White, *Current Issues for Women in the Federal Public Service* (Ottawa: Canadian Advisory Council on the Status of Women, May 1983).

2 *Toronto Star*, October 14, 1982.

3 Canadian Union of Public Employees, *Facts*, August/September 1982, p. 5.

4 Ontario Federation of Labour (OFL), *Parental Rights and Daycare* (Toronto, April 1982).

5 United Nations Convention on the Elimination of All Forms of Discrimination Against Women, Article 11, section 2(b), ratified by Canada, July 1980.

6 Reported in *Toronto Star*, February 25, 1982; reprinted in OFL, *Parental Rights*, p. 6.

7 Summarized OFL, *Parental Rights*, p. 5.

8 National Action Committee on the Status of Women (NAC), Brief to Commission of Inquiry into Part-time Work, January 1983.

9 General Conference of the ILO, Convention No. 100, Convention concerning Equal Remuneration for Men and Women Workers for Work of Equal Value.

10 La Charte des droits et libertés de la personne, Article 19.

11 Lynn Kaye, "A Review of the Enforcement of Equal Pay for Work of Equal Value Legislation in Canada," Presented to the Women, the Law and the Economy Conference, Banff, Alberta, October 14-16, 1983.

12 *Public Sector Compensation Restraint Act*, tabled June 1982, sections 8 and 9.

13 National Action Committee on the Status of Women, "The Impact of New Technology on Women and Employment," Brief presented to the Labour Canada Task Force and the Canada Employment and Immigration Advisory Council, July 1982.

14 White, *Current Issues*, pp. 3-4.

15 Treasury Board of Canada, News Release, June 27, 1983, *Affirmative Action in Federal Public Service*, at p. 4, states:

> The service-wide special measures for women are designed to increase the number of women at managerial levels of the Public Service. Treasury Board will establish service-wide quantitative goals for women in the Management Category and will communicate these to departments in September, 1983. To achieve these goals, the Public Service Commission will be identifying women with management potential and ensuring that departments are aware of them when they staff management positions.

[16] NAC, Brief to the Commission of Inquiry into Part-Time Work, January 1983.

[17] White, *Current Issues*, p. 18.

[18] Canadian Centre for Occupational Health and Safety, News Release, "VDTs — Evidence Incomplete," Hamilton, January 11, 1983.

[19] Minister of Employment and Immigration, News Release, November 10, 1982, on NEEDS program....

[20] Policy Formulation Branch, Ministry of State for Economic Development, January 26, 1983.

[21] This issue is explored further in the section of this submission entitled "Employment and Wage Trends and the Political Impact" that is not reproduced here. — Ed.

[22] *Economist*, October 22, 1983, p. 74.

[23] S. Gustaffson, "Lifetime Patterns of Labour Force Participation," in *Working Papers* (Stockholm: Swedish Centre for Working Life, 1982).

10: *Northern Neglect*

[1] The actual signatories of the agreement are the Northern Quebec Inuit Association (NQIA), the Grand Council of the Crees (of Quebec), the Government of Quebec, the Government of Canada, Hydro-Québec, la Société de développement de la Baie James and la Société d'énergie de la Baie James. Under the agreement, Makivik succeeds NQIA as the Inuit Native party to ensure the full implementation of the agreement and to protect the rights of Inuit beneficiaries.

[2] Inuit aboriginal rights which do not relate to land in Quebec, such as those relating to family law and other customary rights, have not been surrendered or extinguished. In addition, aboriginal rights in the offshore surrounding northern Quebec still exist in favour of northern Quebec Inuit.

[3] The right of Canada's aboriginal peoples to be different, that is, to maintain their own identity, is supported by Quebec's Human Rights Commission. See *Native Rights in Quebec: The Need to Raise the Level of Discussion — A Commentary by La Commission des droits de la personne du Québec* (September 1980), p. 19. See also the working paper of the Commission des droits de la personne entitled, *L'action positive et la charte des droits et libertés de la personne* (March 1981), pp. 34-35.

[4] See the judgment of Mr. Justice Rand in *St.-Ann's Island Shooting and Fishing Club* v. *The King* (1950), S.C.R. 211, where he refers to the federal responsibility as "a political trust of the highest obligation."

[5] For purposes of comparison with the United States, see Hall, *The Federal-Indian Trust Relationship* (Washington, D.C.: Institute for the Development of Indian Law, 1979).

[6] S.C. 1912, c. 45; S.Q. 1912, c. 7.

[7] In regard to nonrenewable resource development, see Nigel Bankes, *Resource-leasing Options and the Settlement of Aboriginal Claims* (Canadian Arctic Resources Committee [CARC], Ottawa, 1983), at page 190 where the author concludes: "The bottom line of the James Bay and Northern Quebec Agreement is that Cree and Inuit are in a very poor position to participate in resource development in their traditional areas," since mineral rights in all land areas remain vested in Quebec and existing rights of third parties are protected.

[8] The Canadian Charter of Rights and Freedoms in Part I of the Constitution Act, 1982, would continue to apply. An aboriginal charter of rights in Part II would deal with aboriginal and treaty rights as well as other funda-

mental rights essential to the ongoing development of Canada's aboriginal peoples, as distinct peoples.

9 See section 35 of the Constitution Act, 1982. Due to the inclusion of section 35 in Canada's Constitution, it is far from certain that Parliament could "extinguish" aboriginal rights in the future without amending the Constitution.

10 See the DIAND pamphlet entitled *In all Fairness: A Native Claims Policy* (Ottawa, 1981), p. 25.

11 See Annex I of this brief where the nature of extent of federal responsibilities in regard to Inuit and the region in and around northern Quebec are listed.

12 For example, section 2.12 of the James Bay and Northern Quebec Agreement clearly provides that existing federal and Quebec programs will continue to apply to northern Quebec Inuit.

13 See page 101 of the DIAND Report.

14 See Quebec Treasury Board decision of July 6, 1982, #140018.

15 This position is often reflected in SAGMAI, Quebec's secretariat concerned with Native affairs (Secretariat des affaires intergouvernmentales en milieu inuit et amérindien).

16 The consent of the Native parties to the agreement is provided for generally in section 2.15, as well as at the end of each chapter, of the agreement.

17 The collective or communal nature of aboriginal rights has been recognized by the Supreme Court of Canada. For example, see *Calder* v. *A.-G. of British Columbia* (1973), 34 D.L.R. (3d) 145.

18 Nonconsumptive uses of resources and habitats include photographic expeditions, nature tours and other recreational and research activities.

19 The above principles on cultural property have been adapted from those found in the Nunavut Agreement-in-Principle respecting Archaeology, which was agreed to in principle by the Office of Native Claims of Indian Affairs and Northern Development on July 23, 1983. No similar recognition of rights or principles exists in favour of northern Quebec Inuit.

20 This view is reinforced in Task Force on Canadian Unity, *A Future Together: Observations and Recommendations* (January 1979), p. 59, which recommends that governments provide increased funding to Native Peoples to "enable them to undertake historical research and to publish histories of their tribes and communities."

21 The right to self-determination is being used here in the domestic (or internal) sense and not in the sense of declaring international sovereignty. For a similar usage under U.S. legislation, see Indian Self-Determination and Education Assistance Act, 25 U.S.C. 450, 455-458.

22 The right to self-determination is proclaimed in the United Nations Charter as well as the International Covenant on Economic, Social and Cultural Rights and the International Convenant on Civil and Political Rights. Canada has ratified these conventions.

23 Inuit do not have any monopoly on neglect. For socioeconomic conditions among status Indians, see Indian Affairs and Northern Development, *Indian Conditions: A Survey* (Ottawa, 1980).

24 Lack of federal-Quebec cooperation continues [1983 — Ed.] to be highly problematic in our region.

25 See the Act Respecting the Organization of the Government (Bill C-152) at sections 15 et seq.

26 See section 33 of Bill C-152 where "economic and regional development agreement" and "general development agreement" are defined to mean agreements with the government of a province.

[27] See sections 2.12 and 29.0.2 of the agreement, which specifically provide that existing federal programs shall continue to be available to northern Quebec Inuit on the same basis as they are available to other Inuit and Indians. In addition, continuing federal responsibility for Inuit was reaffirmed in the preamble to the James Bay and Northern Quebec Native Claims Settlement Act, S.C. 1976-77, c. 32, which act approved and declared valid the agreement.

[28] See section 36(1) (b) of the Constitution Act, 1982.

[29] See sections 6(4) and 15 of the Constitution Act, 1982.

11: The Need for an Industrial Strategy

[1] There was even more foreign capital in Canada than in the United State in 1978.

[2] Statistics Canada, *Canada's International Investment Position, 1977*, Cat. no. 67-202, pp. 33, 36.

[3] Statistics Canada, *Corporations and Labour Unions Returns Act, Report for 1979* (1981), pp. 39-41.

[4] *Bank of Canada Review*, September 1983, T. 70.

[5] Ibid, T. 71.

[6] G. Bruce Doern, "The Mega-Project Episode and the Formulation of Canadian Economic Development Policy," *Canadian Public Administration* 26 (Summer 1983).

[7] A strategy oriented towards market access may determine the activities of a company; in the automotive industry, for example, a firm may give special attention to manufacturing sports cars in order to occupy this market segment. For the economy as a whole, however, such a strategy, instead of enriching the industrial fabric, leaves it more fragile. A technology-oriented approach leading to a vertical integration of all production-related activities would help to avoid these pitfalls and to increase our overall competitiveness.

[8] N. Kaldor, *Causes of the Slow Rate of Growth of the U.K.* (Cambridge University Press, 1966).

[9] Robert Boyer and Jacques Mistral, *Internationalisation, technologie, rapport salarial: quelle(s) issue(s)?*, CEPREMAP, No. 8212, Paris.

[10] *Bank of Canada Review*, October 83, R 71.

[11] Production industries' equipment includes tractors and farm machinery, mining equipment, and other goods, such as those required for production and transport of energy, construction, and machinery transportation. We also include in these sectors the distribution of information, which is necessary to support technical interdependencies and to be able to choose the most productive technologies. A committee of the House of Commons published a report in 1981 entitled "Canada's Trade Challenge," which recommends measures such as furthering the exports of projects involving equipment goods, either in the area of industrial complexes (oil refineries, petrochemical or chemical complexes, pulp and paper plants, and mines) or in the the area of infrastructures (transport systems, telecommunications, electric power plants, hospitals and schools). In these areas Canada's potential has not yet been sufficiently exploited.

[12] *Financial Post*, October 15, 1983.

12: The Pitfalls of Free Trade

[1] Canada, External Affairs, Ministry of Supply and Services Canada, *A Review of Canadian Trade Policy, A Background Document to the Canadian*

Trade Policy for the 1980's (1983), p. 133. This document will be referred to subsequently as *Background*.

[2] U.S. Department of Commerce, Bureau of Economic Analysis, IQ246.

[3] CBC Radio program, "Sunday Morning," April 3, 1983. Further data of a similar kind were presented on this program regarding the Nelson Muffler Company of Canada.

[4] Canada, External Affairs, Ministry of Supply and Services, *Canadian Trade Policy for the 1980's, A Discussion Paper* (1983), p. 49. This document will be referred to subsequently as *Discussion Paper*.

[5] Fred Lazar, *The New Protectionism* (Toronto: James Lorimer, 1982).

[6] *Background*, p. 210.

[7] *Background*, p. 212.

[8] The newly elected Conservative government wasted little time before rendering FIRA "clawless." This seems to be a part of their strategy of appeasing the U.S. — Ed.

[9] *Discussion Paper*, p. 46.

[10] The full brief was published by the vice-chairman of the Canadian Institute for Economic Policy. See Abraham Rotstein, *Rebuilding from Within* (Toronto: James Lorimer, 1984).

14: *The Perpetuation of Regional Disparities*

[1] The Task Force on Canadian Unity. *A Future Together: Observations and Recommendations* (Ottawa: Minister of Supply and Services Canada, January 1979), p. 75.

15: *Can Capital and Labour Cooperate?*

[1] Pierre Elliot Trudeau, *The Asbestos Strike*, 1956.

[2] *Globe and Mail*, October 25, 1983.

[3] Jim Matkin, President of the British Columbia Employers' Council, *Toronto Star*, November 8, 1983.

16: *Going Broke on the Farm*

[1] See Farm Credit Corporation, *Federal Farm Credit Statistics* (1982).

[2] D.D. Hedley and W.J. Anderson, "Problems in Global Agri-Food Development," *Food Market Commentaries* (published by Agriculture Canada), vol. 5, no. 3 (September 1983).

[3] Ibid.

[4] "Top-load" refers to the practice of providing incentives to produce specific agricultural products which are already covered by a price stabilization scheme. This practice has been followed by provincial governments even though federal stabilization programs are already in place. The result is that the producer is getting one set of signals from the provincial authorities and another set from the federal authorities. — Ed.

[5] Bill C-155 was designed to eliminate the preferential rate, charged by the railways, to ship grain. Under what is generally called the "Crow rate" agreement, the railways had guaranteed this low rate. The new bill was meant to allow for upgrading of rail facilities and to improve grain transport, but at the expense of eliminating the preferential Crow rate. — Ed.

17: Economic Development and Social Justice

[1] See Richard J. Barnet and Ronald E. Müller, *Global Reach* (New York: Simon and Schuster, 1974); and John Hutcheson, *Dominance and Dependency* (Toronto: McClelland and Stewart, 1978).

[2] The words *just, participatory* and *sustainable* first came to public attention in this form as a result of the report of the Working Unit on Church and Society of the World Council of Churches to the Fifth General Assembly of the World Council of Churches in 1977. At the World Council of Churches Conference on Faith, Science and the Future held at the Massachusetts Institute of Technology in July 1979, it was stated that "just and sustainable society requires more growth of energy use in poor countries, the curtailment of its use in rich countries and a major shift over time from non-renewable sources (coal, oil, gas and uranium) to renewable ones (direct solar, biomass, hydro, geothermal, tidal and wind) for all nations. A participatory society implies the fuller participation of individuals and groups in decision-making processes concerning energy."

[3] See Bill Ridgers, "Global Restructuring," IDOC *Bulletin 1983*, nos. 3-4 (IDOC International, via S. Maria dell Anima, 30-00186 Rome).

[4] David Hollenbach, *Claims in Conflict: Retrieving and Renewing the Catholic Human Rights Traditions* (New York/Toronto: Paulist Press, 1979), p. 204.

[5] See Federal Budget with "Analysis of Federal Tax Expenditures for Individuals" presented to House of Commons by the Hon. Allan MacEachen, November 1981; also Ed Temagno, "Comparing Direct Spending and Tax Spending," *Canadian Taxation*, vol. 1, no. 4 (Winter 1979).

[6] Taskforce on the Churches and Corporate Responsibility, *Canadian Economic Relations with Countries That Violate Human Rights*, Brief to the Sub-Committee on Latin America and the Caribbean of the Standing Committee on External Affairs and National Defence, presented June 1, 1982.

[7] See Project Ploughshares, *One Problem: Underdevelopment and the Arms Race* (Waterloo, Ont., 1983).

18: The Informal Economy and the Will to Work

[1] Hugh Stretton, "Housing and Government," as quoted in James Robertson, "Seeing the Economy Whole: Satisfying Personal, Familial and Community Needs," Max Bell Lecture, Vanier Institute of the Family, Ottawa, 1979, p. 17.

[2] See William A. Dyson, *Towards a New Work and Income Orientation* (Ottawa: Vanier Institute of the Family, 1976). The concept of the whole economy was first introduced into the work of the Vanier Institute, and to Canadians, through this publication.

[3] Hans J. Alder and Oli Hawrylyshyn, "Estimates of the Value of Household Work in Canada, 1961 and 1971," Statistics Canada (Cat. no. P-003E), Ottawa, 1978; Oli Hawrylyshyn, "Evaluating Household Work: Theoretical and Methodological Approaches," Statistics Canada (Cat. no. H-038E), Ottawa, 1975.

[4] Vanier Institute of the Family, "A Seminar on the Nature of the Economy in a Familial Society," *VIF Perspectives* (Ottawa, 1977), p. 3.

[5] Peter J. Usher, "A Northern Perspective on the Informal Economy," *VIF Perspectives* (Ottawa, 1980).

[6] Jonathan Gershuny, *After Industrial Society? The Emerging Self-Service Economy* (London: Macmillan, 1978), p. 78.

20: Moral Vision and Political Will

[1] Some of the Social Affairs Commission documents are reprinted in Gregory Baum and Duncan Cameron, *Ethics and Economics* (Toronto: James Lorimer, 1984).

[2] Ibid., Appendix 3, p. 175.

[3] For an examination and analysis of the phenomenon of labour devaluation see: John Paul II, *Laborem Exercens*, Part II, no. 7, and Part III, nos. 11-15, 1981; John Paul II, Address to business people and economic managers, "Man and His Values Are the Principle and Aim of Economics," in *L'Osservatore Romano*, June 20, 1983; Gregory Baum, *The Priority of Labour* (New York: Paulist Press, 1982); Canadian Conference of Catholic Bishops, "Unemployment: The Human Costs," January 1980; Harry Braverman, *Labour and Monopoly Capital: The Degradation of Work in the Twentieth Century* (New York: Monthly Review Press, 1974); Walter Johnson, ed., *Working in Canada* (Montreal: Black Rose Books, 1975).

[4] See especially John Paul II, Address to members of the Trilateral Commission, "It Is Not Possible to Separate Technology from Ethics," in *L'Osservatore Romano*, April 25, 1983; David F. Noble, "Present Tense Technology," Parts I and II in *Democracy*, vol. 3, nos. 2 and 3 (1983); Patricia McDermott, "The New Demeaning of Work," *Canadian Dimension*, December 1981.

[5] Baum and Cameron, *Ethics and Economics*, Appendix 2 and Appendix 3.

[6] Ibid., pp. 174-76.

[7] Ibid., pp. 177-78.

[8] See especially John Paul II, *Laborem Exercens*.